Non-State actors in the Middle East

As the recent revolutions in the Middle East have demonstrated, civil society in this part of the world is on the move. The increasingly important role of non-state actors – a phenomenon of globalization – has characterized developments throughout the region, affecting the struggle for democracy and peace.

This volume brings together scholars, primarily from the region, to analyze the varied activities and contributions of NGOs, the private sector, and the new media, from Morocco to Iran, along with the involvement of diaspora groups. The chapter on Facebook in the recent Egyptian revolution captures the role of this new media, while the study on similar technology in Iran outlines the barriers authorities raised in the current struggles there. Even the fledgling process of democratization in Saudi Arabia is driven by non-state actors, while the veteran women's movements in the Maghreb serve as an example for the post–Arab Spring era in those countries.

Providing one of the first assessments of the role of non-state actors in the Middle East, this book will be essential reading for students of political science, sociology, and civil society, among others.

Galia Golan is a leading Israeli political scientist, formerly head of the Political Science Department at the Hebrew University, Jerusalem; currently head of the M.A. and Conflict Resolution Programs at the Interdisciplinary Center, Herzliya (IDC); and the author of 10 books, most recently on the Arab-Israeli conflict: *Israel and Palestine: Peace Plans and Proposals from Oslo to Disengagement* (second edition 2007); and forthcoming *Breakthroughs and Failures in Israeli Peacemaking Since 1967*.

Walid Salem is a lecturer at Al Quds University on the issues of democracy, human rights and conflict resolution. He is also the Director of the Center for Democracy and Community Development (CDCD) in East Jerusalem, a member of the Palestinian National Council of PLO, and a coordinator of Middle East Citizens Assembly (MECA), that aims to promote citizenship and peace in the region since 2001. He is the author of more than thirty books, manuals and research papers on the issues of democracy, peace building, refugees and Jerusalem.

UCLA Center for Middle East Development (CMED)

Series Editors

Steven Spiegel, *UCLA*

Elizabeth Matthews, *California State University, San Marcos*

The UCLA Center for Middle East Development (CMED) series on Middle East security and cooperation is designed to present a variety of perspectives on a specific topic, such as democracy in the Middle East, dynamics of Israeli-Palestinian relations, Gulf security, and the gender factor in the Middle East. The uniqueness of the series is that the authors write from the viewpoint of a variety of countries so that no matter what the issue, articles appear from many different states, both within and beyond the region. No existing series provides a comparable, multinational collection of authors in each volume. Thus, the series presents a combination of writers from countries who, for political reasons, do not always publish in the same volume. The series features a number of sub-themes under a single heading, covering security, social, political, and economic factors affecting the Middle East.

Non-State Actors in the Middle East

Factors for peace and democracy

Edited by Galia Golan and Walid Salem

Routledge
Taylor & Francis Group

LONDON AND NEW YORK

First published 2014
by Routledge
2 Park Square, Milton Park, Abingdon, Oxon OX14 4RN

and by Routledge
711 Third Avenue, New York, NY 10017

Routledge is an imprint of the Taylor & Francis Group, an informa business

© 2014 Galia Golan and Walid Salem

British Library Cataloguing in Publication Data

A catalogue record for this book is available from the British Library

Library of Congress Cataloging in Publication Data

A catalog record for this book has been requested

ISBN: 978-0-415-51704-1 (hbk)
ISBN: 978-0-415-51705-8 (pbk)
ISBN: 978-1-315-85660-5 (ebk)

Typeset in Times New Roman
by Apex CoVantage, LLC

Contents

Contributors

Abdulwahab Alkebsi is the Regional Director for Middle East and Africa at the Center for International Private Enterprise (CIPE). Alkebsi, a native of Yemen, has more than 25 years of experience supporting democracy and market-oriented reform. Prior to his role at CIPE, he served as the MENA Director at the National Endowment for Democracy.

Yossi Alpher is a former Mossad official, former director of the Jaffee Center for Strategic Studies at Tel Aviv University, and a former senior advisor to PM Ehud Barak. From 2001 to 2012, he was coeditor of the *bitterlemons.net* family of internet publications.

Sara Bazoobandi is a lecturer in International Political Economy at Regent's University in London. In her academic career, she has been covering Iran and the GCC countries. She holds a PhD from the Institute for Arab and Islamic Studies of Exeter University.

Galia Golan is Darwin Professor emerita of the Hebrew University of Jerusalem, presently professor and head of the MA Program in Diplomacy and Conflict Studies at the Interdisciplinary Center, Herzliya. The author of 10 books, her forthcoming book is *Breakthroughs and Failures in Israeli Peacemaking.*

Mukhtar Hashemi is an associated researcher at the Newcastle Institute for Research on Sustainability, NIReS, at Newcastle University, where he gained his PhD in water resources engineering and management in 2012 and MSc in Hydraulic Engineering in 1995. He is a visiting lecturer at University of Kurdistan, Iran, a water-resources management consultant and an IWRM specialist working with major international and national projects in Iran and the Middle East and providing consultancy services on IWRM plan, Decision Support Systems (DSSs), wetland ecosystem management, conflict resolutions, trans-boundary waters, and institutional analysis. He has extensively studied the role of ethics, religion, and culture, as well as institutional aspects (water policy, law, and administration), in water management in the West Asia and North African (WANA) region. He is a member of IAHS, Gender Water

Alliance (GWA), and Iran's Engineering Council, Farmers House of Iran and Kurdistan, as well as the editorial board of Iran Water Research Journal.

Raoudha Kammoun was born in 1962 in Sfax, Tunisia. She received her PhD from the Université de Paris VII in 1989 and currently teaches in the English department at the University of Manouba, Tunis. Her research interests include gender issues and language, gender-based violence, political discourse, masculinities, and humor studies.

Charlotte Karouby graduated with a BA in Business and International Management from the Business School of Toulouse in France, and an MA in Diplomacy and Conflict Resolutions at the Interdisciplinary Center of Herzliya in Israel, where she specialized in the study of state security, immigration, and radicalization of minorities. Her research focuses on diasporas as decisive political players in states' internal affairs and on the effects of diasporas' hybrid identities on their political jockeying within their immigration country.

Safi Kaskas is the cofounder of East-West University, Chicago, and chairman of the board of directors for 25 years; the founder and president of Strategic Edge, a management consulting company active in the United States and Saudi Arabia, and the cofounder and president of American Strategic Healthcare Management active in Saudi Arabia. He has 30 years of experience in dialogue and bridge building between followers of Abrahamic religions, and is a public speaker to various congregations in various churches, explaining Islam and focusing on commonalities. He is a peace advocate participating in various forums and conferences to explain the benefits of peace and the dangers involved in a perpetuated conflict in the Middle East.

Yehuda Magid served in the special forces of the Israeli army. He is currently pursuing his PhD in political science at Indiana University/Bloomington, where his research focuses on ethno-religious conflict in the Middle East, with an emphasis on Israeli intrastate politics.

Sherif Mansour is the MENA coordinator at the Committee to Protect Journalists in New York. He worked for Freedom House and other NGOs to advocate democracy and human rights in Egypt and the Middle East. He has a master's in international relations from the Fletcher School at Tufts University, and a bachelor's in education from Cairo's Al-Azhar University.

Benjamin MacQueen is a Senior Lecturer in the Department of Politics and International Relations at Monash University. His research focuses on the role of political institutions during post-conflict transitions, with an emphasis on the Middle East and North Africa.

Fatima Sadiqi is Professor of Linguistics and Gender Studies; author of, among other works, *Women, Gender, and Language in Morocco* (Brill, 2003); editor of *Women and Knowledge in the Mediterranean* (Routledge, 2012), *Women in the Middle East and North Africa: Agents of Change* (Routledge, 2010), *Gender* *and Violence in the Middle East* (Routledge 2011), and *Women Writing Africa: The Northern Region* (The Feminist Press, 2009).

Walid Salem was born in East Jerusalem in 1957. He is a member in the Palestinian National Council of PLO, teaching democracy and human rights at Al Quds University. He is a writer of 30 books and training manuals, and tens of research papers on democracy, civil society, citizenship, refugees, and Jerusalem. He is also a consultant, evaluator, and trainer for several public and private bodies. He trained more than 30,000 Palestinians on these issues since 1990, and, since 1993, he is the director of The Centre for Democracy and Community Development, East Jerusalem. He is the Coordinator of Middle East Citizen Assembly as regional network of experts and activists on citizenship issues that include participants from 19 countries from the region since 2004. He has lectured at several international conferences and seminars about democracy, Jerusalem, refugees, and development in Palestine.

Introduction

Galia Golan and Walid Salem

Citizen activism and the increased role of non-state actors are major phenomena of recent decades, to some degree because of globalization. A number of factors are responsible for these phenomena, not least of which are those factors linked to the extraordinary advancements in technology, communications, and transportation. Time and space have both been telescoped, information has become instantaneous, borders have become porous, and the lines between domestic and foreign groups and institutions blurred. These, in turn, have led to greater awareness of developments around the globe, as well as to a trend toward global responsibility or governance, particularly in connection with human rights. Direct citizen action and organized non-state actors have come to the fore, often playing a key role in numerous events and processes linked with democratization, as well as peace-making. Locally, as part of emerging civil societies in countries moving toward democracy or in conflict/post-conflict situations, non-state actors have assumed importance as a motor for, as well as a consequence of, social and political transformation, complementing, and often substituting, for state actions. This trend has been evident in recent years, particularly in the Middle East and North Africa.

Citizen activism, in its various forms,[1] is conducted for the most part within what is called civil society, itself defined as a non-state actor, encompassing formal and informal actors, in particular, nongovernmental groups or organizations (NGOs). These groups or organizations may be engaged in advocacy or services and educational, political, even spiritual, or other functions. They may include labor unions, religious groups, the epistemological community (universities, research institutes, etc.), even businesses and neighborhood associations; they may be linked to identity, such as ethnicity, gender, or age.[2] As Walid Salem explains in his opening chapter on Palestine, civil society may be defined as "the representative of the society in [the] public sphere, acting for [society's] needs and interests." While civil society groups are generally viewed as active primarily, if not totally, in their local environment, they often have international connections and, increasingly, their actions become linked "virally," not only with each other, but also across borders and globally in the pursuit of resources, support, or power in a broader environment and for their local endeavors.

Thus, NGOs can and often do work in several environments simultaneously, offering relevant information for action, be it of the local scene or the international community. As grass roots, or at the least, unofficial organizations, they tend to be close to the people and therefore usually are credited with having greater access than formal (governmental) agencies. In theory, at least, they possess better knowledge and, most importantly, greater credibility than governmental bodies. Given their placement within society, their role in democratization is doubly important, if not critical, for they may provide not only a voice for people's interests and needs, but also the power to satisfy them.

Yet, representing society's needs and interests (Salem) can be a complex matter, as, indeed, defining these needs and interests may be the object of the very activity of civil society groups. NGOs have been accused of catering to donors' demands, a function often of the tight competition for resources, thereby deviating from their original goals. Issues of accountability and transparency have also been raised against them, given the absence of clear democratic procedures or oversight. Moreover, the positive or negative nature of NGO activities may be a matter of subjective appraisal, whether with regard to peace-making efforts or domestic advocacy. Certainly, government or individual protagonists would appraise the activities of civil society groups according to their own interests and goals. It is also very difficult to assess success or failure of civil society efforts, even when judged by their own objectives. Nonetheless, in the chapter on Israeli NGOs, Galia Golan points to what may be indirect achievements, or at least consequences, of peace NGO activities. Clearer, more direct results are discussed by Fatima Sidiqi with regard to the achievements of NGOs advocating women's rights in Morocco. And, Raoudha Kammoun highlights the critical role played by a leading women's NGO as a major component in the struggle for democracy in Tunisia. For the Palestinians, as pointed out by Walid Salem, civil society has often substituted for government in a prestate situation and under occupation, while, nonetheless constituting a critical watchdog on nascent centers of authority.

What follows in subsequent chapters actually illustrates the significant role NGOs have come to play, even as part of, or in conjunction with, other non-state actors. Diasporas often channel their work through NGOs in their host countries as well as internationally or in their home countries – forming NGOs themselves or linking up with others. Similarly, the private sector may work with various elements of civil society, whether in the democratization process or post-conflict peace-building, while the media – new and old – plays what has often been a critical role in the activities of civil society groups and, also, diasporas, contributing – possibly determining, to some degree – their success or failure. The direct involvement of diasporas, for example, in the search for resolution of conflicts, the mediation or financing by multinational companies with regard to post-conflict reconstruction, or the advocacy efforts of NGOs, particularly with regard to expanding civil society in the areas of human rights or moderate Islam; the use of the internet in promoting democracy, and more, all play roles today that have changed the ways governments and citizens act or are acted upon, in the Middle East no less, possibly even more than elsewhere.

The "new media" constitute both a tool and a central actor in today's globalized world. They not only facilitate the global processes of communications, but they also play a role in the shaping the content and progress of events, thereby, in some ways, becoming actors themselves. The internet is, of course, the vehicle that has flattened space, so to speak, but also opened the world to people everywhere. Even in areas having only low numbers of home computers, other means, particularly mobile phones but also public access facilities (for example, internet cafes), can be found, often in the most otherwise isolated locations. In this way, the internet has served a democratizing function, empowering not only the individual but also the weak, providing men, and women, the means for directly expressing their views and ideas, virtually at will, for all to "hear." Whether by means of blogs, social networks, "tweets," "talk backs," YouTube, reviews, and innumerable frequently unlimited "forums," the new media offer access to the public sphere and to the discourse on issues – sometimes critical – regarding one's life and society.

The new media also contribute to the building of democratic institutions, both directly and indirectly in the creation or facilitation of groups and organizations of civil society. These may well provide a voice for women or minorities previously excluded from the public discourse. Indeed, the various new media platforms actually constitute part of the emerging civil societies essential to democratization, as actors in the democratization process. Moreover, as became amply apparent in the "Arab spring" of 2011, the new media provide both a platform for the exchange of ideas and a powerful mobilizing vehicle for action in the promotion of democracy. Encouraging action, they may themselves undertake viral activities such as online petitions and other online campaigns. Indeed, they may engage in the actual organization of actions on the ground (as distinct from cyber space), providing communication between activists – even to the point of supplying timely information for demonstrations, recruitment, logistics, assistance, and warnings of danger to protests or other activities. Via the internet, pro-democracy activists can take their cause to the world stage, engaging outside media and groups, for assistance. Even simply generating awareness may protect activists, in addition to furthering their cause.

These roles for the new media are apparent in connection with the struggle for peace and conflict resolution, as well with as democratization. They may serve international organizations, NGOs, and diaspora, which seek to apply pressure, provide assistance, or engage in other forms of support for local groups seeking peace or democracy. The internet provides platforms for discussion of alternative solutions, options, or recommendations – even possible peace plans. At the least, they may open the way to communication between protagonists or their supporters, possibly dispelling misinformation or misunderstandings that feed conflict or impede peace-making. This communication may take the form of interactive discussions or debates, which often serve as efforts at "alternative dispute resolution." As conflict researcher Birgit Brauchler has said: the internet "brings together different levels of conflict and authority on the same virtual stage, thus flattening and effectively equalizing those levels and facilitating a discourse between formerly separated levels."[3] This might include facilitation of "citizen diplomacy" or dialogue that brings together people at the grass-roots level. Voices of moderation that may not otherwise be heard can be given exposure and the possibility of engaging protagonists directly. They may provide information helpful to peace-making or protection for peace-makers. The new media have clearly been credited with mobilizing support, both in areas of conflict themselves and beyond, sometimes providing international backing or involvement crucial to peace-making. In actual negotiations, the internet may provide instantaneous connection to advisors and supporters, thereby providing needed information, possibly clarifications that might prevent misinterpretations, or even authorization or feedback of a kind that furthers the chances for agreement. There have been cases in which interested but nonofficial parties, for example women, have been able to provide input from outside the negotiations, thereby gaining access and possibly influence.

Obviously, all of the above uses and roles of the new media can serve negative purposes. They may even enable hate-mongering and engage in net-warfare (cyber war). While Sherif Mansour's chapter on the use of social media in Egypt and Alpher's discussion of *bitterlemons* (in the Israeli-Arab conflict) provide examples of the positive role played with regard to democratization and also peace-making, Sara Bazoobandi's chapter on Iran adds a second dimension. She discusses the use – one might say misuse – of the new media by authorities in Iran to sabotage the pro-democracy movement, restrict freedom of speech, and neutralize protesters. Indeed, it would appear that the greater the role and efficacy of the new media for the promotion of peace and democracy, the more they can also become a tool and platform for impeding this progress.

Immigrant populations have grown significantly over the past 20 years, and their numbers have been swollen to include the growing numbers of foreign workers, as laborers and peasants alike seek a better life due to growing hardships, dislocations and over-crowded cities, reduced safety nets, and growing poverty in their home countries. At the same time, there is the "brain drain" of skilled labor, intellectuals and entrepreneurs seeking opportunities in the more prosperous countries, in addition to students and even long-time visitors. Added to these are political exiles, refugees, and victims of discrimination, to some degree the result of increased intrastate conflicts in recent decades. All of these are added to existing diaspora communities, often similar but also often including many who have been outside their homelands for generations, and some never having stepped foot in the homeland. It is the identification, that is, the consciousness and acceptance of the identification, rather than a direct link, that generally places a person as a member of a diaspora, whether integrated or not into the host country. Moreover, not all these expanding diaspora necessarily actively operate as diaspora; many seek a type of integration in their host societies, eschewing any interest in maintaining contact or a role with their home country. Further, diaspora populations are far from monolithic, often quite mixed with regard to not only the type of diaspora member (immigrant, refugee, etc.), but also with regard to socio-economic status, education, religion, political views, geographic area (of origin or residence), age, gender, and so forth. The degree of integration versus connection, with or interest in, the homeland may vary, just as the circumstances of both their host countries and their homelands may differ and even undergo change over time.

What has changed in recent decades, along with the numbers involved, is the role that diasporas are playing as actors, both in their host countries and home-lands, in connection with the democratization processes or conflicts within their homelands. Indeed, these roles have assumed such importance as to occasion the adoption of "diaspora policy" and representatives by home governments to deal with these groups outside the country. To a large degree, this expanded role has been enabled by globalization, namely, the freeing of financial and currency trans-actions, reduced costs and time of travel and communication, the advent of new media, cyber links, social networks, and the more porous nature of borders, as well as the development of global civil society, which may provide support or facilitation for diaspora activity. All of these may enhance influence in a host country, as well as the homeland, while democratization processes themselves open the way for more involvement of diaspora groups within a home country.

Following an examination of the meaning of the term diaspora, especially as it relates to the various Kurdish groups, Mukhtar Hashemi traces the history and activities of the Kurdish diaspora up to the present. As one of the oldest politi-cally active diasporas, the evolving nature and politics of the Kurdish groups are analyzed, particularly in relation to the controversies and changing situation in the homeland, as well as in Europe – the major stage of Kurdish immigration and activity. One of the largest and oldest diaspora, that of the Jewish diaspora in the United States, is examined by Yehuda Magid. The focus is on the transformation this diaspora has undergone in recent decades, spawning not only a greater num-ber of groups but also a relatively large number of groups specifically dedicated to a resolution of the Israeli-Arab conflict. The chapter deals with the ever-growing "peace camp" and its search both for influence in the American Jewish community and US political circles and for measures and activities designed to promote the possibility of peace between the protagonists of the conflict. Similarly, Charlotte Karouby's chapter on the Maronite Lebanese diaspora highlights the dilemmas and efforts of this group in the face of the sectarian battles in the home country, with an emphasis on the specific ways in which this diaspora became involved in the conflict and sought to assist in the post-conflict efforts to maintain peace.

The private sector has become more than a commercial/economic actor in soci-ety, to some degree because of the economic restructuring, primarily privatization that accompanies globalization. Thus, private companies – local or multinational – gain prominence and often assume new, additional roles. These may in part be linked to a need for public good will or a stable social and political, as well as economic, environment in which to conduct business. The rule of law, an hon-orable judiciary system, and a safe day-to-day functioning of the country, with regular, available channels for the public's expression of grievances, are all part of such an environment and beneficial for business. Moreover, in the new global environment of human rights concerns, and the scrutiny and criticism that may accompany this, private business people may feel a moral obligation to play a positive role in society.

Whatever the motivation, the idea of social responsibility has emerged in recent years as an integral part of private enterprise, often providing the private sector with a role in democratization processes and peace-making. The outsourcing usually connected with peace-building, particularly when local governments are weak, as well as the vacuum created by the abandonment (or reduction) of development and welfare tasks that national governments previously conducted have also opened the way for a greater private sector role. Participation, even leadership of development through investment, along with the provision of other types of assistance, may serve to both promote peace and strengthen the building of new institutions and the foundations of democracy. It is often the case that private businesses are well situated (and respected) within their communities, organizationally and socially, and therefore in a position to provide advice, personnel, facilities, and other services.

This is not to say that all businesses are socially responsible or that the private sector necessarily plays a positive role in processes of peace-making or democratization. Clearly, some companies exploit and benefit from the grievances and conflicts associated with globalization. Private corporations have been guilty of unfair resource exploitation and dislocation of populations. Some business people may believe themselves to be better served by dictatorships (as distinct from democracies and the rule of law) open to corruption and illegal transactions. Some private enterprises may actually thrive on the instability of conflict that renders foods and other essential goods scarce, thus driving up prices, for example, or that promotes even a government demand for their products (such as weapons) or services (as in the case of private security companies), or provides a cheap labor force. All these and more could be noted as the negative role the private sector plays, but that need not be the whole story. Indeed, this is by no means the general picture in the Middle East, as Abdulwhabab al Kabesi points out in his chapter and is substantiated by the examples provided from Saudi Arabia and Iraq in the chapters by Safi Kaskas and Ben MacQueen.

This volume was conceived and, for the most part, written before and during the momentous changes currently taking place in the region. Yet it is useful to look at the region in the light of these changes, coined as "the Arab Dignity Revolutions," better known as "the Arab Spring," "the Arab Awakening," and other names alike. By contrast, some have named it the "Sykes-Picot" of the region, or the Arabic Khamasin, thus highlighting negative perspectives of the events. Generally, the Arabic literature about these changes has not thoroughly examined another approach related to the topic of this volume, namely, an approach based on a democratic transition. Such an approach focuses on citizen activism and non-state actors, such as the role of the media (including the new social media) in the current process of transition, along with the role of diasporas, which include those uprooted by conflicts accompanying the regional changes.

The transition to democracy that we are witnessing starts directly after the introduction of free, transparent, and pluralistic elections. Such a process is very difficult because it includes conflicts (and sometimes violence) between the different groupings, along with many other aspects inherent to the process, exhibiting the complexity of the transition. That makes us realize that a democratic transition is a long-term process, requiring perhaps decades to be completed. France, for example, needed 155 years, from 1789 to 1944 – the year women were accorded the right to vote and be elected. After a sustained transition, a process of consolidation starts, as an ongoing process of democratic development, gradually resolving steadily, but democratically, the problems raised by democracy itself.[4] However, another aspect of the complexity of the transition is the possibility of a setback, with a return to the pre-democratic, authoritarian era. Samuel Huntington described those waves to worldwide democracy, and noted that each of three waves witnessed a counter wave of setbacks and returns to dictatorship. We still have to see if the transition in the region will succeed, while some are already facing setbacks.

In the Arab world, the non-state actors that started the transitions, for the most part, have been citizens themselves, rather than the civil society organizations (as had been the case in a number of Eastern European transitions). In the Arab case, the leading social forces were the young men and women, gathered in the main city squares starting from Tunisia, Egypt, Libya, Yemen, then followed by additional countries. Young people, sharing a concept of liberal democracy garnered to a large degree from the new media, acted outside the scope of political parties. In fact, political parties initially stood aside, assuming a neutral position, only finally joining once it became clear that the protests would succeed.

Various factors enabled the young to initiate and conduct the protest movements. Among them was the role played by new media, which provided access and dissemination of previously hidden information regarding the regimes' despotism and oppression. The new media carried this a step further, as the informed public took to the streets to demand freedom. Beginning with the self-immolation of Mohammed Bu Ezizi in Sidi Buzaid, a poor town of Tunisia, and the Egyptian youth group "We're all Khalid Said," responding to the death of Khalid Said under torture perpetrated in an Alexandrian police station. The new media also exposed the young people to the experience of the stable, liberal, democratic, and free countries of the world. The question that flowed naturally from it was: "Why not us?"

The process began with citizen action due also to the weakness or failure of organized civil society, mainly the political parties, but, in many cases, also non-governmental organizations, as a result of regime oppression and restriction of such groups and the right of association. Moreover, the stronger political parties were often content with "bargaining" with the regimes rather than striving for effective changes in or of the regime.

In a sense, the absence of "citizenship" led people to the streets in the name of freedom and democracy. Theirs was a response to the realization that the regimes were relating to them as subjects (*ra'aya* in Arabic), while viewing themselves as caretakers of the people. People understood that regime policies were designed to divide and rule, by encouraging the patrimonial (familial clannish, tribal, geopolitical) affinities, alongside neo-patrimonial cleavages (denominational, sectarian, and clientele), provoking the people through fragmentation, as an alternative to the move to citizenship and a celebration of diversity as one of the main aspects in a democratic society.

Thus, the transition in the region became in fact a "transition to citizenship." People, particularly the youth, went to the streets to address the regimes directly: "You are not any more our caretakers; we are not your subjects. On the contrary, we want to create a new social contract, recalling that *we*, as citizens, are the source of our government's authority. We are lending it legitimacy by expressing our freewill in direct, transparent, periodical and free elections." Along with this call for democracy, citizens and groups went further in their claims for their rights, extending this to the demand for equal rights for women, and for minorities, in terms of citizenship. In addition, they sought the development of citizen participation in post-election procedures, nurturing participatory democracy that goes beyond simply majority rule and eschews "tyranny of the majority" at the expense of minorities and individual rights. The process that has unfolded in the region may well have reached a point of no return, at which, setbacks notwithstanding, it will be impossible to return to the previous situation. Now, even potentially dictatorial regimes that might arise may not be of a same despotic type. It may well be very difficult to restore what Juan Linz has called the Sultanic Regimes, which prevent any form of pluralism or civil society. Linz distinguished between this type of full authoritarianism (the Sultanic regimes) and mere authoritarianism, which might allow some aspects of pluralism, as had been the case for example in Egypt under Mubarak or Yemen under Ali Abdullah Saleh.

Without delving to the many challenges that are facing both the countries that have started the transition and those that are still on their way to the transition, one can notice the following points about the upcoming role of the non-state actors in the region. First, non-state actors have finally begun to play a central role through civil society organizations and private investment and commercial endeavors, without the restrictive regime control of either the media or the economy. Second, we see the dominance of non-state actors in the socio-political life, previously impossible emergence of a broad and open public sphere. Within this public sphere, pluralism encompasses not only groups promoting liberal democracy and civil rights, but also conservative groups that advocate the rue of the Islamic Sharia or openly practice discrimination against women or non-Muslim minorities.

Beyond these two crucial changes taking place in the role of non-state actors in countries such as Egypt and Tunisia, for example, there is still a long way to go toward them elsewhere in the region. Moreover, the emergence of the free public sphere can create some negative trends, such as struggle between democratic, undemocratic groups, and conflicts along sectarian lines. There are difficult challenges for the creation of cohesive but diverse citizenship necessary for a sustainable public sphere open to freedom of action for non-state actors. There is the danger that instead of a vibrant democratic public sphere, in which different orientations compete and communicate by using peaceful means, there will (and may already be in some places) a deterioration into violence. Fragmentation and internal cleavages, along ethnic, tribal, religious lines are a constant threat.

These are by no means all the challenges facing the transition to democracy in the region, but they are some of the major ones on the path toward creating diverse and equal citizenship, the expansion of the free and democratic public sphere, and therefore the broadening of the role of the non-state actors and citizenship participation at all levels.

Finally, we cannot finish this introduction without some words about the diasporas of the region. The word *diaspora* has several meanings in connection with the region. It includes peoples living outside voluntarily but also those who did not immigrate of their own free will, were forced to leave or uprooted by conflict, namely, refugees such as the Palestinians of the 1948 era and Syrians of today's conflict. Displaced and stateless (*bedon* in Arabic), many of these people of the Middle East are still waiting; we need another book to deal with their plight.

All of the authors of this volume are from the region or directly involved with topics central to the area. Thus, they bring to their studies not only professional or academic knowledge, but also first-hand experience, No less honed in the complexities of the role of non-state actors in the Middle East is Elizabeth Matthews, who has most skillfully shepherded this volume to its completion through invaluable insights and advice. We are deeply indebted to her.

Notes

1 Literature on citizen activism is most often limited to the use of the internet, but our use of the term refers to the multitude of activities by citizens, including, but not only, via the internet.
2 The definition of civil society was greatly debated in the early 1990s, often in response to Michael Walzer's "The Idea of Civil Society," *Dissent*, Spring 1991, pp. 293–304. See also Andrew Arato and Jean Cohen, *Civil Society and Political Theory*, Cambridge, MA, MIT Press, 1990; Charles Taylor, "Modes of Civil Society," *Public Culture*, Fall 1990, pp. 95–118; Adam Seligman, *The Idea of Civil Society*, New York, Simon and Schuster, 1992; Robert Fine and Shirin Rai (eds), *Civil Society-Democratic Perspectives*, New York, Frank Cass, 1997; John Hall, *Civil Society: Theory, History, Comparison*, Cambridge, Polity Press, 1995; John Keane, *Civil Society, Old Images. New Visions*, Paolo Alto, Stanford University Press, 1998.
3 Birgit Brauchler, "Cyberidentities at War: Religion, Identity and the Internet in the Moluccan Conflict," *Indonesia*, 75 (2003), 123–152.
4 There is a vast literature about "transitology" and "consolidology" of democracy as named by Rustow, O'Donnel, Schmitter, Juan Linz, Alfred Stepan, Larry Diamond and others.Author Query

Part I
Civil society – NGOs

1 Civil society in transition

The case of Palestine

Walid Salem

Introduction

The concept of "civil society" became part of the Palestinian political and research discourses in the beginning of the 1990s, during the period of preparation for the establishment of the Palestinian National Authority (referred to here as the Authority or PA), which took place in May 1994.

At that time, the Palestinians went on a thorough exploration process on several questions concerned with state building, including: What should be the structure of the Palestinian National Authority? Can it be democratic? What type of democratic systems should be adopted? What is the relationship between the national tasks for freedom and getting rid of occupation and the democracy building tasks? How should the relationship between the state and the society organizations be empowered? And what type of economy should be established?

Within this context, the Palestinian researchers started to write about the civil society and its relevance and importance to Palestine. Some early studies were written by Mohammed Muslih, Ziad Abu Amre, Azmi Bishara, Said Zeedani, George Giacaman, Walid Salem, Musa Al-Budeiri, and several others who were all a combination of liberal-democratic, left-wing academics and writers, who all were concerned about the possibility of establishing a Palestinian despotic authority. Therefore, they were seeking to find a "shelter" in the so-called Palestinian civil society to balance the power of the state and to find a tool to distribute power resources to different components of the Palestinian society.

The Palestinian academic George Giacaman defined civil society to be "that societal sphere, in which the individual plays the role of a social actor through the society organizations and in relative separation from the state" (Giacaman 1995: 108). Those researchers rediscovered all the classical literature about civil society starting with John Locke and continuing through the 18th century with the likes of Alexis De Tocqueville, Mountsique, Adam Virgson, and Thomas Penn. Then there is the 19th century's Hegel and Marx, along with the 20th century's Antonio Gramsci.

While it is out of the scope of this chapter to review those thinkers' ideas about civil society, we will focus on the development of the Palestinian civil society, starting with an explanatory notes about the meaning of discussing a Palestinian civil society, followed by a historical review of its development in stages, then by the different challenges that the Palestinian civil society has been facing since 2007, when the political division between the West Bank and Gaza occurred. Finally, the paper looks at the role of the Palestinian nongovernment organizations (NGOs) and some conclusion of future perspectives.

The Meaning of Civil Society in Palestine

For this text, the civil society includes the political parties; the grassroots organizations; the community-based organization (CBOs); the unions of labor, women, youth, students; and the voluntary organizations and societies, all of which are characterized by a membership that is open for all citizens regardless of their geographical, familial, clannish, tribal, religious, sectarian, or cliental affinities.

In other words, the civil society includes both the national-based organizations and the CBOs. The latter includes reform committees (Islah Committees), local youth clubs, and all forms of local organizations that act in the sphere extending in the space between the family and the state.

In this sense, the familial associations (called in Palestine as the families' "Dawawin"), are not civil society organizations. State structures and bodies, including the parliament, are political society and have nothing to do with civil society components.

This text adopts a definition of the civil society inclusive of those organizations that are built on a "citizenship bond" and that act in the sphere that is outside of both the family and the state. That sphere, called the public sphere, is not exclusive to the civil society organizations. It also includes the economy and the political society as other actors in it, but the significance of the civil society is that it is the representative of the society in that public sphere, acting for its need and interests, as well as for its future through the visions that the civil society develops and lobbies for on its behalf with the state.

Finally, in the concept of civil society, this paper is interested in the recently added dimension to both the Hebarmasian public sphere and the civil society characterized by the role played by the new virtual public sphere and virtual civil society gatherings, and their impact on widening the "real" public sphere and the "real" civil society. This virtual dimension was expressed in the Arab 2011–2012 public revolutions and in Palestine by new youth movements in 2011, which this text will reference.

With this theoretical background that puts the civil society as an independent actor from the state, can one speak about the Palestinian civil society in the absence of the state? This question was one of the hot issues of the discourses among the Palestinian researchers in the 1990s, and their answers were presented. One had followed the classical literature about civil society and said that the Palestinian civil society had to wait until a Palestinian independent state emerged before it could be formed. Others said that the civil society already emerged in the West Bank, Gaza Strip, and East Jerusalem, in the absence of the state. A third group spoke about a civil society that is under formation.

The first group was represented by the radical left and also a variety of independent thinkers who did not all present the same reasons for rejecting the idea of having a civil society in the absence of the state. Radical left intellectuals like Adel Samara focused on two sets of factors that prevent civil society from emerging. The first set concerns the political aspects of Palestinian life: the prevailing Israeli occupation, the fragmentation of the Palestinians to those who still live inside Israel, those who live in 1967 occupied territories, and the refugees outside. Based on that fragmentation, the question became: If we speak about civil society in the West Bank, Gaza Strip, and East Jerusalem, what then about the Palestinians in Israel and the Palestinian refugees; should we exclude them from the presence of civil society?

The second set of issues this group of intellectuals presented was that its members considered the call for civil society development as a call for the "NGO-ization" of the Palestinian society, leading to the adoption of a Western agenda that would divert the Palestinians' attention from focusing on the task of the national liberation from occupation, to focus instead on societal, communal, and professional agendas within the framework of the Israeli occupation, while also acting within the limits the occupation imposed. In this sense, the NGOs are perceived by this group as the transmitters of the Western culture aiming to penetrate the Palestinian society, and also they help by focusing on professionalism versus liberation on sustaining the Israeli occupation. Adel Samara wrote:

> The Developmental Institutions in the Palestinian Occupied territories were established and still serve the following: spread and concentrate the market mechanism, making the face of the Western imperialism better via the NGO's that it created in order to hide behind during the period of the cold war, while imperialism became able to act directly nowadays. (Samara 1994: 122).

Other independent thinkers who shared the doubts about the presence of the Palestinian civil society, this time also for societal reasons, crystallized in the following questions: How can a society that is structured along patrimonial, familial, clannish, tribal, contradictory, geographical affinities, and cleavages be "civil" therefore create a civil society based on citizenship bond between the citizens, regardless of their familial, geographical, sectarian, and cliental affinities that all express pre-civil structures of fragmentation versus diversity, being the latter a characteristic of the "civil" societies leading to a peaceful rotation of conflict and power, opposites to fragmentation that lead to violence from the groups living parallel to each other without integration, as is the case in the societies that have a level of civility.

According to this group, a society first needs a level of civility as a prerequisite for the establishment of civil society. The absence of this full civility from the Arab World as a whole, and not only Palestine, led an Arab thinker like Burhan Ghalion to talk about the absence of civil society in the Arab World. Alternatively, this world has what Ghalion called the "Domestic Society" or "Al Mujtama'a Al-Ahli" (Ghalion 1990). This means that its organizations build on lines of the patrimonial and neo-patrimonial structures. Moreover, Musa Al-Budeiri wrote that the idea of the creation of the civil society in Palestine is not "possible without a national consensus, and a joint vision of the political and economic system to be established" (Budeiri 1994: 88). Budeiri, in this sense, was not seeing that such a consensus was possible. Later, in the next year, he wrote in another paper about civil society in Palestine, referring to the writings of Israelis Edward Kaufman and Moshe Moaz, that the Israeli occupation itself "embraced the civil society, and sponsored a Palestinian pluralistic democracy, and that the military rule in the occupied territories encouraged the democratic fidgets of the people that was ruled undemocratically" (Budeiri 1995: 69).

This opinion has two possible implications. The first is that the civil society emergence in Palestine has to wait until the national liberation is achieved, and that any talk about it during the national liberation period will help the Western and the Israeli agenda against the Palestinians. The other possible implication is that in order to create a civil society in Palestine, it is not necessary to wait for the state to be established, but a minimum consensus about the political and economic systems for Palestine still is needed.

Opposite to the opinion above, another one presented is the idea that the Palestinian civil society does exist in West Bank, Gaza, and East Jerusalem. Others went even further to talk about the historical presence of such a civil society starting from the late period of the Ottomans in Palestine until 1917. In this regard, Ziad Abu Amre wrote in 1995,

> The Civil society in West Bank and Gaza is considered to be the only Palestinian civil society. The Palestinians in the Diaspora do not form one civil society and they did not form special civil societies for them, despite the state of organization that the Palestinian collectives abroad had represented by the formation or joining political parties or factions, the formation of labour trade unions, professional societies, or other organizations that are included originally in the framework of civil society. (Abu Amre 1995: 27)

He added later that the Palestinian collectives in the Diaspora are "part of the civil societies of the countries that they live in, based on the fact that the Diaspora Palestinians do not have a special political or geographical sphere for them." This is "despite the relative differences of their integration in the host societies" (Ibid: 17).

Beyond this area that excludes the Palestinian civil society to the Palestinian territories that were occupied in 1967, there are others who spoke about the existence of the Palestinian civil society and did not constrain it to only those territories. They spoke about the concept of a civil society in the absence of the state. Opposite to the classical literature that links the civil society to the presence of the state, those Palestinian thinkers and activists spoke about the Palestinian civil society as being the holder of the burdens of the Palestinian state in its absence. In this regard, they carried health, agricultural, educational, and other tasks that the state is supposed to carry on and they managed these tasks successfully.

Mustafa Al-Barghouthi, a leader of NGOs in Palestine, considered in this regard that "the existences of Democracy basis, pluralism, and the role of the civil society organizations, are not just a luxury or accessories that the Palestinian people can live without in the coming period, but it is a vital condition for the Palestinian people survival and continuation as a people that are eager to achieve their self determination and national independence" (Al-Barghouthi and Giacaman 1995: 15).

The PLO was looked at as the "National Entity" of the Palestinians as if it were the symbol of the state and its political regime. When PLO leadership was still outside the 1967 occupied territories, those occupied territories' NGOs understood and expressed their roles to be as complimentary to the PLO, helping it reach its people in the occupied territories and provide them with services. In this sense, the agricultural, health, educational, and other activities of that period were understood not only as services, but also as political tasks aiming to create trust between the people and leadership by presenting that leadership as being capable of providing the people with their needs through services. In this regard, it should be mentioned that most of those new NGOs established in the 1980s were connected to the Palestinian factions, mainly the PLO left-wing factions. Therefore, on one hand, their activities were in line with the political agenda, but on the other hand, because they were leftist organizations, they focused on the link between the political agenda for liberation and the social-economic agenda for development and for the communities' democratic participation. They were very critical of the PLO leadership for its inability to work on a developmental agenda that they felt was necessary to sustain people's presence (Sumud) and to empower them to meet the liberation's requirements and sacrifices.

Opposite to the previous opinion that saw the NGOs' emergence as a deviation from politics, these new NGOs of the 1980s envisioned their role as being both political and developmental. Seeing the link between both, and in order to achieve political gains, the people must first be empowered to make them capable of sacrifice. This cannot be done without developmental projects.

Since 1994, when the PNA was established, a new period started when the NGOs found themselves facing new tasks. They found that they could no longer continue carrying the full burden of the state in some fields, namely: health, agriculture, and education because the PA had started building the whole national structure of those sectors. Much discussion about the strategies of working with the PA took place in which parts of the NGOs decided to work fully separate from the PA. Others considered their role to be both independent and complimentary, which required coordination with the PA. A third group selected the path of being just complimentary to the PA. The latter represents those organizations that were established by Fateh, during the PA period. A full analysis of those positions between the NGOs and PA can be found in a book published by the author in 1999 (Salem 1999).

Ezzat Abdel Hadi, another NGO leader of that period, defended the right of the NGO's for independency in the framework of the role of law and social contract. He wrote:

> In order for the NGO's to contribute to the ongoing developmental processes aiming to build the civil society, they should enjoy real independence, including in the designation of their aims and programs that they consider appropriate and fit with the interest and the needs of the groups that they represent, and also in their institutional organizations that enable them to achieve their required visions. Also they should be free to create regional and international relations, all in accordance with the rule of law and the social contract that is agreed upon between the different social groups. (Abdel Hadi 1995: 3)

This is the idea of those who analyzed that civil society existed in Palestine, carrying the burden of the state, and working with, as well as independently of, the PA after its establishment. Yet still there are others, such as Muhammed Muslih (1993), who went back to history since the beginning of the 20th century to show that the Palestinian civil society has existed since then. According to Ibrahim Abu Loghoud and others, historical civil society was characterized three main characteristics, pluralism, participation, and elections (Abu Loghoud et al. 1993).

The coming part of this text will shed light on the historical development of the Palestinian civil society and its roles as a non-state actor in different stages until present day.

In addition to the first approach that denies the presence of a Palestinian civil society and the second that says it exists, a third one was presented in the same period, talking about a "Palestinian civil society in transition" or "in formation" under a continuous occupation and dependent authority. This approach spoke about the Palestinian civil society as being in transition or formation in two meanings: The first is the Palestinian internal meaning, which shows the presence of both new civil, modern organizations that are open for all Palestinian citizens, regardless of the patrimonial and neo-patrimonial affiliations, combined with old domestic society (Ahli) and represented by the CBOs and other localized organizations. In this sense, a period of transition of the latter to the first is still required. The second deals with the movement toward national independence from the occupation, leading to the transformation of the civil society from one that is under formation to a full one that acts in the presence of a Palestinian state (Salem 1995: 27–35).

Historical glance

Regarding its overall role, the Palestinian Civil Society primarily focused its work during all the periods on the issue of national liberation, while the social issues were always marginalized. It witnessed two periods of richness in its organizations and actions: One before 1948, and the second after 1967. Hereinafter is a short historical review of the development of the Palestinian civil society.

1920s–1940s: Focus was mainly on the national issue by the Islamic-Christian Societies, labor unions, youth clubs, women's organizations, and charitable societies in the 1920s. The 1930s witnessed the emergence of six political parties who joined the national struggle against the British Mandate and the Jewish Emigration to Palestine (see details in Salem 1999; Nakhleh 1994).

1948–1964: This was a period of dispersion for the Palestinian Civil Society. Those who continued to exist in Israel worked for the preservation of their national culture and national identity. Those dispersed in the Arab countries joined the Arab political parties and NGOs. A few also organized few Palestinian organizations, such as the Palestinian General Federation of Students, which was established in 1959. The Arab-National issues and the liberation of Palestine were the main two points on the agendas of these organizations. In the West Bank and Gaza Strip, the Palestinians joined the Arab parties, organized labor unions, and charitable societies. While the labor unions concentrated more on the national issue than on workers' rights, the charitable societies concentrated, as their name implies, on social charity, but not on social change or social transformation, avoiding there any frictions with despotic regimes.

During this period, the West Bank was annexed to Jordan, who named it the "West Bank of Jordan." Meanwhile, the Gaza Strip was put under Egyptian administration, but without annexation to Egypt. This situation led to a difference between the West Bank and Gaza Strip. Gaza witnessed the emergence of the Palestinian Communist Party of Gaza, the Muslim Brotherhood's Gaza Branch, and also the Gaza Branch of the Arab Nationalist Ba'ath Party. In comparison to the situation in Gaza, these same parties worked secretly in the West Bank during the same period. Moreover, Gaza witnessed the emergence of the First Palestinian National Council in 1948, which worked for two weeks before being dissolved by the Egyptians. Elections were first held in Gaza for a Palestinian Legislative Council, created solely for the Gaza Strip in 1963. This all means that the Palestinians in Gaza were able to act as Palestinians at this time. In the West Bank, Jordanian citizenship had been imposed on them, unlike in Gaza. Therefore, the Palestinian civil society organizations in Gaza were more independent than those in the West Bank.

The only organizations that were allowed the right to work in the West Bank were nonpolitical organizations such as the charitable societies who established a federation in 1958. It is worth mentioning that these societies were obliged to follow the Jordanian law: To request a permit for every activity they wanted to conduct, even an indoor lecture.

1964–1988: The PLO-led civil society was composed of the PLO itself as an organization that had semi-state and semi-civil society structures. It also included PLO factions such as the so-called Popular Federations that acted outside Palestine, including those of students, women, teachers, writers, journalists, farmers, and other. The PLO also supported voluntary work committees, grassroots youth and women organizations, and health and education NGOs in the West Bank and Gaza Strip during the 1970s and 1980s. The work of such civil society at that period began to provide services like the health and education NGOs. This PLO supported civil society was accompanied by the continuation of the work of the non-PLO supported organizations of the charitable societies and the Islamic Christian endowments in the field of services.

The activities of this period can be categorized as being services or relief. The people were considered either as receivers of these services and relief activities, or as fuel for revolution. No developmental participatory approach had yet emerged when it came to dealing with the people.

1988–1994: With the eruption of the Intifada at the end of 1987, the focus of the Palestinian national work was transferred from outside to inside Palestine. This transfer was accompanied with changes on the work of the civil society toward more participation and more professionalism, and also more combination between the national liberation agenda and the social agenda. The social agenda included the design of developmental vision to be implemented within the framework of protracted conflict and long-continuing occupation, and the priority of defending human rights, mainly against the violations committed by the Israeli occupation. In this period, the PLO faction-supported grassroots organizations of women, youth, and others were ineffective. In their place, new grassroots participatory organizations emerged represented by the different types of the so-called popular committees that represent the main holders of the Intifada.

1994–2000: For the first time, the social internal agenda became the priority in the work of the Palestinian civil society. Despite the reality that political parties began to show weaknesses and signs of crisis, the role of the NGOs grew in this period. The NGOs health and kindergarten education sectors services were bigger than those of the PA in this period. Moreover, the internal agenda of the civil society began to include deeper issues such as democracy building, institutional building, and different approaches to development; PA violations to human rights; advocacy and lobbying; antimilitarization vision; peace and nonviolence projects. The PA–civil society relations were tense at this time (while the PA-supported NGOs were ineffective), but within this tension the civil society was able to advocate policies toward development, the disabled, youth, women's rights, and also regarding the civil society–PA relations. The Islamic organizations exploited the concentration on the social and internal agendas in order to increase its status among the Palestinian public, using Islamic Charity (Zakah system) to promote their support.

During this time, the PA tried its best to control the civil society, mainly the areas of NGO involvement, and a conflict ensued for several years around the content of the NGOs law. In 2000, a relatively democratic law for NGOs in response to the struggle of the NGO's networks was inaugurated. The law came to include the right of the NGOs to work via registration and not by permit, as the PA had insisted. This essentially meant that the people had the right to organize themselves freely in civil society organizations, and the PA must register these organizations. According to the law, the PA has no legal basis to claim that such NGOs are prohibited or otherwise not allowed. Additionally, the law gave independence to the NGOs to make their decisions solely according to their governing boards without the imposition of policies and decisions on them from outside.

2000–2005: Due to the militarized Intifada, a setback occurred in the work of the civil society. While its main political parties retuned to armed struggle, some NGOs were obliged to return to relief activities called "emergency aid programs." The work on the fields of development, democracy, education, and democracy building retreated, while new fields of work emerged, such as extending the work aiming for demilitarization, the promotion of nonviolence, and confronting security chaos. The civil society also presented its agenda for financial, administrative, and legal reform in the PA and participated in the national committee for reform that included the PA.

This period also witnessed a setback on the work of the Palestinian peace organizations because of the problem of "normalization." The Islamic civil society organization witnessed a boom in its membership and activities, mainly giving support to the poor families. The work of these organizations is characterized as being done with clean and uncorrupted hands, in comparison with the work of the PA and some corrupted civil society organizations.

2006–2012: With Hamas's success in the Palestinian Legislative Council (PLC) elections of 2006, followed by their takeover of Gaza in June 2007, the Palestinian civil society became fragmented into three trends: Of the three, one is supportive of Hamas, the second supports the PA in Ramallah, and the third is composed of the liberal and democratic independent organizations.

The Hamas-affiliated civil society witnessed a boom in the Gaza Strip in this period and tried to increase the professional aspect of its work in order to contribute to the legitimization of Hamas. Meanwhile, the same organizations witnessed a retreat in the West Bank because the PA government there closed down dozens of organizations affiliated with Hamas in different cities of the West Bank in 2007. The PA-Ramallah affiliated civil society witnessed a boom in the West Bank, while it faced restrictions to its activities by the Hamas-led government in Gaza Strip. Beyond these two, the liberal of democratic civil society organizations faced restrictions from both authorities ruling in West Bank and Gaza.

These changes led to deeper and more significant ones. One of these changes was the growth of the domestic-sector divided civil society, in line with the factional split between Fateh and Hamas, on the expense of the civil society that has all the Palestinian citizen as potential members without reservations for any reason that concerns all the predemocratic system cleavages. The noncivil "civil society" grew, and the civil society witnessed a setback.

Another reason for such a setback concerns the political thought of both ruling powers in Gaza and the West Bank, which can be seen more clearly in Gaza, which is against people participating in designing policies that meet their needs and interests. In Gaza, Hamas focused on the Muslim Brotherhoods' well-known approach of characterized by the "Islamizing the society more than Islamizing the political system." The Islamization of the latter will be the product of the Islamization of the society and not because of an imposed policy by Hamas. Based on such an approach, Islamization is the priority. What will be practiced is a top-down approach with the society. It will be against democratic participation, the freedom of expression, association, and organization. With that known, one can understand all the restrictions that Hamas made on the civil society in Gaza, including closing some organizations and preventing all to hold any activity without getting a permit in advance from the Hamas government in Gaza.

In the West Bank, the PA practiced restrictions on the freedom of expression, restricted the media freedom, and also practiced extensive censorship on the NGOs. (All these violations can be reviewed in the website of the Palestinian rights organizations such as: the Palestinian Center of Human Rights, Al-Haq, and others.)

The split between Fatah and Hamas became like the split between the West Bank and Gaza. Within this framework, a despotic ruling authority emerged in Gaza, one that rules by presidential decrees in the West Bank. The PLC was paralyzed because of the split. With growing despotism in the absence of the PLC, the civil society organizations paid the price in both the West Bank and Gaza.

As other results of the growing despotism, the public sphere was closed for participation in Gaza and diminished in the West Bank. With the impasse in the political process toward Palestinian statehood, this was another reason to close up the open public sphere for participation. In this situation, the independent civil society organizations found themselves facing a very difficult situation for their work in Gaza, excluding their activities in the West Bank to the classic ones (monitoring human rights violations, training the PA staff to develop policies and strategies for different fields, raising public awareness, and providing public services). These organizations also began organizing and conducting nonviolence activities in scattered areas. The developmental agenda of the civil society organizations witnessed a cutback in this period due to the heavy restrictions imposed on the implementation of agendas in area C (two-thirds of the West Bank), East Jerusalem, and Gaza, due to its closure and the failure to fulfill the promises to rebuild Gaza after the 2008 war on it, including the allocated $4.7 billion by the donor countries for that reconstruction process in the beginning of 2009. No penny of this amount was spent ever since.

> The close up of the public sphere was confronted starting in 2011 by two new civil society processes: one from the new youth movement, and the second from East Jerusalem that was separate from the Hamas-Fateh power struggle.

New youth movements emerged as a result of the Arab Spring. In March 2011, more than 60 new youth groups organized themselves on Facebook. In March–April 2011, they acted against the split between Hamas and Fateh. In May, June, and July, they organized activities against occupation and for the right of return. After July 2011, they allied with President Abbas in his bid to the United Nations. During the previous months, those youth movements received cruel treatment from Hamas against their activities in Gaza, while the PA and the West tried to use them to work for their interests, They temporarily stopped their activities after starting a national discussion about a "new national contract" that concerns the democratization of the PLO, PA, and their relations with the Palestinian society (see the contract on the Sharek website: www.sharek.org).

The other challenge to the closing public sphere came from Jerusalem. The Jerusalemites, excluded from both Palestinian authorities, found themselves obliged to organize themselves in CBOs emerging in East Jerusalem's 21 communities by composing committees in their communities that plan and work together for their needs (more on that in Salem 2010).

What will be the future of the Palestinian civil society? Will they be able to re-open the public sphere for essential participation by them? These are questions for another text.

Palestinian NGOs: Structure and the Understanding of the Roles

In moving from discussing the role of the civil society in Palestine to the more specific role of the NGOs as one of the components of the Palestinian civil society, it will first be found that there are different estimations of the number of NGOs in Palestine based on different definitions. For instance MAS Institute concluded in a study conducted in 2007 that the number of NGOs in Palestine is 1,388 organizations (951 in West Bank and 437 in Gaza) (MAS 2003). This number did not include the CBOs that existed in West Bank, Gaza, and East Jerusalem communities.

In 2000, Walid Salem presented other numbers of the different NGO networks. Those networks and their membership were as follows:

- The National Union of NGOs was established in 1997, has 1,200 member institutes, and depends mainly on local funds. It coordinates its work with the offices of the PNA.
- The Forum of NGOs Union in the Gaza Strip, established in 1997, is composed of 200 institutions, the majority of which depend on local funds. It coordinates its work with the PNA offices.
- The Palestinian Union of Charitable Societies, established in 1958, is composed of 391 member organizations in the West Bank and Gaza. It and depends primarily on local funds, and it coordinates its work with the Ministry of Social Affairs.
- The Cooperatives Union, established in 1993, has 1,000 member corporations and depends mainly on local funds. It coordinates with the Ministry of Labor.
- Palestinian NGOs Network, established in 1993, is composed of 70 institutions, the majority of which depend on external sources of funding.
- The Forum of the NGOs Union in Gaza Strip, which is composed of nine syndicate Institutions, established in 1996, it coordinates with the PNA offices. (Salem 2000: 59)

There are about 2,700 organizations, not including the youth clubs coordinating with the Ministry of Youth, Zakat committees, and youth and women centers, as well as the Chambers of Commerce Industry, and others (Ibid: 60).

In 2009, the Palestinian Ministry of Interior records presented 2,126 registered organizations by them (Constantini and Jamal Athamneh 2011: 35). This number is not inclusive of the 1,000 Cooperative Union member organizations mentioned above.

Despite their differences, the roles of these networks were concentrated generally in the following fields: First, monitoring Israel and the PA's violations of human rights and also monitoring the PA and the local authorities' elections. Second, training the PA civil and security departments, the CBOs' staffs, activists, and the citizenship in general. Third, raising awareness amongst the Palestinian public on different issues ranging from democracy, human rights, and gender, to agricultural and health information. Fourth, service delivery including charity health, relief, farming, and educational services (mainly to kindergartens). Fifth, international lobbying through distributing information, and the participation in the international conferences. Finally, organizing nonviolent activities against the occupation with the participation of international and Israeli activists.

These roles are conducted in cooperation with or independent of the PA, based on the nature of their relationship with the PA, which differs from one network to another.

The Palestinian NGOs practiced these roles differently during the stages of their development and based on changes on the ground. Until the 1970s, the NGOs were focused on providing charity and relief services more than on any other role. At the end of 1970s, the strategy of Sumud (Steadfastness) emerged, which would change the way that NGOs viewed their interventions.

During the 1980s and through the first Intifada, the NGOs aimed their interventions at promoting "Sumud, resistance, and bottom-up state building." The latter was done during the first Intifada through land reclamation, support campaigns to the national products while boycotting the Israeli ones, interventions in education, and what was called "popular education."

After the first Intifada, and with the formation of the PA in 1994, the NGOs continued to focus on "Sumud, resistance, state building, and the content of building." There was an additional focus as well, though on increased professionalism that needed to be developed in order to ensure an institutional building that is transparent, integrative, and accountable leading to a democratic state-building process (see more in Abdel Hadi 1997).

This last stage of the NGOs' focus on the content of state building reached its end by 2007. The first reason for this was that the political process to statehood reached an impasse. A second reason was the splits between Fateh/Hamas as well as Gaza/West Bank, and the ramifications on the NGOs' freedom of work. Third, the composition of the Salam Fayyad government, composed of professionals since June 2007, will no longer need any more of the NGOs' services in order to promote professionalism in the PA structure.

By August 2011, the Fayyad government plan for statehood building reached its end in its attempt to create facts on the ground in area C and East Jerusalem in order to prepare for statehood. All the NGOs in the same two areas also reached the same results. When that happened, the Palestinian NGO community faced large external and internal challenges to moving forward.

Challenges Ahead

The first important challenge concerns the leading vision of the Palestinian NGOs. So far, they have focused practically on development and state building, while they focused verbally and in writings only, on confrontations with the Israeli occupation policies.

This created unbalanced activities, which some of the NGOs discovered in the last few years. Therefore, they started to shift attention to nonviolence activities organization and promotion with international and Israeli activists' participation. Others still did not discover this dilemma, leading to de-politicized positions and types of activities that result in further marginalization of them in the Palestinian society.

Beyond that, and also at the visionary level, taking a political approach led these NGOs to minimize the impact of the patrimonial and new-patrimonial pre-democratic cleavages. Thus, the Fateh-Hamas 2007 fight in Gaza was a shocking event that they did not ever expect to happen. They were then unable to deal with its ramifications, creating another reason for the NGOs marginalization by the two authorities in West Bank and Gaza.

In order to meet the new situation then, the Palestinian NGOs need to develop a firmer and more clear-cut political position and to practice it toward the issues that are related to the Israeli occupation, as well as the issues that are related to the split among the Palestinian people. Additionally, this political position needs to be accompanied by a developmental approach that goes beyond just focusing on the micro-level projects. In this sense, a community based, macro-developmental approach needs to be developed for all the Palestinian territories, and specifically for Gaza, Area C, and East Jerusalem. This approach should be based on working with the people, more than just working for them as Robert Chambers wrote:

> Enable local and marginalized people to share enhance and analyse their knowledge of life conditions, and to plan, act, monitor and evaluate. (Chambers 2004: 7)

To engage with these political and developmental challenges, some changes in the structure of the NGOs' work need to take place. A balance between the global and the national must be achieved. One of the results of NGOs' development in Palestine was the emergence of what was called by Sari Hanafi and Linda Taber as "the Palestinian globalized elite" that "consist of an important group of the leaders and local offices of the international NGOs" (Hanafi and Taber 2006: 17). While this elite is globalized, it is also disconnected from the Palestinian people and do not have the time or the energy to create links with the communities. The ramifications of such a phenomenon are the absence of sustainable constituencies of the Palestinian NGOs' temporary contracts with "target groups" until the end of the projects with them. One of the reasons for that is the dependency on funded projects that have beginning and finishing times rather than developing sustainable and continuous programs.

Contrary to the above, the globalized nature of the Palestinian NGOs' activists did not mean that they are capable of influencing the international level for the sake of Palestinian rights. There are few who become international public figures through their work with the NGOs and most of these moved from the NGOs to politics. Aside from those few, the others who act internationally have different levels of influence.

Palestinian NGO activists need to persuade the international community to become more involved for the sake of Palestinian rights, while at the same time, to continue to be influenced and bring the international knowledge and values to the Palestinian society. In order to achieve this, they need strong contacts with the local communities to have influence and to be influenced by these communities. The strong contacts will also enable the NGOs to contribute to the revival of the political parties, grassroots organizations, and the citizen movements that faded away in the in last decade, such as the students' and women's earlier, stronger movements. The new youth movements mentioned earlier are one of the attempts to revive citizens' movements, but it is too early to predict where it will lead.

In order to reoccupy and reorganize the public sphere, the Palestinian NGOs have reached a point that they also need a reform process toward more institution-alization, internal democratic processes, and transparency, integrity, and account-ability procedures. They need more networking and partnership among them, along with more lobbying toward the two authorities in West Bank and Gaza to counter the attempts for their marginalization. With all of this above, the goal is building a civil society in Palestine, opposed to the retreat to domestic society based on clientelism to the two authorities.
Arabic references

Arabic references

George Giacaman (1995), The Civil Society and the Authority. In Musa Al Budeiri et al. (eds.), *Palestinian Democracy: Critical Overview.* Ramallah: Muwatin Center.
Burhan Ghalion (1990), Building the Arab Civil Society: the Role of the Internal and the External Factors, pp. 733–755. In Al-Alawi Sa'eed Ben Sa'eed (1990), *The Civil Society in the Arab World, and Its Role in Democratization.* Beirut: The Center of Arab Unity Studies.
Saad Eddin Ibrahim (1995), Preface, pp. 5–41. In Amani Qandeel (1995), *Democratic Transformation in Egypt.* Cairo: Ibn Khaldoun Center.
Musa Al Budeiri et al. (1995), *Palestinian Democracy: Critical Overview.* Ramallah: Muwatin Center.
Adel Samara (1994), *Democracy, Political Islam and the Left.* Jerusalem: Al-Zahara'a Center.
Mustafa Al-Bargouthi and George Giacaman (1995), *The Civil Society Organizations and Their Role in the Coming Period.* Paper presented to the Civil society organizations and their role in the coming period Conference, Birzeit University.
Ezzat Abdel Hadi (1995), *Preliminary Notes about the Relationship between the NGOs and the Palestinian Authority.* Unpublished manuscript, can be found at Bisan Center Library, Ramallah.

Ezzat Abdel Hadi (1997), The Palestinian non governmental organization experience of transition from relief to development, *Shoun Tanmawiyyah* Magazine, pp.76–90.

Walid Salem (1999, June), *The Societal Voluntary Organizations and the PA, towards an Integrative Relationship.* Ramallah: The Forum of Social And Economic Policies Studies in Palestine.

Walid Salem (1995, July), "Methological Comments about Civil Society in the context of a Continuous Occupation and Dependent Authority." *Al-Taybeh Can'an Magazine* 66: 27–34.

Khalil Nakhleh (1994, September). "Our National Institutions in Palestine, Jerusalem." The Arab Thought Forum, Jerusalem.

Ezzat Abdel Hadi (1997), "The Palestinian NGOs and the Management of Transition from Relief to Development." *The Developmental Issues Magazine* 3–4: 76–90.

Musa Al Budeiri (1994), The Concept of Authority and Democracy, pp. 77–85. In *Challenges of the Transitional Period of the Palestinian Society*, Jerusalem: The Jerusalem Center for Media and Communication.

Ziad Abu Amre (1995), *Civil Society and Democratic Transition in Palestine*. Ramallah: Muwatin Center.

Ibrahim Abu Loghoud et al. (1994), *The Palestinian Elections*. Nablus: The Center for Palestinian Researches and Studies.

English references

Mohammad Muslih (1995, Spring), "Palestine Civil Society." *Middle East Journal,* 77: 258–74.

Palestine Economic Policy Research Institute (MAS) (2007), *Mapping Palestinian Nongovernmental Organization in West Bank and Gaza*. Ramallah: MAS.

Walid Salem (2000), "Relationships between the PNA and the Palestine Voluntary Societies: Reality and Prospects." In *Palestinian Governmental NGO: Cooperation and Partnership*. Ramallah: Welfare Association Consortium.

Robert Chambers (1994), *Ideas for Development: Reflections Forwards*. Brighton: Sussex: Institute of Development Studies.

Sari Hanafi and Linda Tabar (2006), *The Emergence of the Palestinian Globalization Elite: The Donors, International Organization, and the Local NGOs*. Ramallah: Muwatin Center.

Walid Salem (2010), *Jerusalem: Monitoring Reported a Human Security Community-based Agenda for Change.* Jerusalem: The Center for Democracy and Community Development.

2 The impact of peace and human rights NGOs on Israeli policy

Galia Golan

Following the elections of 2009, Israeli civil society, more specifically, the peace and human rights elements of civil society, began to come under serious attack from the Knesset and various members of the Israeli government.[1] This attack appeared to culminate in a preliminary decision by the Knesset, by means of a large majority, to create a committee to investigate left-wing NGOs with regard to their foreign resources on the grounds that they were contributing to the "delegitimization" campaign against Israel outside. Though never implemented, this proposal in the Knesset, initiated by a party belonging to the government coalition, had the support of almost all members of the government coalition, along with some members even of the opposition (three members of Kadima, at the time the leading opposition party). Criticism of NGOs, specifically of peace NGOs, is nothing new for right-wing Israeli parties, whether in or out of power. Efforts to discredit peace NGOs were evident in the 1980s when right-wing politicians accused Peace Now of being financed by Saudi Arabia, or the CIA.[2] Far more serious were accusations that the peace movement constituted a fifth column, expressed during the months of protest against the Lebanon War in 1982. An atmosphere of incitement against the movement led to the throwing of a grenade on a demonstration, killing one and wounding seven others.

The difference today is, first, that such accusations have become a high-profile campaign, virtually blaming peace and human rights NGOs for Israel's growing isolation in the world, as well as making accusations that they are weakening the country's will or ability to stand up to its enemies. Secondly, these accusations are the basis for demands upon the government to curb these organizations. While these developments should be seen as part of the disturbing trend (in the form of legislative proposals and actual laws) directed against various elements of Israeli society (e.g., refugees, Arab citizens, foreign workers), not unlike xenophobic or racist currents in various European countries today, the attacks on the peace NGOs and those groups working against the occupation in one form or another attests to a specific link to Israeli policy regarding the Arab-Israeli conflict. Moreover, both the persistence and intensity of this onslaught suggest that the majority of the Knesset and the government believe these NGOs to be powerful—possibly even critical with regard to Israeli policy. In any case, the organizations (themselves NGOs) and individuals spearheading the campaign against the groups, and demanding action to restrain them, appear to believe that the peace and human rights NGOs have had, and will continue to have, an impact on matters of war and peace.

It is interesting that such a fear, if that is what it is, comes not only at a time when there is no peace process of which to speak, but also at a time when what is called the "peace camp" (usually identified as the "left"), namely the supporters of the peace and anti-occupation[3] groups, is the weakest it has ever been—electorally or otherwise. There have been numerous articles on the demise of the left, the disappearance of the peace camp, and the swing to the right amongst the Israeli public as a whole. Indeed, evidence of this is not only the electoral losses of the last national elections, or the emergence of the nationalist, right-wing party of Avigdor Lieberman as the third largest party in the country, but also the disintegration of the once powerful Labor party as it split, one part blending indistinguishably into the right-wing coalition government and the remaining part limiting itself to purely domestic-welfare issues.

Even one of the most prominent leaders of the once-massive peace movement, Peace Now, recently told a meeting of the group's leadership that the movement had simply failed.[4] Not only has peace not been achieved, nor the abuses of human rights under the occupation eliminated, but also the situation has in fact become worse, from the point of view of prospects for peace and human rights. For example, the settlement enterprise has grown to the point that some half million Jewish Israelis are living beyond the green line (including East Jerusalem) with continued expropriation of land, including privately owned Palestinian land; residence and movement for Palestinians living under occupation is more restricted than 30 or 40 years ago; permits are needed for West Bank or Gaza Palestinians to enter Jerusalem and barred from living there even if married to a Jerusalemite; Gaza remains under almost total siege; and daily abuses, including harassment, settler violence, and occasional killings, are the lot of the Palestinians. And while today, Israelis are living (within the green line) in relative safety, the previous decade saw the worst years of terrorism since the creation of the state, the Islamist takeover of Gaza occasionally results in rocket fire on Israel's southern border, and another Islamist group is steadily arming just beyond Israel's northern border. Thus, it would appear impossible to discern an impact of the peace or human rights NGOs with regard to government policy in connection with the conflict.

Nevertheless, such judgments depend upon the criteria, and clear, objective means for judging the efficacy of civil society groups or social movements are difficult to come by. One can look to the expressed goals of a movement or organization, but often such goals are so general or all-encompassing (peace, for example) that anything short of this overall objective may be considered failure. More problematic perhaps, is the impossibility generally to ascribe causality to an act by the NGO and the decision of a government, given the myriad of factors that enter into any decision. Theories on resolution of intractable conflicts posit a number of events or developments that may bring about a decision that ends a conflict, such as a change in leadership, the loss of popular support, high costs of continuing, and so forth.[5] However, it is far more difficult to prove a link between the actions of an NGO and such events. Rare are the incidents of relatively certain causality, such as a decisive battle, an election or revolution, or the like, and the contribution of NGOs to such developments themselves would be hard to prove. Equally difficult to prove would be connections between what Zartman calls "ripeness" for resolution, on the one hand, and the actions of NGOs, on the other. Furthermore, it is generally unlikely that causality with regard to the role of an NGO in the decision taken by a government could be empirically tested short of statements by the decision-makers themselves acknowledging the connection. Yet, such statements are rare, constituting, as it were, an admission that something other than the wisdom of the decision-maker was at play

In her detailed study of the Israeli peace movement, Tamar Hermann maintains that no Israeli leader has even mentioned the peace movement in connection with any decision regarding steps toward ending the conflict or improving the situation for those under occupation. In fact, she argues, governments undertaking peace initiatives have been careful to avoid or deny any such connection. To some degree, this may be explained in general by the inherent tension between governments and nongovernment actors that are often formed in response or opposition to government actions or perceived lacunae. Acknowledgement of their role might therefore be construed as an admission of government failure. More specifically to Israel, a number of additional factors may account for the reluctance to acknowledge any impact of the peace movement and related human rights NGOs.

First, the political culture in Israel centers on political parties, with significant civil society groups having emerged only in the late 1960s to early 1970s. The collective ethos of the early years, notwithstanding, participatory democracy such as that characteristic of British and American traditions, was not an integral part of the essentially East European political culture of Israelis. Even after NGOs began to proliferate, and the peace movement itself gained mass strength, many believed that only parties could in fact influence policy. For this reason, groups were often urged to form a party when elections approached. Second, the electoral system in Israel leaves little room for the idea of individual responsibility to constituents (except in certain cases, for example, ethnic parties). Thus, responding to public demands was not necessarily seen as more important than demonstrating party leadership. Third, in Israel, possibly in any country engaged in a prolonged conflict, the public as well as the leadership accord the highest priority to security considerations. Association of government decisions with considerations other than security needs, for example, association with concerns usually raised by peace movements, namely, humanitarian or emotional, or possibly even moral, concerns, might discredit the perceived value of the government's efforts. Even Peace Now played into this prioritization of security, in order to gain public legitimacy, by using the "combatant" motif in its creation (1978) through the "officers' letter." In fact, no woman officer was permitted to sign to avoid impairing the "warrior" image. More recently, a Combatants for Peace movement was started, also using this motif, along with Breaking the Silence—the implication being that as fighters they have "legitimacy" as well as experience behind their protest.

Thus, both prime ministers Yitzhak Rabin and Ehud Barak in the Oslo period and Arik Sharon with regard to his disengagement policy all shunned any connection with the peace camp, preferring to identify themselves with the broadest possible public and a concern only for Israel's security.[6] While willing to meet with Peace Now leaders (on the issue of settlements), for example, Rabin had little regard for the peace movement and only reluctantly agreed to appear at events or demonstrations (such as the one at which he was assassinated) in support of the peace process he had begun. He would not even permit a speaker from the peace movement at that fatal demonstration on 4 November 1995. Sharon, for his part, totally ignored the campaign waged in support of disengagement and sought, rather, to keep himself and even his party far away from demonstrations of support for his own policy of disengagement.

It is not entirely true, however, that no leader ever credited the peace movement with having played a role in decisions regarding resolution of the conflict. Menachem Begin, in the course of peace-making with Egypt, acknowledged that the Peace Now demonstration on the eve of his trip to Camp David in September 1978 did impact positively on his interest in reaching an agreement there. This is not to say that the movement was responsible for the Framework for Peace that emerged from the Camp David meeting (the basis for the peace agreement signed one year later). Obviously, a very large number of factors brought about this meeting, which had been preceded first by Begin's efforts to meet with Sadat, then by Sadat's historic visit to Jerusalem, months of negotiations, and, finally, American mediation. Nonetheless, some credit was given the peace movement, if only for creating Begin's sense of responsibility that he could not return home empty-handed.[7] Later, as prime minister, Barak was to acknowledge the role played by public pressure, as expressed by the Four Mothers group regarding the withdrawal from Lebanon in May 2000; still later, Prime Minister Sharon revealed that one of the factors that led him to devise the disengagement plan was the appearance of other "dangerous" plans, such as the Geneva Initiative, thereby acknowledging the role of what was in fact a civil society endeavor, the Geneva Initiative, with regard to his decision.[8] Here and there, other such pronouncements may be found, though they are infrequent.

If statements indicating some connection are rare, one might seek empirical evidence of direct connections, presuming, or at least suggesting, causality between an NGO action and a government decision. One step removed, an indirect connection may be perceived in the linking of NGO action with public opinion, which then may be connected with a government step or policy change. Social movement theory posits such indirect impact, for example, maintaining that civil society more generally affects the social and political landscape—the domestic environment in which government decision-making takes place. Movements, groups in civil society, introduce language, ideas, options into the public discourse, in this manner contributing to the shaping of public opinion, perhaps even values. In these ways, movements can operate as agents of change, even if influencing government decision-making only indirectly.

Moving from the general to the specific, the public discourse and public opinion in Israel today are light-years away from what they were as recently as the

1980s, and certainly the 1960s. Ideas proposed only by the very extreme fringes of society in 1967, such as "two states for two peoples," or even the existence of a "Palestinian people" are today not only part of the daily discourse but also supported by the majority of Israelis, including the majority of Israeli Jews.[9] The Israeli army (IDF) and its actions—once sacrosanct—are openly criticized and even investigated, while induction figures have dropped dramatically. Similarly, a majority of the public supported the dismantling of settlements in the disengagement and continue to support evacuation of most of the settlements.[10]

Moreover, most of these changes, specifically, support for the creation of a Palestinian state, have been adopted by the Israeli government, including, and most notably, the Likud-led government of Sharon and verbally, at least, that of Prime Minister Netanyahu's government of 2009, though missing from the coalition he formed in March 2013. The first official adoption of the two-state solution by an Israeli leader was in fact expressed by Sharon in a February 2002 press conference at the White House, and reiterated to the Israeli Knesset in May the next year. Subsequently, the Road Map, which explicitly posits the two-state solution as the goal, was adopted by the government, and later, Olmert negotiated with the Palestinians at the Annapolis conference for such a solution. Even Netanyahu has given at least verbal support to the proposition in his speech June 2010 (Bar Ilan speech). To what degree these changes were the result of the pressure of public opinion, and to what degree the NGOs played a role, is only speculative given the undoubted importance of other factors, most notably American pressure in 2010.

The changes in public opinion are well documented, demonstrating the public's gradual move over the years to the dovish positions of the peace camp, though, obviously, many factors were at play. Globalization may have played a role as Israelis moved from a welfare state to capitalism and individualism, and an accompanying interest in simply getting on with their lives, and livelihoods. Additionally important were the first intifada, with its revelation of the impossibility of maintaining the status quo in the territories. All this was reflected in the graphs of opinion polls, which spiked in the direction of support for compromise during the first intifada. Additionally, under Rabin, the government itself was acutely aware of opportunities created by the changing international environment (the collapse of the USSR, the "new world order" of American dominance – particularly important for the Arab world, and the 1988 PLO acceptance of the two-state solution). In addition, the growing danger of the spread of weapons of mass destruction in the region (particularly Iran) added a further incentive for ending the conflict with the Palestinians, who themselves were in a weakened position because of their support for Saddam in the 1991 Iraq war. And, later, Likud leaders like Sharon ultimately became concerned over the demographic implications of continuing the occupation. All of these may well have been the factors behind the Israeli decision, but, at the very least, one might argue, the moves by Rabin (Oslo), Sharon (disengagement, adoption of the two-state solution), and Olmert (Annapolis) – possibly even Netanyahu (Bar Ilan speech) – would not have been undertaken without at least some conviction that there would be public support for these policies. This support was in fact present in the opinion polls. But, it was the expanding peace movement and a burgeoning number of related NGOs that had shifted these ideas from the fringes to the mainstream of Israeli discourse, expounding these policies and lobbying politicians to adopt them, particularly throughout the 1980s.

One may look to more specific incidences of possible impact. The first Lebanon War began what became the erosion of the popular view of the IDF as a sacred cow, opening the way to what has become relatively commonplace criticism and ultimately, in the second intifada, refusal to serve in the occupied territories by persons who were mainstream Zionist reservists and would-be recruits. Without exaggerating their numbers, one may assume that such critics perceived at least implicit backing by the many demonstrations that occurred during the Lebanon War and over the ensuing years. Demonstrations and publicity were organized by the peace movements. But, more directly, it was large demonstrations organized by Peace Now that contributed to Begin's hesitation, and delay, of the army's move into West Beirut until late in the war (along with smaller demonstrations that probably contributed to the timing of the ending of the second Lebanon War in 2006). Begin himself explained his 1983 resignation in part as the result of the daily demonstrations against him by opponents of the war.[11]

Far easier to discern is the direct connection between the massive peace demonstration demanding a state commission of inquiry into Israeli's role in the Lebanese Sabra and Chatila refugee camp killings and the formation of such a commission in 1982 (the Kahan Commission). The findings of that Commission led to Sharon's removal as defense minister by Begin. Similarly, post-war demonstrations such as those of 1974 and 2006 also had an effect, in the first case, contributing to the resignation of Golda Meir, Abba Eban, and Moshe Dayan in April 1974, and in 2006, the creation of the Vinograd Commission after the second Lebanon War and the resignation of Amir Peretz as defense minister in June 2007, shortly after the Commission's Interim Report. In both of these post-war cases, ad hoc groups led the protests. The withdrawal of the IDF in May 2000 from southern Lebanon has often been attributed to the NGO "Four Mothers," which focused attention on the diffuse but prevalent opposition to the continued losses of soldiers in Lebanon, leading to the Barak election-night promise to take the IDF out of Lebanon within one year (which he did). Barak's decision was not necessarily the result of the public's position, but, again, at the very least, that position provided support for the decision and, in fact, it may well have contributed – in the form of pressure from below – to Barak's promise. Indeed, as noted above, Barak even acknowledged this.

A clearer connection may be drawn between an NGO and Sharon's decision to withdraw from the Gaza Strip, dismantling the settlements there and also four small settlements in the northern part of the West Bank. There was clearly public pressure, expressed mainly by the media, with regard to the danger to soldiers serving in the Gaza Strip, and there was also pressure upon Sharon to take action toward peace (most notably a public letter by air force reservists; interview by four former heads of Israeli security services). Sharon's advisor Dov Weisglass also claimed that Sharon's decision to disengage from Gaza was due to "internal erosion" as expressed in the public demands of various (ad hoc) groups.[12]

There are other examples of Israeli NGO actions resulting in at least some change or recognition of the need for change. A number of NGOs, particularly Yesh Din (There Is a Law), Peace Now, Ir Amim (City of Peoples), Association for Civil Rights in Israel, have all petitioned the Supreme Court of Israel regarding matters such as the separation barrier and illegal settlement building (including the outposts, building in East Jerusalem, and the like). The Public Committee Against Torture, Gisha (Legal Center for Freedom of Movement), and other NGOs have also turned to the court. Some of these petitions have been successful, with decisions to move the location of the separation fence or wall in some places and to dismantle outposts or parts of West Bank settlements, as well as orders limiting the investigative methods employed by the Security Services. Only some of these judgments have been implemented, however, since the government has resisted change. Nonetheless, there are cases in which government crises have even resulted due to pressure to implement court rulings, for example, the 2012 crisis over illegally built houses on private Palestinian land in the Ulpana section of the Bet El settlement in the West Bank.

Of a different nature, the activities of Machsom Watch (Checkpoint Watch), which monitors IDF behavior at check-points in the occupied territories, has led to some improvement, and reports of Breaking the Silence (de-mobbed soldiers and reservists reporting on abuses conducted by the army in the occupied territories)[13] have been credited with some of the IDF investigations of actions conducted during the war on Gaza ("Cast Lead"), despite early denials by the army of any wrong doing.[14] There are other instances of response to specific protests, in the case of a house demolition or settler activity, but it can also be said that the vast majority of such protests have in fact failed to produce results.[15] With the exception of isolated successes, such as abandonment of the plan to build a settlement near the Flowers Gate of the Old City or the more recent withdrawal of a tender for luxury development in the former (destroyed) Palestinian village of Lifta – both in East Jerusalem,[16] the many demonstrations and protests against settlement building have resulted at most in delaying but not preventing government action. This was the case, for example, regarding the Har Homa and Ras al-Amud projects, both in East Jerusalem,[17] and apparently, the E-1 project just outside Jerusalem.

The last two examples bring to fore the matter of joint actions. The rare but positive decision regarding a settlement in Lifta was the result of efforts by joint Israeli and Palestinian NGOs. Such NGOs have been dwindling, primarily as the result of the absence of negotiations and the deterioration of the situation (and hopes) since the failure of the Oslo Accords, the devastating violence of the post-Oslo period (2000–2005) and a resultant opposition of some Palestinian groups to continue to engage in joint efforts on the grounds that such cooperation creates the impression of a "normalcy" that certainly does not exist today. Nonetheless, joint groups such as Ta'ayush and Solidarity – grassroots protest groups of mainly young Israelis and Palestinians, may be able to point to some success at least in drawing public interest to such issues as the settler takeover of

Palestinian homes in Sheikh Jarrah (East Jerusalem). Similar are the joint actions by the Israeli "Anarchists" along with occasional participation of the joint Combatants for Peace protests against the fence in Bil'in and elsewhere – sometimes successful via court action taken by other NGOs. In the context of joint groups, both the Bereaved Parents Circle and the now-defunct women's NGOs the Jerusalem Link and the International Women's Commission for a Just and Sustainable Israel-Palestinian Peace were able to involve previously unengaged populations.[18] They may be credited with bringing a somewhat greater understanding of the situation to leaders such as Tzippy Livny or even Condoleezza Rice, but it would be hard to identify an impact even on public opinion, much less on the government. The value of joint people-to-people groups, such as the Parents Circle or women's groups, for example, has been in creating a modicum of trust, understanding, and communication between the conflicting communities – something that is even harder to evaluate than the work of the more visible peace groups.[19]

Also characteristic of some of the above efforts has been international involvement. In the case of the delayed settlement building in Ras al Amud and Har Homa, for example, the interaction between Israeli NGOs (primarily Peace Now) and their counterparts in the diaspora led to behind-the-scenes US government intervention. Similar interaction was apparent when Peace Now revealed the building of outposts during the Barak administration, leading ultimately to US opposition and the demand in the Road Map, along with American communications to the Sharon government, not only to freeze settlement building but also to dismantle the outposts.[20] Many Israeli NGOs (like most institutions) have support groups abroad, such as Americans for Peace Now (APN, perhaps the oldest), French Friends of Peace Now, American Friends of B'tzelem (amongst the newest), and similar groups in a number of countries. In addition, diaspora groups in the United States and Europe deal with the conflict, such as the very recently created J St. in the United States, J-Call in Europe, Jews for Palestine, and more.[21] These often work with Palestinian groups in these countries.

Some results of such cooperation in lobbying may be seen in the US decision in 1991 to link a freeze on settlement building to US government loan guarantees for Israel (to finance the absorption in Israel of the large immigration from the former Soviet Union). APN lobbied in favor of the settlement freeze, and it is likely that their efforts contributed to the US decision. The move did not result in a change in the Likud-led government's settlement policy, but the US-Israel falling out over the issue did factor into the 1992 election of the Labor party (and Yitzhak Rabin), which campaigned on a promise to freeze the settlements. Similarly, APN lobbied successfully several times for renewals of US aid to the Palestinians – which was an important element for maintaining continuation of the peace process, and, in addition, it initiated letters and meetings with members of Congress in support of the peace process, particularly during the Oslo period and later, in September 2010, when Secretary of State Hillary Clinton hosted direct Israeli-Palestinian talks. In this last instance, APN were joined by the newer J St., as well as others. The Jewish-American peace NGOs – working in conjunction with Israeli NGOs, do appear to have been successful in placing the settlement issue on the agenda of Jewish public opinion and perhaps even into the general public discourse, as well as that of various US administrations. And when the US administration has adopted the issue, for example, with the Road Map or the settlement freeze demanded by Obama in 2009, the government of Israel has been forced to make certain commitments.

The impact of other NGOs abroad and international NGOs (INGOs) is a difficult topic and one that warrants a much larger study than intended in this chapter. Activities of many non-diaspora NGOs and INGOs, mainly in Europe, seek to influence public opinion, if not actual governmental positions, of both their own governments and that of Israel. Some have acted as mediators or at least conduits for peace proposal, most notably FAFO (which led to the Oslo talks and Declaration of Principles), or Pugwash, which conveyed peace proposals to Israel in the 1970s and since has organized many track-two type meetings of Israelis and Arabs.[22] Other groups as well, such as OXFAM and Pax Christi in particular, have been active in organizing track-two and track-three (grass roots dialogue) meetings, and many fund as well as assist Israeli-Palestinian meetings and joint Israeli-Palestinian projects. International women's groups, such as the Global Women's Fund, the Swedish Kvinna Till Kvinna (Women to Women), have played similar roles, in some cases supporting the work of the afore-mentioned Jerusalem Link and IWC and other local groups, assisting them in bringing their issues and proposals to governments and international bodies. Often the role of such outside NGOs or INGOs is indirect, however, making it still more difficult to discern their contribution to actual decisions.[23] Those INGOs such as Human Rights Watch, Amnesty International, or Children International that act more directly – pressing for governmental action in very specific, usually individual, cases, have had only the most minimal success. It is possible, however, to make a case for the easing of the siege on Gaza because of INGO and Turkish NGO action, namely, the flotilla effort of 2010. This may actually be the only example of such an impact, inasmuch as efforts by many INGOs, specifically solidarity groups working against the occupation in Gaza and the West Bank, have not succeeded in changing Israeli policies. These and many other INGOs in the occupied territories have, of course, had an effect in assisting communities and the Palestinian Authority there on a daily basis, easing somewhat life under occupation, providing advice and guidance on many matters, including those of political value in negotiations, for example.

Similarly, INGOs have been very effective in focusing international attention on the conflict and on the Palestinian cause. Reflecting the phenomenon of globalization, INGOs dealing with the conflict are most active on the internet, via blogs, the social networks, YouTube, and simply their own websites. They have spawned the growing BDS campaign, calling for not only academic boycotts of Israel but also boycotts of specific products, and especially goods produced in the settlements as well as in Israel itself. In some cases, they have been successful in obtaining sanctions; for example, the company producing Caterpillar machinery suspended of deliveries to Israel, Norwegian companies boycott the Israeli medical equipment firm Elbit, and South Africa is working against imports of products made in the settlements. Their importance in building support for the Palestinian cause can be seen in the reaction of the Israeli government to what it views, with alarm, as a growing "de-legitimization" of Israel in the world. However, this growth of the BDS campaign has not had the effect it had intended; the campaign has not moved the government of Israel to change its policies. Indeed, this work of the INGOs has led to a counter domestic campaign in Israel – an attempt by the Israeli government to restrain and repress Israeli peace and human rights organizations, creating a pretext for xenophobic and extreme nationalist government policies that the public may well embrace. Linking the outside efforts to cooperation with local Israeli NGOs, the explicit accusation by Israeli officials has been that Israeli NGOs are providing the material (information) with which INGOs are castigating the country, and, incidentally, also weakening the army's ability to defend the country.

Such accusations, and Knesset proposals to investigate the peace and human rights NGOs, were spearheaded by Israeli NGOs of another type, which, slightly later than their targets, emerged with the development of Israeli civil society. Looking at the actions of right-wing NGOs over the years, the impact on policy is no clearer than that of the peace groups. Some groups, like the Land of Israel movement, were created just after the 1967 war, with the goal of ensuring that Israel hold onto the newly acquired territories in the West Bank. Later, a right-wing NGO, Gush Emunim, organized the settler movement, taking advantage of the then Labor government's support for settlement construction, but also often forcing the government's hand by action on the ground. Later, settler NGOs such as Ateret Cohenim organized appropriation or the purchase (by American supporters) of land in East Jerusalem. Almost all of these can be said to have been successful in achieving their goals, namely, the building of settlements, but just what their contribution was to this development is difficult to ascertain inasmuch as left-wing as well as right-wing governments favored the enterprise, allowing it to progress even in as it declared the outposts, for example, illegal. Moreover, their essential goal of permanently ensuring Israeli control over all of the occupied territories has yet to be achieved, or indeed supported by the majority of Israelis, though many may claim just the opposite given the large numbers of settlers and their ongoing efforts to demonstrate how difficult evacuation would be.

Aside from settler groups, advocacy NGOs were created to counter the peace groups, for example, Women in Green who demonstrated in reaction to Women in Black in the late 1980s or Zu Artzeinu (This Is Our Country) that conducted civil disobedience and demonstrations against the Oslo Accords in the late 1990s. Without a specific identifying NGO, massive numbers of people identified as supporters of the "National Home" conducted large campaigns against the disengagement from Gaza in 2005. This last group was no more successful than its predecessor had been in the movement to prevent the withdrawal from Sinai and the evacuation of the Sinai settlements in 1982. In these two cases, the decisions for evacuation of settlements were those of right-wing (Likud) prime ministers, but the absence of significant public support for the settler opposition to the disengagement may also have been attributable, at least in small part, to the years of left-wing NGO publicity of the negative effects of the settlement enterprise.[24]

However, while it would appear that these right-wing NGOs did not succeed in changing policy regarding Israeli engagement in peace processes, they may have had an effect on the lack of progress. In the case of efforts for an Israeli-Syrian peace agreement, both Rabin and Barak were confronted by strong NGO led campaigns against returning the Golan Heights. According to one of the Israeli negotiators involved in both sets of negotiations, a major factor for Rabin and particularly (according to President William Clinton) for Barak was concern over public opinion, in other words, that the Israeli public would not accept a return of the Golan to Syria.[25] It may be argued that the public pressure on the Labor government against Oslo played a key role in weakening both Rabin and Barak's coalitions, to the point, perhaps, of limiting their perception of how far they might compromise in negotiations with the Palestinians. One might even go further and argue that that the right-wing NGO campaign against Oslo led to the 1995 assassination of Rabin, an act that many view as having spelled the end of the possibility of completing the Oslo process despite subsequent efforts. The assassination was not, however, the only reason for the continuing problems in reaching a peace agreement between Israelis and the Palestinians, nor could the assassination be interpreted as a major factor in changing policy, unless it could be demonstrated that subsequent leaders viewed the act as proof that the public would not accept similar attempts to seek a peace agreement in the future.

Following the 2005 disengagement, settler groups targeted right-wing as well as left-wing governments. Even under the far-right coalition of Netanyahu, the settlers were not able to change policy regarding a 10-month freeze of settlement construction beginning in 2009. Their efforts were not a total failure, however, inasmuch as the government allowed some construction to continue, particularly in East Jerusalem. Moreover, the settlers' subsequent campaign may be said to have had some impact on the government's decision to resist US pressure (and incentive offers) for an extension of the freeze in 2010. The decision itself was most likely dictated by coalition considerations, but the public campaign of the settler groups against the extension fueled the coalition divisions that ultimately led to the negative decision. Some might say that the public campaign provided Netanyahu with a justification – to the Americans – for rejecting the extension because it would lead to a collapse of his coalition.[26]

Since the government coalition at the time of this writing is composed of a right-wing and extreme right-wing parties, the work of right-wing advocacy NGOs is not so much in opposition on peace-related issues, because, rather, their work is designed to strengthen the ability of the government to withstand internal or external pressures to give up territory or limit settlement building, etc. Thus, groups such as Im Tirtzu (If You Will It),[27] NGO Watch, Media Watch, for example, target domestic criticism and critics, notably the peace and human rights NGOs but also the universities and other institutions. As noted above, the main contention is that such criticism strengthens Israel's enemies, harming Israel's efforts to defend itself. Given the government's orientation, this argument is well received by the government and Knesset, for the most part, prompting measures to restrain criticism and the activities of the peace and human rights NGOs, as noted at the beginning of this chapter. Perhaps the greatest success of the right-wing NGOs, however, lies not in their direct influence upon a government ideologically in tune with them, but, rather, their indirect but important impact on the public discourse and public opinion in Israel. Accusing the peace and human rights NGOs of disloyalty and linking them to what are portrayed as nefarious, foreign (even Arab) outsiders, not only serves the government's offensive against what it calls the "delegitimization campaign against Israel" abroad. It also diverts opinion away from the Israeli government's policies regarding the conflict, and it introduces (in juxtaposition) the issues of loyalty (to Zionism) into the public discourse on peace.

While these may be the effects of the efforts of the right-wing NGOs, their major purpose would appear to be to restrain if not eliminate the peace and human rights NGOs by means of legislation, intimidation, and public pressure. Why they seek to do this derives apparently from their belief and concern (from their point of view) that the latter have had the power to turn the Israeli public in favor of the two-state solution, in other words, away from the idea of "greater Israel," and even influence past Israeli governments to give up land, along with the power, today, to create international pressure that may force the government to adopt "capitulationist" policies. In contrast, the peace and human rights NGOs are far from viewing themselves as possessing such power, particularly in view of their dwindling numbers and weak showing in opinion polls and, indirectly, in recent Knesset elections. Indeed, there has been a general atmosphere of discouragement and even despair as well as powerlessness among most of these groups over the past few years, given not only the failure of the various peace processes that have been conducted but what they perceive as their – the NGOs – failure to change government action.

It may be, as this chapter has sought to demonstrate, that a more accurate appraisal of the impact of the peace and human rights NGOs lies somewhere in between that of the right-wing in Israel and that of the NGOs themselves. Small achievements notwithstanding, the most important accomplishment may well be what the right wing has indeed perceived – the impact of these groups on the public discourse and public opinion in Israel. Their contribution cannot be denied with regard to the enormous changes that have taken place in public opinion over the years, but also even in the positions of recent governments, including Likud governments. There has not just been acceptance. but actually advocacy, of the two-state solution, recognition that there is a Palestinian people and they have the right to a state, acceptance of the Green Line as the more or less logical border (used as the reference line in negotiations, as well as a guide for the Supreme Court), with the idea of land swaps accepted for border corrections. Settlements have been disbanded, and the future status of East Jerusalem, to accommodate a future Palestinian capital, has been placed on the negotiating table (prior to Netanyahu's government). There has been a steady change in the positions of Israeli governments, all in the overall direction of ending the occupation and achieving peace based on the two-state solution. That it is taking too long, that the goal has not been achieved, that the present government has stopped at the declarative stage and retreated on Jerusalem and other issues (proving that reversibility is possible), may all justify discouragement. But these negative signs – from the point of view of the peace and human rights NGOs – do not indicate total failure. And even if NGOs' contribution to all this cannot be clearly determined, one might wonder if any or all of these changes would have taken place had these groups not existed.

Notes

1 Civil society is defined as non-state groups, voluntary organizations but distinct from state, political, private (family), and economic spheres. See Thania Paffenholz, *Civil Society and Peace-building* (Boulder: Lynne Reinner Publishers, 2010), 43. I use NGOs generally in reference to civil-society groups.
2 E.g., Ronnie Milo, at the time, a member of Knesset.
3 Not all the human-rights groups can be called anti-occupation. Many merely deal with the abuse of rights caused by the occupation, among other issues, (e.g., the Association for Civil Rights), or limit themselves to humanitarian work without addressing the occupation as such (e.g., Machsom Watch).
4 Name withheld; Tel Aviv meeting January 2011.
5 Louis Kriesberg, "Nature, Dynamics, and Phases of Intractability," in Chester A. Crocker, Fen Osler Hampson, Pamela Aall (eds.), *Grasping the Nettle: Analyzing Cases of Intractable Conflict* (Washington DC: US Institute of Peace Press, 2003).
6 Tamar Hermann, *The Israeli Peace Movement* (Cambridge: Cambridge University Press, 2009), 243–244; Lev Luis Grinberg, *Politics and Violence in Israel/Palestine* (London: Routledge, 2010), 85–88.
7 An often referred to but not necessarily accurate statement attributed to former President Ezer Weizman referring to Begin. See, for example, Mordecai Bar, *Peace Now: A Portrait of a Movement*, (Tel Aviv: Kibbutz Meuchad Press, 1985; Hebrew), 31–32; Weizman himself says categorically that while he was "charmed" by Peace Now, no cabinet decision was influenced by its protests (*The Battle for Peace* [Toronto: Bantam Books, 1981], 306).
8 Sharon speech to the Knesset, 15 March 2004; his comments to William Safire, *New York Times*, 16 April 2004. See also Ehud Olmert with regard to Sharon's decision, *Yediot Ahranot*, 28 January 2011.
9 Michal Shamir and Jacob Shamir, *The Anatomy of Public Opinion* (Ann Arbor: University of Michigan Press, 2003), 187–194.
10 Truman Institute of the Hebrew University, *Israeli-Palestinian Surveys*, April 2010.
11 *Haaretz* (weekend magazine), 24 February 2012.
12 *Ha'aretz*, 21 June 2012.
13 De-mobbed soldiers and reservists reporting on abuses conducted by the army in the occupied territories. [This type of activity has actually been criticized by opponents to the occupation on the grounds that they are contributing to a "beautification" of the occupation (Amira Hass, *Haaretz*, 20 January 2012) or "making the occupation more convenient" (Yagil Levy, *Haaretz*, 11 January 2011).]
14 *Haaretz*, 11 January 2011.
15 The only appeal to the Court that resulted in actual prevention of the building of a settlement was the landmark case of Alon Moreh. The court rejected the government's claim of security reasons for the expropriation of private land. However, the settlement of Alon Moreh was subsequently built elsewhere in the West Bank.
16 *Ha'aretz*, 8 February 2012.

17 Har Homa, like many other settlements in East Jerusalem, is in fact located in the environs of East Jerusalem that were added to the municipality by Israel when it annexed East Jerusalem after the 1967 war.

18 There are many, many more groups than mentioned here, from the well-known Women in Black to the joint groups such as the Peace NGO Forum or IPCRI, bitterlemons.com or the more academic *Palestine-Israel Journal*, to name but a few.

19 Called creating a "culture of peace." See Oliver Ramsbotham, Tom Woodward, and Hugh Miall, *Contemporary Conflict Resolution* (London: Polity, 2011), 356–358. In the Israeli context, see, for example, Aviva Shemesh, "Citizen Diplomacy – Creating a Culture of Peace: The Israeli-Palestinian Case" (unpublished paper, 2012).

20 There have also been multinational groups with an Israeli counterpart, that have come and gone over the years, such as the International Center for Peace in the Middle East. The purpose of these, like the diaspora groups, has been to influence Israeli policy directly by means of appeals to or meetings with Israeli officials, but the main avenue of influence has often been indirect: lobbying and advocacy outside Israel.

21 Road Map, published April 2003; George W. Bush letter to Sharon, April 2004.

22 Academic institutions, think-tanks, policy institutes, such as the Norwegian FAFO, along with foundations in a number of countries are very involved in the same types of activities.

23 Beyond the scope of this paper, it would be interesting to examine the activities of peace and human rights NGOs and INGOs in Europe with regard to EU, particularly European Parliament decisions.

24 In his 1992 electoral campaign, Rabin used Peace Now's figures on the costs of the settlements.

25 On Rabin: Uri Saguy, *Lights Within the Fog* (Tel Aviv: Yedioth Ahronoth Books, 1998); on Barak: Uri Saguy, *The Frozen Hand* (Tel Aviv: Yedioth Ahronoth Books, 2011), 142; Bill Clinton, *My Life* (New York: Vintage, 2004), 886.

26 Right-wing protests provided Golda Meir's government with justification for a degree of inflexibility (or negotiating advantage) in the 1974 mediation efforts of Kissinger for the disengagement agreement with Syria.

27 A use of the slogan of the originator of the Zionist movement, Theodore Herzl.

3 Women's NGOs and the struggle for democracy in Morocco

Fatima Sadiqi

Introduction

The story of women's NGOs and the struggle for democracy in Morocco is an interesting one. The beginnings go back to 1946, when *The Sisters of Purity* association, the first ever women's NGO in Morocco, publically issued what they called *Al Wathiqa* (Document) in which they enclosed a set of demands including the abolition of polygamy, full and equal political rights, and increased visibility of women in the public sphere (Sadiqi et al 2009). These demands, legal and political in nature, have constituted the pool of subsequent women's NGOs' missions ever since, hence ensuring continuity in the overarching Moroccan feminist movement. Women's NGOs' gains have culminated in the recent institutionalization of gender equality in the June 17, 2011 new constitution. The nature of these demands makes them directly linked to the process of democratization that Morocco embarked on in the 1990s. As such, women's NGOs have had to negotiate power and strategize with both society and the decision-makers. They succeeded largely on these fronts. The result is that in spite of high percentages of women's illiteracy and poverty, Moroccan women's NGOs helped to propel both women and Morocco to the forefront of the Arab world. However, with recent Islamization of the region, women's NGOs fear the loss of the hard-won rights and struggle to maintain these rights.

The sections of this text tell the story of women's NGOs along six decades and the ways in which they struggled for democracy.

The period 1956 to the end of the twentieth century

The demands of the first Moroccan NGO were taken up by female journalists, academics, and civil society in the decades after Morocco gained independence from France in 1956. During this period, through journalistic and academic discourse, feminists started to question gender divisions, examine historical and ideological roots of gender inequality, and promote the recognition of women's labor. They depicted women's condition not as a "natural state," but as a state that stems from historical practices, and women's work, not as merely reproduction, but as production.

The women's movement was bitterly disappointed by the first Mudawana, or personal status code regulating all matters pertaining to family life, enacted in 1957. This legal text was based on the Maliki school of Islamic jurisprudence, whereas other laws, such as the penal code and the constitution, were based on civil law. Women obtained the right to vote in 1962 and the right to a free education under the constitution, but even female cabinet members and entrepreneurs were considered the dependents of their husbands or fathers and treated like minors under the law. The fundamental principle of marriage required a wife's obedience to her husband in exchange for financial maintenance, and the husband retained the power to abandon his wife without a judge's authorization. Not surprisingly, the Moroccan feminist movement focused its efforts on the Mudawana, which was seen as the prime locus of legal and civil discrimination against women.

From the 1980s onward, the feminist movement also had to contend with growing support for Islamism. The Islamists' ideology appealed particularly to young, unemployed males who were easily led to believe that women working outside the home robbed them of opportunities. In response, feminists also began to push for women's rights from a religious perspective. They implemented new strategies, including a gradual downplaying in their writings and practices of the "religious" role of the veil; increased use of Arabic and references to the Qur'an and Hadith (the Sayings of the Prophet Muhammad); a gradual inclusion of children's rights within women's issues; and reinforcement of Islam as culture and spirituality.

Moroccan women activists also endeavored to draw attention to the problems that women faced because of their lack of legal protection. They made excellent use of the media in depicting the misery of women and children who were victimized by divorce, thus reclaiming such social issues from the Islamists and reiterating the necessity of reforming the personal-status law. Nonetheless, a package of reforms the government proposed in 1999, including the abolition of polygamy, ultimately failed in the face of Islamist and conservative opposition. Despite this setback, feminist activists continued their campaign, increasingly concentrating on the "goals of Shari'a" rather than Shari'a itself. They also forged an alliance with King Mohamed VI, who took the throne that year and did not welcome increased control by Islamists.

The 21st century

When King Mohamed VI took power in July 1999, he had to deal with of three main issues, each of which constituting a social movement: the Amazigh (Berber) issue, the Islamist issue, and the women's issue. Only one month after he took power, the king said in his August 20, 1999, address:

> "How can society achieve progress, while women, who represent half the nation, see their rights violated and suffer as a result of injustice, violence, and marginalization, notwithstanding the dignity and justice granted them by our glorious religion?"

A series of high-profile female royal appointments followed this statement: in March 2000, for the first time in the country's history, the king appointed a female royal counselor; in August 2000, the king appointed a woman to head the National Office of Oil Research and Exploration; in September 2000, he confirmed the first-ever female ministerial appointment, and in October 2000, he appointed the first woman to head the National Office of Tourism. Similar appointments at political and religious posts followed in subsequent years.

In addition to the king's disposition to enhance women's position in the public sphere, the Socialist Party, led by Abderrahmane Youssoufi, set the ground in May 2002 for the democratization of the Parliament by approving a proposal, backed by the king, that sets aside 30 seats for the election of women in the national elections of September 2002.

These top-level political actions greatly boosted the work of women's NGOs in Morocco and forced their recognition as a genuine democratizing tool in the public sphere. Although feminist journalists and writers continued to focus their efforts on legal demands, NGO activists varied their domains of action and endeavored to reach more and more women, especially in the marginalized rural areas. By so doing, these activists succeeded in asserting that inequality and social relations are socially constructed, and that the law itself is a social construction that can be deconstructed and reconstructed based on equality. In light of these ideas, activists demanded a re-examination of the social, political, and economic structures, and an analysis of the judicial norms with respect to men-women relations in order to fight the ambivalence in men-women social relations. On other fronts, secular feminists reduplicated efforts to introduce gender as a powerful tool of analysis in various public institutions, including the country's ministries.

As for women's associations, they became more and more active, proving themselves more accessible to women than the institutional political parties because they do not require extensive material resources or influential connections. Two main types of women's associations may be discerned at the eve of the 21st century: the ones that focus on service provision by filling gaps left by the deficient state structures in terms of social and economic development, such as addressing concrete problems on the ground using available means, and the ones that focus on advocacy and lobbying with the aim of defending a vision of society where women's legal and civil rights are respected. Both types of women's associations kept a dialectical relationship with the broader civil society (human rights associations, youth organizations that involve women's issues, etc.). This advocacy and lobbying tightened the link between women's associations and other actors of civil society.

Overall, women's associative work started to assume political, social, and economic functions, hence strengthening institutional politics. Politically, local activism bridges the gap between women and the institutional political sphere, mainly through local activists' networks with more urban/political women's NGOs. Socially, the increasing proliferation of women's associations allowed women to assume more powerful social roles as leaders and managers of public affairs.

Economically, NGOs have allowed many women to acquire economic independence through self-generating incomes such as micro-credits.

On a more general level, women's associations started to become carriers of alternative projects of transformative gender roles in Moroccan society, and this protects and guarantees an effective exercise of public freedoms favoring the emergence of pluralist collective identity based on the universal values of the culture of citizenship, for bottom-up development and for empowerment (Kandiyoti 1991, Joseph 2000). Indeed, women's associations endeavored to promote participation, social mobilization, and associative lobbying that encourage good governance and a culture of responsible citizens, not passive subjects, thus working toward a dynamic participatory and equitable democracy (Moghadam 1995; Chadli 2001; Roque 2004). They have become real schools of democracy, which encourage women to get involved in decision-making in local public affairs and to empower women at all levels of governance. NGOs have enabled women to critically assess their own situation, create and shape a transformation of society.

Because of the social, economic, and political issues they persistently address, women's NGOs, and civil society in general, gradually became the raison d'être of the Moroccan political class, not only because of the disposition of the latter, as mentioned above, but also because of external pressure and pressure from political parties and other human rights NGOs. The government and political parties have realised the need to take account of these new areas of participation and mobilization. The challenge facing the women's NGOs is to elaborate autonomous strategies and establish themselves as forces for innovation, political pressure, and proposals, to push the state to revise its policies. The NGOs autonomy is a basis for genuine partnership with the state and for cooperation with political parties. For the time being, Morocco is perhaps a unique example in the Arab world – a country where the battle led by feminine NGO activists has begun to have a tangible impact on national human rights and development policies. Support for these movements remains essential, not just for Morocco, but also for the sake of social development throughout the region. Moroccan women's activism helps to promote awareness and knowledge of legal rights among women, to develop networks between women's NGOs and community-based groups, and to ensure a broader spectrum of participation in the public sphere.

Overall, the dialectic relationship between the monarch, political parties, the Parliament, and human rights NGOs, on the one hand, and the feminist movement, on the other hand, led to the promulgation of the new Family Law. In April 2001, the king formed a commission to study the possibility of revising the Mudawana, but the final push for reform came after May 2003 terrorist attacks in Casablanca stoked widespread antifundamentalist sentiment. The king announced a draft family law in Parliament in October 2003. During the next few months, women's rights organizations, organized within the Spring of Equality network, analyzed the details of the draft legislation and organized workshops, roundtables, and discussion groups to prepare for renewed lobbying efforts in Parliament and to educate the public about the reforms.

The final text was adopted in January 2004. It secured several important rights for women, including the right to self-guardianship, the right to divorce, and the right to child custody. It also placed new restrictions on polygamy, raised the legal age of marriage from 15 to 18, and made sexual harassment punishable by law. However, it did not completely abolish polygamy, unilateral repudiation of the wife by the husband, separation by compensation (*khula*), or discrimination in inheritance rules. This was in part because literal readings of the Qur'an explicitly authorize such provisions.

Whereas a flurry of ideological and political debates about women and their rights in Morocco characterized the 1998–2003 period, a calmer legal discussion over the gains and implementation of the new family law, the new labor code (promulgated in December 2003), and the revised nationality code (which took effect in April 2008) characterized the period extending from 2004 to 2009.

The implementation of the family law in particular varies from region to region, but it has generally been met with resistance. It is still very poorly understood in rural, and sometimes even urban, areas, and many male judges are reluctant to apply it. Moreover, the ongoing societal influences of patriarchy, tradition, illiteracy, and ignorance may prevent women from invoking their rights or reporting crimes such as rape, child abuse, sexual exploitation, and domestic violence. Existing efforts to overcome this societal resistance, such as education campaigns conducted in the mother tongues (Berber and Moroccan Arabic), have proven insufficient. Many feminists argue that the new family law can be adequately implemented only in a democratic context, while some advocate a purely secular government system. Another issue is that the law does not adequately address the problems of single women and the non-Moroccan wives of Moroccan men.

Nevertheless, Moroccan women have achieved considerable progress in consolidating legal equality and access to justice in the last five years, and the autonomy, security, and personal freedom of women has also improved. Women now have more freedom to travel, obtain employment and education, greater equality at home, and more leeway to negotiate their marriage rights. They are spearheading business ventures and advancing to higher levels of education. Important progress has also been made in protecting women from domestic violence, and support networks are getting stronger despite restrictive social norms. Women are increasingly taking up national and local political posts and becoming more involved with the judiciary. Most recently, a 12 percent quota for women was applied to the June 2009 local elections, substantially increasing female political representation.

Women's rights groups and individual activists have collaborated with the government to improve the rights of all women, but true equality remains a distant goal. While the recent legal reforms have allowed the government to promote a modern and democratic image of Morocco at the international level, bringing certain benefits to society at large, more needs to be done to translate these changes into tangible gains for individual women in their daily lives.

An assessment of women's NGOs and Moroccan women's gains

Moroccan women's rights have achieved the most significant gains at the level of law, and the last six years have been particularly rich in this regard. A revised nationality code passed in 2007 eased women's ability to pass citizenship to their children, the country lifted its reservations to CEDAW in 2008, and the Mudawana enacted in 2004 is now considered one of the most progressive legal texts in the Arab world. Thanks in part to the efforts of women's groups, particularly the Democratic Association of Moroccan Women, a new nationality code was passed in January 2007, thereby improving gender equality with respect to citizenship rights. Article 7 of the new law, which came into force in April 2008, enables women married to noncitizen men to pass their nationality to their children. However, the only children eligible for citizenship under this provision are those of a Moroccan woman and a Muslim noncitizen man who married in accordance with the Mudawana. In practical terms, the code excludes Moroccan women married to non-Muslim men and those married outside of the country and its laws. Furthermore, while foreign wives may receive Moroccan citizenship within five years of marriage to a Moroccan man,[1] the foreign husbands of Moroccan women remain altogether ineligible for Moroccan citizenship. Although imperfect, the amendments to the code provide significant benefits for children with Moroccan mothers and noncitizen fathers who were previously excluded from receiving the free education and health care available to citizens. These gains partly spared Morocco the deep upheavals of the recent Arab Spring. Indeed, the 2011 constitution institutionalizes gender equality.

However, the implementation of that law is still problematic, and little headway is being made despite the sustained efforts of both women's rights activists and the government. Of course, social and cultural constraints, as well as a certain reluctance to implement the laws fully, have yet to be overcome (Sadiqi 2010). Legal and societal barriers often obstruct women's access to the justice system, especially in rural areas. Although women enjoy equal testimony rights in most civil and criminal cases, the court gives their testimony half the weight of a man's testimony when it comes to family matters. In addition, many women are reluctant to defend their rights in court, particularly if male family members are responsible for the violations or if it is perceived that their legal action could damage their family reputation (Ennaji 2011). It is also customary for men to file court papers on behalf of women in rural areas, where illiteracy rates remain high. However, in some aspects, access to justice has improved in recent years. Family courts and the training of judges to staff these courts have served to create a friendlier environment for women. In addition, a fund has been established to guarantee payment of alimony and child support pursuant to an enforceable judgment.

On the other hand, autonomy, security, and freedom of the person are in principle guaranteed by law in Morocco, and much progress has been made in these domains over the last five years. In addition to the advances associated with the new family law, women have begun to serve as trained religious authorities, and the government is now tracking data on violence against women. However, social and cultural norms still prevent women from fully enjoying their legal rights or receiving adequate protection from domestic abuse.

Freedom of worship is guaranteed by Article 6 of the constitution. Although most Moroccans are Sunni Muslims, the country is also home to small Christian and Jewish communities. Christian and Jewish women are subject to separate family laws, though they are generally similar to the family law for Muslims. A Muslim's conversion to another religion is socially stigmatized but not illegal. Under Article 39 of the family law, Muslim women may not marry non-Muslims, while Muslim men may marry women of Christian or Jewish faith. The logic behind this policy is that children usually follow the religion of their father, and the government would like to encourage an increased Muslim population.

Women are allowed to pray in mosques, lead women-only prayers, and practice their religious rites freely. They have been steadily increasing their religious freedom in recent years. In May 2006, the first cohort of 50 female *Murchidat*, or Islamic guides, graduated from a government-backed program and were empowered to perform all of the same functions as male imams, except leading the Friday prayers. The program was part of the government's drive to promote a more tolerant version of Islam.

The 2004 reforms to the family law improved Muslim women's freedom of movement. Women now have the legal right to travel freely both domestically and abroad, but deeply ingrained social and cultural norms restricting women's ability to travel alone have hardly changed. In their implementation of the new family law, some judges tend to adhere to the traditional divisions between the male-dominated public space and the private space assigned to females.

Despite improvements, it remains difficult for women to negotiate their full and equal marriage rights. Article 19 of the 2004 family law fixes the minimum age for marriage at 18 for both men and women, in accordance with certain provisions of the Maliki school of Sunni jurisprudence. Women who have attained this age may contract their own marriages without the consent of their fathers. However, judges are empowered to waive the minimum age rule, and as a practical matter, they are very reluctant to uphold it. About 10 percent of marriages in Morocco involve underage girls, according to the Democratic League for the Rights of Women (LDDF), and such unions have increased in rural areas. The LDDF also warned against what it described as "too many exceptions" in the case of polygamy. The family law (Articles 40–46) allows polygamy only when it is approved by a judge, who must verify that the husband can provide equally for each wife and their respective children. Women have the right to forbid polygamy as a condition in their marriage contracts. Moreover, the first wife must give her consent for a second marriage, and the prospective new wife must be informed of the husband's marital status. In practice, however, a first wife who lacks financial independence may feel compelled to agree to polygamy.

On the economic level, since the mid-1970s, Moroccan women have increasingly worked outside their homes, thereby significantly raising the quality of life in Morocco and contributing to the economic transformation of the country. As of

2007, nearly 27 percent of women participated in the workforce, compared with participation rates in the single digits in the 1970s. However, a combination of patriarchy, illiteracy, and discrimination in the workplace preclude women from fully enjoying their economic rights. More than five years after the enactment of the 2003 Labor Code, men still have better employment opportunities, make more money, and hold higher-level positions than women hold.

Article 15 of the constitution guarantees the right of private property. Moroccan women have the right to own and make full and independent use of their land and property, and various articles of the 2004 family law protect women's property rights within marriage. Article 29, for example, safeguards a woman's control over her dowry, while Article 34 protects the possessions she brings with her into the marriage. Article 49 allows couples to draw up a document separate from the marriage contract to govern the management of property acquired during the marriage. Without such an agreement, contribution to the family property is evaluated by judges according to the paperwork provided by each one of the parties. However, by encouraging women's financial dependence on men, social norms restrict women's property rights in practice, and it is not common for women to own land. Similarly, women have full legal access to their own income, but it is often the case that male family members manage women's finances.

The 2004 family law made progressive changes to the rules of inheritance, although inequalities remain. As noted in the law's preamble, the children of a man's daughters, as well as those of his sons, may now inherit from him. Previously, only the grandchildren on the son's side were eligible for inheritance from their grandfather. However, women are still disadvantaged in a number of inheritance situations, with daughters typically receiving half the amount set aside for sons. Moreover, women, especially in rural areas, often give up their already unequal share of inheritance to male relatives.

The Moroccan commercial code was revised in 1995 to give a woman the right to enter into a contract of employment or initiate a business without her husband's authorization. While women are able to sign their own business contracts and obtain loans, high-level business contracts still usually go to men. In addition, social norms inhibit the interaction of male and female entrepreneurs, and women, especially in rural areas, face difficulty in securing loans because they often do not have bank accounts or assets in their names. Only about 1 percent of the total female workforce owns their own businesses, compared with 6 percent of the male workforce. A 2004 study by the Women Business Managers' Association of Morocco (AFEM) identified 2,283 companies that were run or managed by women.

The main cause of the vulnerability of working women is a lack of education. The combination of poor education and societal pressure to work in certain professions or industries has led most working women to take up low-paying jobs. For example, many women work in the textile industry (where they represent 71 percent of the workforce), the agricultural sector (which employed 61.4 percent of working women as of 2007), or as domestic servants. Morocco's failure to ratify the International Labor Organization's Convention 87 on freedom of association and collective bargaining has permitted a hostile environment for organized efforts to defend these workers' rights. The 2003 labor code does not apply to domestic and agricultural workers, meaning they do not have the right to form unions. Furthermore, social norms discourage women from working at night, and to the extent that trade unions are able to operate and secure better working conditions and benefits, women are often excluded because union activities take place at night.

On the political level, Moroccan women have come a long way in the field of politics. In the last decade, many women have been appointed as cabinet ministers, diplomats, and judges, and thanks to implementation of a quota system, the number of women in the 325-seat lower house of Parliament rose from two in 1997 to 34 after the 2007 elections. Another quota rule recently boosted women's representation in local government, as well. However, more than five decades after independence, women's participation in political life is still hampered by socio-cultural constraints, including the conservative notion that women's voices are *awrah* (not to be exposed in public, as with certain parts of the body). In addition, patriarchal and undemocratic structures within political parties tend to exclude women and youth, limiting their access to politics.

Morocco is a constitutional monarchy with a royally appointed government, a popularly elected lower house of Parliament (the Chamber of Representatives), and an indirectly elected upper house (the Chamber of Counselors). Women have had the right to vote and compete for office since 1956, but the character of their engagement has been heavily influenced by traditionalist and Islamist political trends. After their disillusionment with the 1957 family law, women's rights advocates generally aligned themselves with leftist parties. They later grew frustrated with the heavily patriarchal structure of political parties in general, choosing instead to organize within NGOs, first with connections to leftist parties and then as independent groups. Zouhour Chekkafi, elected to lead the Democratic Society Party in 2007, was the first woman to head a political party, but women today continue to participate more in NGOs than in political parties directly.

Despite recent successes, women in decision-making positions frequently face various social challenges. Although they are generally seen as less corrupt than men are, women leaders are forced to prove their credibility and accountability more than men do. Women who do succeed as leaders within politics and the government, however, provide strong role models and help to dispel negative stereotypes (Sadiqi 2010).

Grassroots women's rights NGOs have been steadily proliferating in recent years. Although their ideological backgrounds sometimes conflict, they tend to share the goal of promoting women's dignity in and outside the home, and have had a beneficial overall effect on Moroccan society. The government and women's rights NGOs have collaborated to increase women's involvement in local civic life. In March 2009, the government allocated 10 million dirhams (US$1.14 million) to boost women's political participation.

In the recent years, women have increasingly gained access to information with the aim of empowering themselves in different spheres of life. Various associations, such as Tadros in Fes and Rabat, are offering computer training and instruction on how to protect oneself on the internet. They are also helping rural women artists and carpet weavers to sell their products online. Moreover, women in academia have been particularly instrumental in disseminating democratic ideas through the university system. Most current civil society leaders are university professors, as well. Postgraduate programs in women's and gender studies are gaining some popularity, and the first cohorts of students have begun to receive advanced degrees in these areas.

Nevertheless, women generally, and rural women in particular, are frequently unaware of their political rights. There is a genuine communication problem in Morocco. Most literature regarding women's rights, political or otherwise, is written in Arabic and French, meaning it is inaccessible to large numbers of women. Some NGOs use Moroccan Arabic (Darija) and Berber in their outreach campaigns, but these efforts are insufficient, particularly in light of the high illiteracy rates among women.

The recent years constitute a turning point for women's rights activists and the feminist movement. Hard-won gains have been realized, but there is a clear need to reassess priorities for the future. The generational tensions that inevitably accompany a renewal of leadership present a major obstacle. The youth's opinions regarding women's rights are complex, ranging from outright support of the gains the older generations have achieved to a sense of skepticism. The feminist movement will have to address this ambivalence and improve its ties with young people.

Up to now, illiteracy, socioeconomic exclusion, fundamentalist ideologies, and the use of women's issues by the state to combat radicalization have been highlighted as the main challenges for the Moroccan feminist movement. However, urgent attention must be paid to educated, nonradicalized men and women who are politically savvy but cynical, and those who are university educated but unemployed. These groups are important because, while they readily adhere to human rights and social justice principles, they do not appreciate the relevance of gender equity within the larger project of democratization. Fewer still see the many links between poverty and gender discrimination.

The actually current developments linked to the Arab Spring are yet further evidence that Moroccan women's NGOs are pivotal in their struggle for struggle for democracy. Across ideological borders, secular and Islamic women's NGOs pushed and succeeded in institutionalizing gender equality by including it in the July 2011 new constitution, including more women and youth in the new parliament: the number of women in November 2011 new parliament is 67 (percent) and are now lobbying to have more women in the upcoming local elections.

Conclusions

The aim of this text is to underline the struggle of women's NGOs for democracy in Morocco. This relentless struggle has had difficulties, but it has succeeded in inscribing itself as a major actor in the overarching process of democratization that Morocco launched in the 1990s.

The central role of women's NGOs in democratizing the Moroccan political discourse has been achieved through constant critiquing of the government's decisions with respect to gender issues, dissemination of information through communication channels that the majority of women (often illiterate) understand, reaching to global feminist NGOs, etc. The value of NGO aspect of Moroccan women's struggle to democratize the public sphere and public discourse may be understood if compared to the hierarchical and heavily patriarchal structure of political parties where women's voices are hardly heard. The structure of NGOs and its positioning between the state and the people gives women more space to act. Thus, beyond their achievements, the NGO aspect of Moroccan women's struggle for democracy is a formidable tool.

Having started various reforms in the 1990s, Morocco is considered an exception in the Middle East and North Africa region. However, it has not escaped political Islamization, and though the country has been propelled to the forefront of the Arab-Muslim countries in what concerns women's legal rights, it is at this level that women's security is seriously threatened. A teenager, Amina Filali, took her life on March 10, 2012, at the age of 16 because she was obliged to marry her rapist; two other girls followed suit for the same reason. Amina Filali's death galvanized women's rights activists, who took to the streets asking for the repeal Article 475 of the penal code, which allows the rapist to marry his victim. This, in turn, ignited a nationwide debate that brought violence against women center stage.

Although the Morocco House of Councillors (the upper house of Parliament) approved the proposal to change Article 475 and deleted the statement "the kidnapper cannot be prosecuted if he marries his victim on the complaint of persons entitled to request the annulment of marriage and cannot be ordered until such annulment is pronounced," the government has recently proposed to revise Articles 20, 21, and 22 of the Family Code in order to set the minimum age for marriage at 16 years instead of 18.

This proposed amendment is in blunt contradiction to the Convention on the Rights of the Child that Morocco ratified. The danger of this proposal resides in the fact that it will allow guardians to use it to marry their girls even younger than 16. Statistics show that 12 percent of current marriages (more than 40,000 cases) were marriages of girls under 18 years old, although the current legislation stipulates that the legal age of marriage is 18 years. Changing the age of marriage for girls will have a serious negative impact on the modern and democratic society that Morocco is trying to build. Early marriage will have disastrous implications for the education of girls in a country where the majority of females (more than 60 percent) are illiterate.

Overall, Moroccan feminist NGOs know that a woman's security in present Morocco has a name: legal security. The Moroccan feminist movement has always prided itself on its legal achievements and its capacity to negotiate legal rights. Indeed, legal rights constitute the pool of the Moroccan feminist movement with its three heads: academe, activism, and politics. The regression in legal rights constitutes a serious blow to this movement. This regression is a genuine challenge to the promise of the new Islamist government to protect women's rights.

Note

1 See Article 10 of the nationality code, available (in French) at http://www.consulatdu maroc.ca/natma2007.pdf.

References

Chadli, El-Mostafa. 2001. *La société Civile ou la Quête de l'Association Citoyenne*. Publications Faculté des Lettres et des Sciences Humaines, Rabat.

Ennaji, Moha. 2011. "Gender-Based Discrimination in Morocco: Strategies to Fight Violence against Women," in *Gender and Violence in the Middle East* (edited by Moha Ennaji and Fatima Sadiqi). Routledge: London.

Joseph, Suad, ed. 2000. *Gender and Citizenship in the Middle East*. Syracuse: Syracuse University Press.

Kandiyoti, Deniz, ed. 1991. *Women, Islam and the State: Women in the Political Economy*. Philadelphia: Temple University Press.

Moghadam, Valentine. 1995. *Modernizing Women: Gender and Social Change in the Middle East*. Boulder, CO: Lynne Reinner Publishers.

Roque, Maria-Angels. 2004. *La Société Civile au Maroc*. Barcelona, Spain : IEMed Publications.

Sadiqi, Fatima et al., ed. 2009. *Women Writing Africa. The Northern Region*. The Feminist Press, New York.

Sadiqi, Fatima 2010. "Women and Stereotypes in Morocco," in *Women in the Middle East and North Africa. Agents of Change* (Edited by Fatima Sadiqi and Moha Ennaji). London: Routledge.

4 NGOs and women's rights in Tunisia

The case of ATFD[1]

Raoudha Kammoun

Introduction

Tunisia has long been known for having the most progressive policies on women, for being a secular nation-state and the standard-bearer for the emancipated woman in the MENA region (the Greater Middle East). The ground-breaking phase occurred in 1956 with the promulgation of the Code of Personal Status (CPS) in the aftermath of independence from French colonial rule. The legislative change eradicated most patriarchal prerogatives regarding family law. It expanded women's rights by reforming marriage and abolishing polygamy. It redefined divorce by elimination of the husband's unilateral right of repudiation, entitling both husband and wife equal rights and obligations within a judicial frame. It regulated custody and established the principle of alimony.

The newly born national state had a large building program for a modern state and faced no political challenger since the remaining tribes and the religious establishment had no voice in politics after the independence (Charrad 2007). Though the CPS represented a sharp reform, President Bourguiba had a large support from most factions, and reticent factions withheld their resentment, particularly when the whole population was celebrating the victory over the colonizer considering the initiator of women's rights as the nation's greatest savior.

Bourguiba, the father of the nation, western educated, took great delight in comparing himself to Jugurtha (King of Numidia c. 160–104 BC) and did not hold a very high opinion of the Arab and Muslim world. Unlike his economic and political strategies (where he believed firmly in *la politique des étapes*, the "step by step" policy, which functioned perfectly well with France), in gender matters, he did not proceed gradually, believing the whole package to be indivisible. He also felt the moment was particularly propitious, the timing perfect and the opportunity to be seized immediately.

In addition to his pro-Western stance, Bourguiba benefited from previous local women defenders, such as Tahar Haddad, a theology scholar educated at the Zaituna University in Tunis, and his controversial publication of *The Status of Women in Islamic Law and Society* in 1930. The book met with a storm of indignation and very violent reactions from his faculty peers, who labeled him a heretic and, without reading his book, considered it an outrageous attack against Islam. They published back *Mourning over Haddad's Wife,* which led him to self-imposed exile. Haddad drew upon Islamic principles to develop an argument for the liberation of woman and insisted that in emancipating women, they would contribute to the stability of the family and the education of future generations by being better mothers and wives (*Ibid,* 2001). Haddad's work produced considerable debate, proved to have an enormous impact on the advancement of Tunisian women and to be incredibly significant over the later feminist discourse.

The participation and activism of several women in the social and political arena not only initiated Bourguiba's position, but also prepared, more or less willingly, the whole society for a radical change regarding family law. Bchira Ben Mrad used the banner of nationalism, religion and good manners, more acceptable arguments to resist gender discrimination, and oppressive customs and laws, and founded "the Muslim Women's Union of Tunisia" in 1936.[2] Tawhida Ben Cheikh,[3] first woman doctor in Tunisia in 1934, who studied medicine in Paris, argued "elections are not a matter of science, but of awareness-taking" (Marzouki 1993: 165). In 1924, while delivering a speech on "Muslim Women of the Future-For or Against the Veil," Habiba Menchari, while removing her own veil, urged the women to drop the veil,[4] causing a great stir among the male audience. A few years later, she asked for the liberation of women and the abolition of polygamy.

It is worth noting that all women activists in this pre-independence period preferred to align themselves first to the nationalist cause, putting aside the feminist agenda and, most particularly, the *hijab* issue. This issue featured predominantly in the struggle for independence (by both women and men) and some women wore it deliberately as an identity marker (Tchaicha and Arfaoui 2012). Women's demands were always pushed aside, allegedly to address more urgent and serious issues first.[5] During the next 50 years, it was either the democratic process, which, though in a totally stagnating state, was nonetheless considered a more urgent priority than women's issues. The Palestinian-Israeli conflict was considered a top-priority issue, presented as the most irrefutable and intimidating argument by politics ready to topple not only the comparatively 'trivial' question of women's rights but also the issue of the struggle for democracy.

State feminism: CPS of 1956

The nationalist rhetoric prevented the then still soft feminist movement from being vocal until the independence and, quite unexpectedly, no feminist movement or any form of social contestation had called for reforms of Tunisian family law now that the country was free. Gilman argues that "although women's organizations may have existed prior to independence, Tunisian women played no role in the promulgation of the family law legislation that ultimately propelled them, rather ironically, into the spotlight as symbols of the 'emancipated' Arab woman." (Gilman 2007: 97) Bourguiba believed he had to nurse and foster Tunisian women, who were his responsibility. In fact, considering himself the father of the nation, he felt responsible for all Tunisian people, but most particularly for women, toward whom he felt great sentimental affection, calling himself the father of Tunisian women's liberation. He often attributed his feminist side to his deep love for his mother, who died when he was six and who suffered under bad living conditions while raising her children.

Granting women more rights was not a victory of feminism. According to Charrad (2007: 1518), "The CPS was part and parcel of a larger state building program that aimed at developing a modern centralized state and marginalizing tribal or kin-based communities in local areas. . . The political groups that could have spoken for a conservative interpretation of Islamic law and blocked the reforms had lost all political leverage at that particular time." Bourguiba is personally credited with the radical reform brought to family law and the advancement of women's status, which led numerous Tunisian men to believe that Tunisian women did not struggle or fight for their gains and rights, that they received their freedom and rights on a 'tray.' In other words, the men believed women had been waited on, hand and foot, regarding their freedom and their progressive status, which was effortlessly brought to them. According to many, this is the reason why the gap between their legal status and progressive rights and their effective implementation in the process of everyday life remained so wide, particularly when applied to the patriarchal family structure and society as a whole, and also when facing gender-biased mentalities.[6]

Undeniably, Bourguiba had a soft spot for women in general. When greeting them, he often patted them on the cheek in a paternalistic way (a gesture he never shared with men). Yet the reform he planned was not fuelled by feminist and gender equality motives, it was rather prompted by a nationalist agenda, because he wanted women to fully participate in the construction of the new independent sovereign nation state and not be an impediment. He believed both men and women were equally needed to build a modern Tunisia. Under his rule, the only legal women's association was the state-affiliated National Union of Tunisian Women (UNFT). Women activists who fought for the independence and supported Bourguiba during his difficult years became active members of the UNFT. Radhia Haddad, chairwoman of the UNFT, declared that the members, and particularly the women, with leadership positions belonging to any other party but the *Neo-Destour*, Bourguiba's political party, could not be accepted (Marzouki 1993: 166–167).

The members of this union totally depended on the president, and became known as 'Bourguiba's organization,'[7] in as much as it was heaving with the president's relatives (Arfaoui 2007). It had no autonomy and was progovernmental, embodying Bourguiba's stance on women in civil society. Its activities ranged from welfare and mobilization to birth control. Sarah Gilman (2007) asserts that the UNFT secured state control of formal women's organization and maintained monolithic state feminism until the 1970s.

The CPS, oft-amended, certainly offered pioneering legislation, giving further protection to women with legal rights, but their status, nonetheless, remained inferior and maintained gender inequality in inheritance, giving a woman half a man's share; in guardianship, with greater rights to husbands; and, above all, required women's obedience to the husband.[8] These 'woman friendly' reforms were revolutionary in the Arab world in the 1950s. With the massive education programs and the compulsory schooling for boys and girls from all regions of the country and all social backgrounds, some awareness arose to object to the short-comings of the CPS via women's voices and movements, which emerged and developed in the late 1970s (Charrad 2007).

A cultural club, which bore the name of Club Tahar Haddad, named after the aforementioned Tunisian scholar who asked for the emancipation of women in the 1930s, was created in 1978 and gathered students in the beginning. However, with the establishment of a charter that included objectives such as the support of women to actively participate in socioeconomic life and to empower them by fighting against gender-biased stereotypes and social practices, it grew into a forum where lawyers, artists, journalists, and women academics joined to meet regularly for discussions and hot debates.

The club's activities were crucial to the development of feminist and autono-mous movements and associations, which became officially legal in 1989 (ATFD and AFTURD).[9] These associations grew very actively, "called themselves 'the daughters of Tahar Haddad' and developed a sense of solidarity" (*Ibid*: 1525). An informal network of women called themselves NISSA (Women) and published a monthly, independent, and bilingual magazine of the same name in 1985. It tackled important women's issues, such as women's discrimination, female self-empowerment, and the necessity to eliminate the concept of victimization, trade-union and women's affiliation, and particularly, the defense of the CPS from any backlash against women's rights. This magazine, which gained popularity on the media scene, disappeared in 1987 due to the absence of professional writing and journalism, the informal work conditions and the lack of efficiency in organiza-tion and management, the lack of cohesion among its members, and the attempt to respect the rules of democracy by allowing all members absolute freedom in the choice of subject, writing, and expression, regardless of their differences and divergence of their political orientations (Zoughlami 1989). All these weaknesses persisted and prevailed in the future work, projects, and also activities of the ATFD (The Tunisian Association of Women Democrats) which, one week before Tunisian Women's Day, became legal in August 1989, two years after Bourguiba, the 'president for life' was deposed by his then–prime minister and successor, Ben Ali, in 1987.

The Ben Ali period: Repression and persecution

The first signs of democratic openness initiated by Ben Ali were soon to wane, and tight state control and hegemony were applied to all civil society movements and autonomous associations. The new regime clearly and largely was based on corporatist-bureaucratic agreements. Taking advantage of the vulnerability and the unstable socio-political situation in the aftermath of Bourguiba's deposition, many voices were raised in protest against the CPS considering the document not sacred. Twenty-three years later, after the fall of Ben Ali and in the midst of a social turmoil and political unrest, the same reaction is repeated again today, only with more fervent vehemence since a new constitution is to be written within a Muslim majority at the Constituent Assembly. This unstable atmosphere awoke all the dormant male-domineering reflexes that called for the establishment of the *Sharia*, invoking the same argument as in 1988, in other words, the Arab-Muslim identity, while referring implicitly to the CPS.[10] Hence, insinuating the hotly debated and seemingly obsessional issue of polygamy and its rehabilitation which, not so amazingly, the first thing some males from different social categories and lifestyles claimed after the uprising. After weeks of huge and increasingly polarized social tension, the Islamist majority party chairman Rached Ghannouchi unemotionally declared on March 27, 2012, that the Islamic *Sharia* law would not be enshrined within the new constitution.[11]

In 1988, Ben Ali had decided to follow Bourguiba's commitment and principles in maintaining the CPS, and created in 1992 a state cabinet for Women and the Family. In 1993, he founded the Ministry of Women, Family and Children's Affairs, to which even the affairs of the elderly were later added; in other words, all the vulnerable communities were lumped together, with the woman in charge of the rest, her time divided between taking care of and looking after the family, the children, and the elderly, hence enhancing the patriarchal nature of the Arab and Muslim society.

The state feminism was largely maintained and reinforced under Ben Ali's reign, making women's rights the major theme of his policy. With the exception of the ATFD and the AFTURD (*L'Assocation de la femme Tunisienne pour la recherche et le développement* / The Association of Tunisian Women for Development and Research), the only autonomous women's associations, the Ministry of Women coordinated the activities of various government institutions, such as the UNFT, the Women and Development Committee, and the National Council of Women and Family, founded in 1992 and reinforced in 1997 with the creation of three commissions – the Commission on the Image of Women in the Media, the Commission on the Promotion of Equal Opportunities for All and for the Application of the Law, and the Commission of National and International Deadlines Pertaining to Women and the Family. The CREDIF (*Le Centre de recherches, d'études, de documentation et d'information sur la femme* / Center for Studies, Research, Documentation, and Information for Women),[12] "the respected Women's Research Institute" (Moghadam 2004: 49), which operates under the Ministry of Women's Affairs, as well as the National Commission on Working Women, set up in 1991 as part of the state-controlled The Tunisian General Federation of Workers (UGTT), carried out surveys and studies pertaining to women and the workplace. Yet, not one woman has been elected in the UGTT elections and its 27 branches throughout Tunisia since 1946 – and, more surprisingly, in the recent December elections – for the executive committee members, though several women candidates were confident and firmly believed more than one would be elected, particularly after the January uprising and the support of the UGTT for the gender-parity law. Some sociopolitical analysts simply declared, with no further insightful analysis, the fatalist and presumably convincing deduction that, traditionally, unionists are sexist and any different result would have been a total surprise and a profound change in their mindset.

Women's associations were particularly active in the 1990s. They created "a climate in which women's rights and women's issues were prominent" (Charrad 2007), which led to the 1993 reforms making mothers a source of *jus sanguinis*.[13] Conversely, Moghadam (2004) believes that Tunisian feminists and women's NGOs have been somewhat more successful than women activists elsewhere in working with government agencies, calling this "critical realism." She recognizes that in neo-patriarchal societies, women activists are aware that the authoritarian state reinforces their subordinate status and "limits the political participation of citizens, including women's rights activists" (49–50), which causes a great deal of tension and creates a serious dilemma between their constant yearning for independence and autonomy and the necessary and unavoidable negotiation with the state to implement the signed conventions to improve women's status.

The ATFD encountered several difficulties during Ben Ali's regime, unlike other NGOs. Generally called *Les Femmes Démocrates*, there is some consensus that they were the principal feminist organization of the Tunisian women's movement. Their field of advocacy included women's issues, as well as democracy, human rights, and dignity. The ATFD activists had to work and carry out their programs in an atmosphere of concentrated power overwhelmed with state-sponsored and party-affiliated associations. Their mission proved particularly difficult as they combined an agenda for improving women's condition in a democratic state where human rights are fully respected. The objectives of the association aim at eliminating all forms of gender discrimination, defending the CPS to reach total gender equality, transforming the patriarchal mindset, enhancing women's empowerment and their participation in social and political life, and finally, recognizing women's full citizenship. These objectives would have certainly pleased the regime had the ATFD restricted its activities to women's conditions and their empowerment. But, what the ruling power considered inacceptable was the interference of the *Femmes Démocrates* in the governance as well as the governmental decisions, based on the AFTD's inalienable principles, mentioned in their chart, which proclaim that women's rights are part and parcel of human rights. This entails, above all, the struggle against all forms of discrimination, but also the inevitable struggle for real democracy in both public and private spheres. They proclaimed out loud, much to the government's dismay, that the cause of women and the cause of democracy are inseparable, which infuriated the regime. The interference of the association activities in the regime's policy was not tolerated and was considered a serious encroachment on the general rules of NGOs. Ben Ali's government and institutions sent several warnings ordering the ATFD to restrict its activities to women's issues and to immediately stop releasing bulletins and reports, as well as publishing articles and interviews in foreign papers condemning the politics and decisions of the regime, which not only tainted the country's image overseas but seriously questioned their independence and required political neutrality demanded from a lucky license-granted feminist NGO. The standoff was continuous, and the final warning issued was that women activists could not possibly reach both objectives. They had to make a choice; it was either women's rights or democracy, and if they insisted on carrying on acting as political activists alongside their feminist advocacy, they would be considered hostile opponents and be subject to the same treatment inflicted to the illegal opposition.

Contrary to Ben Ali regime's wishes, the association's activities varied increasingly. Its advocates invested great efforts in combating gender-based violence[14] and even if they started without any strategy and faced difficulties in handling the issue, they appointed a person to assist the women victims of violence. Before the great inflow of women seeking help, they created a center in Tunis (*Centre d'Ecoute et d'Orientation des Femmes Victimes de Violence*) in 1993 for counseling and legal assistance. In 2000, a campaign was launched against sexual harassment of women in schools and the workplace in order to shatter the silence over this problem and motivate women to face and denounce it. On March 8, 2004, a bill was presented to parliament. A law criminalizing sexual harassment was passed, but with a very limited definition of sexual harassment and also with a provision that if a woman failed to provide proof of the aggression, she could be sued by her aggressor (ATFD 2008: 75).

The clash with the deciders was based on a divergence on the principles and the goals. The Ben Ali government upheld and maintained Bourguiba's commitment to the CPS and state feminism with the deliberate absence of women's involvement and participation in the promulgation or betterment in family law. By imposing autonomy, women's organizations that chose this mode of activism paid too high a price and their ability to effect change in the status of women was not significant. Ben Ali had no interest in developing women's rights and gains, and during his rule, very little was achieved to further advance the social, political, or economic status of women. It was news to no one that women's emancipation in Tunisia had been achieved more in theory than in practice, but nonetheless, "has always represented a source of pride which the government constantly highlighted nationally and internationally, even when it is used to short-circuit embarrassing questions (generally related to democracy and human rights) or to combat religious extremism. Women's rights and female success are manipulated to hide shortcomings which, with unceasing media overkill, became part of everyday speech, 'deadwood' discourse, or what is commonly called in Tunisia as 'langue de bois'" (Kammoun 2010: 202). While women's NGOs were fighting for gender equal chances and equal pay, the government cynically insisted that Tunisian women had gone past the equality phase and had pioneered the revolutionary stage of women's partnership, a slogan that was massively taken up by the media, intended to make everybody believe in the concept of Ben Ali's era of 'Excellence.'

The government kept on widely spreading the postulation that Tunisian women were enviable, their condition unequalled, their rights inviolable, and that there was no need for women's organizations to protect the women because their conditions or rights were all safeguarded in the CPS. In total disagreement with the ATFD on their causes and solutions, the government denied the existence of gender-based violence, rape, sexual harassment, incest, and pedophilia, claiming these plagues could not exist in a Muslim country (unlike in the depraved and the debauched West), let alone in a modern country like Tunisia, with such an avant-guardist women's status. The government insisted that all the indicated cases were isolated, reckoned as miscellaneous short news items or '*faits divers*' and reported only among the lower classes, which would naturally be solved once the problem of poverty had been eradicated. Therefore, these rare cases should resolutely not be considered serious or urgent enough to make studies or conduct any surveys, especially after all the unceasing and laudable efforts made to beautify and protect the immaculate image of Tunisia abroad and particularly across the West (ATFD 2008: 109–111). The Ministry of Social Affairs, however, never refrained from transferring, shrouded in the greatest secrecy, embarrassing cases of single mothers, incest, procuring, or pedophilia to the care of the ATFD on the basis that they had more experience in handling such social cases.

The organization also highlighted politically incorrect issues such as the removal of the CEDAW (Committee on the Elimination of Discrimination against Women) reservations and the gender equality in inheritance through the publication of several books and booklets and the organization of conferences, round-tables, seminars, and training courses. Criticism came from official sources, which blamed the women activists for being gluttonous hardliners, and also from the unofficial ones, which blamed them for mixing up feminism and democracy, accusing them of 'political shift,' 'overpoliticization,' and 'over-valorization' of the political over the feminine cause (*Ibid*: 26). In view of their unrelenting determination to achieve their goals, harsher official pressure and harassment, executed by Ben Ali's secret police, followed through blocking meetings and instructing hotels not to rent space to ATFD for public events, deploying routine sentinels in front of their headquarters, preventing the women activists from accessing their offices occasionally, and beating them when they showed resentment. Their telephones and/or internet connections were very often cut off, and funds from overseas sponsors blocked (Arfaoui 2011). Several initiatives undertaken by the *Femmes Démocrates*, for instance, providing a needy woman with a volunteer lawyer,[15] a social worker, psycho-analyst, or doctor, or sending immediately needed help to women hundreds of kilometers away infuriated Ben Ali, who felt these women were parading and acting ostentatiously replacing the government in order to show and prove its incompetence and inefficiency. To further silence the ATFD activists, the regime prohibited any access to the media for them, which were under its authority. Untamable, the women activists denounced the government's insidious practices of marginalizing and oppressing the organization, while offloading some of its responsibilities to its members (ATFD: 112).

It is undeniable that the fact of having no access to the media restricted and reduced the AFTD activities tremendously and left them with no communication strategies, but many other factors also contributed. The organization decided from the start it was an elitist one and would not be open to the public. Its rhetoric and literature were aimed at the elite and educated women, and therefore, a very limited number of women and men were aware of the organization's activities, generally limited to the capital since there were no representations in the other cities or in rural areas. For many years, the same persons and the same team ran the association in a rather archaic mode of management where some activists from the older generation unwilling to bring any technological change or more efficient innovations were maintained even after their retirement, grounding their motives on gratitude to long careers, loyal services, as well as respect of their age.

On the other hand, there were, and still are, many divergences among the organization's members regarding several issues, such as the male participation in the activist agenda or the hot issue of the veil. Veiled women were not accepted in the association, and in order not to create any clash or crisis, those who were in favor preferred to align with the hardliners. However, the position of the latter seems to have changed toward more flexibility, especially after the January uprising. The association's broad outline has been resolutely secular and liberal, and some hard core advocates would not make any concession which created a disagreement among the members as in the case of the Islamists' wives when they were brought before the court in the mid-1990s and were in need for more feminist support.[16] Furthermore, some members consider the association's political approach somewhat harsh and advise to bring more focus on the feminist struggle. All members were, and are, aware of these weaknesses and drawbacks, but have kept the status quo in the absence of any consensus.[17]

The January uprising: A wintery spring for Tunisian women

Unable to quell the insurrection against his regime, Ben Ali fled the country on January 14, leaving the population in a state of euphoria and excitement. Men and women took to the streets, calling for work, freedom, and dignity. Soon the situation became uncontrollable and insecurity reigned, urging the people to organize neighborhood watches. At the grassroots levels, women's contribution was very significant in combating food shortage and providing assistance for neighbors, demonstrators, and spotters.

The women participation in the uprising and the images of women on men's shoulders that traveled the world over were soon swept aside. An enormous movement involving the different media, the civil society, and the political parties – yet with a very low participation of women – reorganized the new political and social context of the Tunisian people. During the LTDH (Tunisian League for Human Rights) election in September 2011, an old ATFD partner, 5 women out of 25 members were elected, which was strangely considered by its head members as a slate with high female participation. The social participation of women went in decrescendo, and their absence went almost unnoticed had it not been for the ATFD and some new-born women's organization reports, which tried relentlessly to remind the media and the political activists of the women's participation in the uprising and to counteract this current by participating in TV panels and taking part in meetings. It is interesting to note that among the slogans heard and the banners raised by the protesters, no reference was made to gender equality or rights. There was also no sign of religious slogans or radical groups among the demonstrators. The Islamists played no role in the uprising; they were invisible, but this did not constitute, to them, any lack or absence of legitimacy. On the contrary, they invaded the public space in the aftermath, ostentatiously, in an attempt to test the reaction of the people, bragging about their years in jail, considered henceforth as the sole requisite for legitimacy and eligibility at all levels. The motives of the uprising have been sidelined, and the core of the issue has become the Arab and Muslim identity, providing a cover for gender issues.

Not unexpectedly, the first and major question raised was not unemployment, poverty, or freedom, it was women's issues, which resulted in unending and impassioned heated discussions, questioning the entirety of the CPS in an undermining and ironic way and according to many, it was not *Quran*, and was therefore liable to change or suppression. Tunisia all of a sudden had no other problems or deficits except the condition of Tunisian women. This new picture took most women by surprise, which led to the founding of many new feminist associations. The association *Egalité et Parité* (Equality and Parity), which grew out of a Facebook page, accepted both men's and women's memberships, had a significant impact on the electoral process and made one of its main objectives the gender parity law, which was enacted in the electoral code. Another grassroots women's association that was founded shortly after the uprising, *La Ligue des Electrices Tunisiennes* (The League of Tunisian Women Voters), chose to contribute to the democratic transition by mainly focusing on women's participation in the election as voters, candidates, and election observers.

Alongside these young associations, *The Femmes Démocrates* benefited for the first time from the impact of the media, which did not always have positive repercussions. They organized several national and international seminars and invited members of the interim government, pointing out the threats jeopardizing women's gains, as well as Tunisia's modernist way of life; a great number of women have started to wear the veil, and later the *niqab,* not fearing Ben Ali's state police any longer. There were reports of women harassed or insulted in the street by Islamists, who ordered them to wear the veil and dress properly, in other words, according to *Sharia* tenets. All this was encouraged by the bill adopted by the Minister of the Interior, which grants women the right to wear the veil on ID cards, as well as the general amnesty law promulgated on March 2011 about opinion and political prisoners, hence releasing, in a revolutionary élan and without distinction, thousands of *Salafis* (radical Islamists), who quickly reorganized and restructured themselves. Regularly, the AFTD issues reports and bulletins to express its refusal and condemnation of the practices contrary to the principles of freedom of dress, opinion, and belief. As to the events of the University of Manouba and the *niqab* issue, the organization created an "emergency unit" to receive statements of women who suffered assaults and offer them support and solidarity. It also issues communiqués to condemn firmly all the ignominious acts inflicted on the premises of the General Union of Tunisian Workers (UGTT). On March 8, 2012, a conference held around the crucial subject of the 'constitutionalization' of women's rights released recommendations about the drafting of the constitution, insisting Tunisia was at a turning point and hammering the unequivocal demand of the 'constitutionalization' of gender equality, which must become a fundamental nonnegotiable principle not subject to revision. The senior members of the Islamist majority party (*Nahdha*), who ascribed themselves as moderate Islamists, as well as their chief have from the very beginning reassured the women, as well as their Western partners, that they were going to opt for a civil state and that the CPS was not going to be altered, but 'improved.' All the feminist activists, old and young, from various organizations are very cautious about the double talk of the *Nahdha* members, who regularly flirt with the *Salafis* and give contradictory speeches insinuating, when addressing their party members, that their ultimate goal is an Islamist regime with the full implementation of the *Sharia* and that it all needs a soft and gradual psychological and social preparation and training over time of the secularized Tunisian society.

Some Islamist women's associations have also been founded particularly since the *Nahdha* took over in October 2011 (as a majority party in a tri-partite coalition). The old state-affiliated UNFT has been infused by the Islamist female members from the *Nahdha* party. A new women's association '*Tunissiyet*' (Tunisian Women) recently founded, aims at defending the Arab Muslim identity, enhancing the condition of women, particularly the veiled ones, and protecting them against all forms of discrimination.

Since the uprising, the press, the public and private television channels have begun to cover the ATFD activities and many of their members have become known to the public, which was not always in accordance with the conservative mounting movement. A violent smear campaign has been launched ever since, particularly against the *Femmes Démocrates,* reaching all the media and social networks. They have been called all the names imaginable, ranging from whores and prostitutes to 'loose drunkard atheists,' and Bourguiba's and France's orphans. Some fierce ATFD critics spread the rumors that their so-called feminist program and objectives encourage, besides equality in inheritance rights (which has become an act of blasphemy and heresy since the Islamists took power), premarital sex, homosexuality, and calls for the legalization of gay and lesbian marriage, which caused huge waves of social indignation. Notes and bulletins denouncing these smear campaigns are regularly issued by all the women's NGOs, condemning the violation of basic human rights as well as women's rights, insisting that these slandering and vilifying acts toward women's rights activists will only serve to reinforce the feminist NGOs' determination to struggle for more gains in a true democratic state within a progressive and woman-friendly society project and vision.

Women's rights at risk

When the Constituent Assembly unveiled a draft constitution in August 2012, referring to women as "complementary to men" instead of "equal to" as the 1956 constitution stipulates, women's reactions diverged. The *Nahdha* MPs refuted gender equality and argued women were not equal to men but are "complementary," adding that "complementarity" encompasses equality. The liberal and democratic MPs disagreed and insisted to include the rights of women, their full equality to men and universal rights in the constitution, which was rejected by both Islamist genders, who argued that drawing on the Universal Declaration of Human Rights and using it as the main reference insinuated it was superior to the Qu'ran, which they considered the supreme and highest source of law.[18]

Moreover, women's rights associations, activists, and supporters reacted in mass protest, took to the streets (as this has become a regular form of protest), calling it a setback from the earlier constitution, which was considered progressive relative to others in the region and with regards to women's rights. The *Femmes Démocrates,* suspecting the Assembly of deliberately excluding them from the process of drafting the Constitution while numerous organizations had attended several assembly meetings to present their views, complained vigorously and required to be among other women associations to express their demands. They finally met with the president of the Republic and the CA chair to sensitize them on gender inequality and to invite them to 'constitutionalize' women's rights. The ATFD members finally succeeded in removing the 'complementarity' issue from the draft and obtained the solemn commitment from *Nahdha* leaders that the final document would unambiguously endorse gender equality and universal rights.[19]

Besides the *Sharia* issue as the only source of law, other issues divided the women's opinion at the CA.[20] A *Nahdha* MP claimed that "single mothers were a disgrace to Tunisian society, do not have the right to exist and should not benefit from state protection".[21] Her comment clearly divided the population. Secular women expressed deep shock and outrage and took to the street, which made the Islamist MP reconsider her position, denying the allegations and arguing she was deliberately misunderstood and her comment extracted from its original context.[22] In the same line, giving the patronymic name to abandoned children or those of unknown parentage, though supported by the law,[23] was rejected by the *Nahdha* women in the name of Islam and caused an enormous public outcry.

Other issues, such as the *niqab* or rape, provoked national polemics and fiery debates. Wearing the *niqab* (full-face veil) in class and during exams has become highly controversial (the *niqab* issue) causing a university dean to appear in court.[24] Furthermore, Islamist MPs expressed their full support to the children educators in kindergartens who wear the *niqab* and considered its ban grounded on child psychology a form of discrimination and exclusion. This contentious issue was objected to by the Liberal Democrat MPs and the *Femmes Démocrates,* who were accused of partisanship for refusing to defend the Islamist Women in court under Ben Ali's rule only because they wore the veil.

The 27-year-old woman who was reportedly raped by two policemen in October 2012 was subsequently charged with "outraging public decency." This issue raised very hot debates, particularly the gender-based violence question. As a reaction, the ATFD announced a campaign to fight sexual violence against women in Tunisia and organized a conference entitled "Put an End to Sexual Assaults against Women." The ATFD chair declared "the recent rape case exemplifies the sexual violence experienced by women in Tunisia; the victim has become the accused. She had to go to five police stations in order to report her rape and three hospitals to get a medical examination. This shows the amount of difficulties women who experience sexual assault face in order to report their incident. Women give up eventually." She also stressed the importance of 'constitutionalizing' women's rights in order to fight gender-based violence insisting "medical, security, and judicial institutions should have a strategy to facilitate procedures for women who report their cases."[25]

Conclusion

There is a general impression today that many dangers are still threatening Tunisian women's status. Most women feel they must remain vigilant and not drop their guard because the situation is critical, despite the repeated reassuring promises of the Islamist party. There is also a lack of awareness of the high importance of maintaining women's status among the younger generation, and especially the young women. This is even more the case since most of them never heard of the CPS and believe that the risk of any regression of their rights and privileges could not occur to them. Numerous feminists and activists express many regrets today; they realize their work was not transmitted down to the younger generations and there have been no writings or literature on the Tunisian feminist movement, perspectives, and strategies. Many questions on women's issues were not raised, such as the religious one and the place of women in the Qu'ran, which was always avoided in the name of secularism, and consequently, the Tunisian feminists have no answer to offer, today, to the younger generation that is asking, among other questions, about the position of feminism regarding the Muslim woman. Tchaicha and Arfaoui (2012) point out the absence of dialogue between the different generations and the privileging of the autonomous organizations of topics required by funders and sponsors. Other critics believe feminine NGOs and mainly the ATFD imported the issues and locally debated them in order to keep up with the gender issues mainstream, neglecting the specificity of the Tunisian feminist movement. The ATFD has always refused to address the theme of cultural specificities, arguing that this was the regime's excuse to overlook their democratic demands.

What seems urgent according to Bochra Belhaj Hmida, one of the most prominent figures of the ATFD, is not whether the *Femmes Démocrates* are accountable today, but rather the necessity to unify all Tunisian women. The situation is transitional, the work conditions different, and the atmosphere of democracy and freedom of expression must be taken advantage of in order to establish a different relationship with the state. Several meetings have been held with the president of the Republic and the chair of the CA, both secular, but not with the Islamist head of state who, in all likelihood, would seek to establish a good relationship with the ATFD, at least for the time being, if only to prove that he stands out from the politics of Ben Ali. In addition to that, he would also want to show the West his progressive vision, because he has often reiterated in his speeches that he is the prime minister of all Tunisians and not of a particular party.

There are clearly many unknowns. and what lies ahead for Tunisian women is not easily predictable, but women's NGOs must reckon with all the progressive and less-progressive forces and rebuild new strategies of communication with the secular and the Islamists, with a special focus on the 65 women (30 percent) in the CA, among whom 42 are members of the ruling Islamist party who have declared the CPS would not be amended. The *Nahdha* women need to be trusted, supported, coached, and partnered to benefit from them. Recently, some of them have stopped being party-blind followers and expressed their disappointment and disagreement, but were immediately hushed. The barrier of elitism and the taboo of nonsecularism must be removed in order to reduce the widening social divide between staunch secularists and ardent conservatives. This could only be conducted by women from diverse movements. Women, together, can definitively foil any obscurantist project regarding women and society, given that the cornerstone of the Islamist ideology is the unavowed open secret: the woman and the feminine body.

It may be too early to assess the uprising's consequences on women's rights and gains. It is undeniable that women's rights activists still suffer harassment and oppression and that attacks against artists and journalists and militants in general have increased, yet the freedom of expression newly gained represents a significant and very useful asset to help civil society advocates to be vocal, express their opinions, and mobilize openly and freely. As to the women's, although the only substantial gain seems to be the parity law (though partially respected in the 2011 electoral lists), which allowed for the presence of 65 women (30 percent) in the CA with an Islamist majority (42 *Nahdha* women), it is now implemented regarding the call for candidates to the Independent High Electoral Commission for the coming elections. This law could also assist women's rights NGOs and work toward greater gender equality in the future if applied appropriately.

Notes

1 Acronym from the French *Association Tunisienne des Femmes Démocrates* (The Tunisian Association of Women Democrats).
2 "I regret," said B'chira Ben M'rad, that women are increasingly losing their personality. Islam that was a guarantee against this, is considered by some to be a backward religion but they are mistaken; I am profoundly Moslem, but I have demonstrated in the streets, organized courses, participated in collections, discussed with men . . . and equality was to demonstrate in the streets, to help the ignorant and to spread true knowledge. This is reaction!"
3 Tawhida Ben cheikh, « La Tunisienne doit-elle voter ? » ("Should the Tunisian Woman Vote?") In *L'Action*, 26 December 1955.
4 Bourguiba repeated the same gesture to a veiled woman.
5 Even after the uprising, women's issues seem to be of a low priority on the parties' agenda, considering the democratic process and the transitional justice as top priorities in negotiations.
6 Tunisian women's activists attributed the discrepancy between women's advanced status and the conservative society to the democracy deficit and the absence of the freedom of expression and of the media, which did not allow for a profound awareness-raising in order to change the mentalities through various mechanisms.

7   Radhia Haddad declared in October 1971: "Our strength is first in the President's support . . . the Party's and men's support as a whole. We would have been power-less without their understanding. I am against an extreme feminism: we mustn't fight against men but against all forms of underdevelopment" (Marzouki 1993).

8   Amendments occurred in 1993 and 2007.

9   See note 1. For ATFD. AFTURD (The Association of Tunisian Women for Develop-ment and Research).

10   Strangely enough, the whole code of family law, questioned and reconsidered today, is reduced to the issue of polygamy. In fact, when men mention the revival of the Arab and Muslim identity, it is women's rights, and more precisely polygamy, that is targeted.

11   He simply argued that there is no need to mention the *Sharia* law as main source of legislation since the first clause of the previous constitution, which will be maintained, already mentions the Muslim faith of the state.

12   Center for Studies, Research, Documentation, and Information for Women.

13   This reform allows the Tunisian mother to give her nationality to her child, regardless of its place of birth.

14   ATFD published a book in 1995: "Les violences à l'égard des femmes" (Forms of Violence against Women). It is the proceedings of the International seminar organized in Tunis by ATFD on 11, 12 and 13 November 1993 released for publication 14 years later, in 2008.

15   Many of the *Femmes Démocrates* were lawyers and volunteered as such to men and women, including the Islamists (men) who had difficulties at all levels.

16   Bochra Belhaj Hmida, former ATFD chair and current member, in a personal commu-nication on March 18, 2012.

17   *Id.* xvi

18   *Gender and Political Discourse in Tunisia*, R. Kammoun (Forthcoming).

19   The final constitution is expected on December 2013, at the latest.

20   http://www.tuniscope.com/index.php/article/20094/actualites/politique/enfants-abandonnes-252914, accessed on February 10, 2013.

21   www.magharebia.com/cocoon/awi/xhtml1/fr/features/awi/features/2011/11/18/feature-02, accessed on December 12, 2012.

22   There is no certainty that this will be truly applied until the constitution is formally adopted.

23   Law n° 98–75 of October 28, 1998, supplemented by law n° 2003–51 of July 7, 2003.

24   http://elizabethbuckner.com/2012/11/28/the-niqab-debate-at-al-manouba/, accessed on March 6th 2012.

25   www.facebook.com/notes/ . . . /a . . . women/433349970058451, accessed on Novem-ber 2012.

References

Arfaoui, Khedija. 2007. "The Development of the Feminist Movement in Tunisia 1920s–2000s," *The International Journal of the Humanities* 4(8): 53–60.

Arfaoui, Khedija. 2011. "Women and Education in Tunisia: From Independence to the Jas-mine Revolution," *Women's Studies North and South* International Conference, Bellagio Center, Italy, September 13–17, 2011.

ATFD (Association tunisienne des femmes democrats). 2008. *"Femmes et République: un combat pour l'égalité et la démocratie,"* Tunis: Imprimerie Signes, La Charguia.

Charrad, Maya. 2007. "Tunisia at the Forefront of the Arab World: Two Major Waves of Gender Legislation," *Washington and Lee Law Review* 64(4): 1513–1527.

Gilman, Sarah. 2007. "Feminist Organizing in Tunisia: Negotiating Transnational Link-ages and the State" in *From Patriarchy to Empowerment: Women's Participation,*

Rights, and Movements in the Middle East, North Africa, and South Asia, ed. Valentine M. Moghadam. New York: Syracuse University Press, 97–119.

Kammoun, Raoudha. 2010. "Women and Language in Tunisia." *Women in the Middle East and North Africa: Agents of Change,* ed. Fatima Sadiqi and Moha Ennaji. London: Routledge (UCLA CMED Series), 188–214.

Marzouki, Ilhem. 1993. *Le mouvement des femmes en Tunisie au XXème siècle: féminisme et politique*: Cérès Productions, "Enjeux" Tunis.

Moghadam, V. 2000. "Transnational Feminist Networks: Collective Action in an Era of Globalization." *International Sociology* 15(1): 57–85.

Moghadam, V. 2004. "*Towards Gender Equality in the Arab/Middle East Region: Islam, Culture, and Feminist Activism.*" Human Development Report Office. United Nations Development Program.

Tchaicha, J. and K. Arfaoui. 2012. "Tunisian Women in the Twenty-First Century: Past Achievements and Present Uncertainties in the Wake of the Jasmine Revolution," *Journal of North African Studies* 17(2): 215–238.

Zoughlami, Neila. 1989. "Quel féminisme dans les Groupes-femmes des années 80 en Tunisie," *Annuaire de l'Afrique du Nord*, Tome XXVIII. CNRS, 443–53

Part II
New media

5   *bitterlemons*

Internet dialogue in the Middle East

Yossi Alpher

The concept of *bitterlemons* and the experience of producing and disseminating it for a decade offer lessons regarding both the substance and the culture of Israeli-Palestinian and broader Middle East dialogue. They also tell us something about uses of the internet in fostering dialogue and the dissemination of ideas on Middle East issues of controversy.

Evolution of the *bitterlemons* concept

The *bitterlemons* family of internet publications was born in early 2000, when Ghassan Khatib and Yossi Alpher began to flesh out the idea in a series of meetings in Khatib's office in East Jerusalem. They had become acquainted during the 1990s in unofficial or "track II" meetings that brought Israelis and Arabs together for informal discussion of the conflict and its resolution. Their relationship was characterized by near total disagreement on issues of substance, along with a strong mutual respect at the personal level.

By 2000, Alpher, formerly a Mossad official and then director of the Jaffee Center for Strategic Studies at Tel Aviv University, had just left a five-year post representing the American Jewish Committee in Israel and the Middle East. Khatib, a former Palestinian peace negotiator, was running the Jerusalem Media and Communications Center, specializing in polling, research, and briefing the media regarding Palestinian affairs, and was teaching at Bir Zeit University in Ramallah.

The concept they formulated in their discussions was to use the internet to, in effect, expand the track II idea of a civilized airing of differences between Israelis and Palestinians, with the entire world able to listen in. They would appeal to an elite audience with short and sophisticated articles in polished English – a product that could easily be read off the screen or printed for reading in a taxi or on a train. Each week, they would discuss a new topic. They would each write about it in around 800 words, and each would recruit a compatriot with a different point of view to write also. Readers would be offered four articles embodying a broad spectrum of Palestinian and Israeli views – from Hamas to the settlers – on the week's subject. Readers would thus be informed, and they would also receive a subtle message about civilized discourse among enemies. The project would make a virtue out of its founders' policy disagreements.

At the personal level, both cofounders would presumably also acknowledge that they sought a vehicle that would allow them to present their own specific views on Israel-Arab issues on a regular basis to a large audience.

Would there be enough topics to sustain the project over time? Enough qualified Israeli and Palestinian writers, especially given a decision to avoid recruiting Israelis and Palestinians living permanently abroad? In the course of the ensuing years, Khatib and Alpher would be surprised at the seemingly unlimited bounty of topics and writers their conflict could produce. And what if peace broke out; would a project that in effect capitalizes on differences between enemies be able to adapt to peace-related topics? Sadly, that question has never been tested.

A division of labor was quickly established: Khatib and his JMCC team had the internet expertise; Alpher would be in charge of fundraising, with all funds recruited beyond the bounds of Israel/Palestine to avoid local pressures concerning content. The project would only be launched when there was money in the bank to pay editors, translators, and especially writers, for whom financial compensation was understood as a necessary incentive given the stigma that might, in certain circles, be associated with participation.

In searching for a name for the project, the cofounders agreed that it had to be catchy, like Amazon, somehow suggestive of the Arab-Israel conflict, and of course, available as a URL. Alpher had an epiphany while sitting under the lemon tree in his garden north of Tel Aviv: *bitterlemons* was the title of Lawrence Durell's seminal book about the EOKA revolt against the British in Cyprus in the late 1950s. Incredibly, *bitterlemons.com* was taken at the time by a pun-loving New Jersey used car salesman, but *bitterlemons.org* was available. (Years later, the project would buy out the dot.com site for $1,000 from entrepreneurs who had converted it into a knock-off variety sales site, capitalizing on the popularity of the *bitterlemons* name but failing to sell very much, while confusing *bitterlemons* readers.)

It took over a year to raise funds, initially from the European Union and the US State Department. *bitterlemons.org* was launched in late November 2001. By then, the second intifada was well into its second year, peace was not likely to break out, and Khatib was being forced to move the JMCC main offices into Ramallah. In retrospect, had he and Alpher not been able to meet frequently in Jerusalem in 2000 to develop the project, it might never have been born. Luckily, by the time it was born, it had become possible for the two partners to manage it without direct contact, using phone and internet hookups. While parallel Israeli-Palestinian dialogue projects collapsed under the weight of renewed conflict because the two sides could not easily meet, *bitterlemons* flourished.

Still, intifada, suicide bombings, and IDF incursions into Palestinian cities did not necessarily provide a congenial atmosphere for managing *bitterlemons*. It is not surprising that this project remains unique in the annals of Palestinian-Israeli collaborative enterprises. It required courage on the part of both partners, but particularly on the Palestinian side and particularly during the intifada.

Both Khatib and Alpher were already well-known figures locally and internationally prior to launching the project, thus giving *bitterlemons* a head start among readers and rendering it attractive to writers. Both had the broad contacts as well as the intellectual independence needed to make it work. And both apparently had the capacity to compromise and find creative solutions to problems, insofar as every topic and every major policy decision has to be agreed by both sides.

The first edition of *bitterlemons.org*, on "The significance of the Palestinian Authority," was posted on the web and emailed on November 19, 2001, to JMCC's subscription list of some 2,000 media and diplomatic figures and a list of some 400 that Alpher had compiled. Readership and internet attention began to grow immediately.

Developing and refining a series of related *bitterlemons* projects

The perception of success prompted Alpher and Khatib to expand the project. Not everything worked, and a lot of trial and error was involved. A yearlong experiment in publishing Hebrew and Arabic versions on the web in 2001–2002 was eventually abandoned when it became clear that *bitterlemons'* elite readership preferred the English version, to the extent that over 98 percent of website visits from Saudi Arabia during this period chose the English rather than the Arabic site.

But *bitterlemons-international.org* succeeded. Launched in July 2002, it featured a weekly discussion of a specific Middle East issue, analyzed in short articles by four writers from diverse backgrounds – either from the region or expert in its conflicts and problems. By 2011, its weekly editions were devoted almost entirely to a wide spectrum of issues emanating from the revolutionary wave sweeping the Arab world. A third project, *bitterlemons-dialogue.org*, launched in March 2005, attempted to present in-depth discussion of a Middle East issue, back-and-forth in dialogue form, between two experts with differing views. It lost momentum after 10 editions; it simply proved too complex to manage the dialogues over a three-way internet connection (editor and two participants) in the course of weeks or months. Today, *bitterlemons-dialogue* remains available as an archive: its contents have proven to have an extended relevancy. A similar fate awaited *bitterlemons-api.org*, which was launched in late 2010 and ceased publication half a year later (see below, case study 2).

An online book, *The Best of bitterlemons*, was published in 2007, summarizing the project's first five years. It enjoyed considerable success in the form of thousands of downloads.

In late 2010, *bitterlemons.net* was created as the web gateway to the then three active sites, *bitterlemons*, *bitterlemons-international,* and *bitterlemons-api*, and for the *bitterlemons-dialogue* archive. All the sites have search, archive, "about," and documents files. Facebook and Twitter links were also added. In the ensuing year, plans were laid to publish three new *bitterlemons* virtual books and to develop bitterlemons apps for the I-phone and I-pad.

Measuring Success

Within a few years of its launching, *bitterlemons.org* had around 11,000 email subscribers and about 6,000 daily unique visits to the website, or around two million a year. *bitterlemons-international* lagged slightly behind. Considering that the websites are updated once a week at most, these are positive figures. Consistently, *bitterlemons*' readership has peaked at times of crisis in Israeli-Palestinian relations.

Overall, in recent years, subscriptions have tended to level out while website visits have increased. This trend apparently reflects reader frustration with widespread (and often unannounced) spam filters that "catch" *bitterlemons*' email editions unless programmed otherwise – something many readers are either not aware of or are not comfortable with. This difficulty reflects a challenge confronting many distributors of legitimate material by email: more than 90 percent of email traffic is now spam or junk mail, rendering it that much more difficult to get one's message through to potential readers.

A second measure of success is reprinting and redistribution of *bitterlemons* articles by additional websites and the print media, and of source resending by recipients to their "lists." All *bitterlemons* material may be reproduced freely and without permission, as long as proper credit is given. Alpher and Khatib estimate that this circulation multiplier, which they encourage, brings their weekly readership into the hundreds of thousands. It is in the nature of the internet that, while there is no need to advertise your product – the system itself takes care of that – it is also difficult to keep track of who reads your product. Over the years, the cofounders have sporadically tracked reproduction of their articles, for example, in the Saudi, Lebanese, Egyptian, and Israeli print press, and on numerous Arabic websites in Syria and Urdu sites in Pakistan. A Portuguese version of *bitterlemons* appears in Brazil; a German reader translates articles into Germany and sends them to journalists and members of the Bundestag; Italian, Turkish, Spanish, French, and Russian translations have also made themselves known.

Yet a third way of judging success is emulation. Readers have reported plans to establish projects similar to *bitterlemons* in Iraq, Iraqi Kurdistan, Georgia/Abkhazia, and elsewhere. University professors use it as a teaching aide. Fourth, there are reader and writer responses: when writers see their *bitterlemons* articles bouncing around the web and the print press throughout the region, they are more than willing, sometimes even anxious, to write again. Increasingly, topics for editions are suggested by veteran writers and readers.

Fifth, and sadly, there is evidence of the extent of circulation and influence from the persecution of *bitterlemons-international* writers. In 2006–2007, two Iranian scholars, Ramin Jahanbegloo and Haleh Esfandiari, were each imprisoned for several months in Iran, after which their television "confessions" featured their having written for *bitterlemons* – which despite its totally pluralistic approach and editorial independence was portrayed as a Zionist, anti-Islamist tool. On the other hand, as far as is known, access to *bitterlemons* is not blocked anywhere.

Finally, success or failure can be measured by donor response. Here, the reaction is far from uniform. Over the years, *bitterlemons* has been supported primarily by the European Union, as well as by the United States, Norwegian, and Swiss governments, Swedish SIDA and Canadian CIDA, the Ford Foundation, Open Society Institute, National Endowment of Democracy, Rockefeller Brothers Fund, and one private donor. For every donor that agreed to provide support, two refused. Donors (and, for that matter, readers) who expect *bitterlemons* to "solve the conflict" or demand "proof" that the project has mitigated it, are quickly disillusioned. Then, too, because of its elite content, language, and format, *bitterlemons* is occasionally criticized by donors as old-fashioned and lacking in interactive features. Indeed, from the outset, Khatib and Alpher have shunned forums, chats, and talkbacks because they tend very quickly to descend to a vulgar and unsophisticated level, while *bitterlemons* writers are generally reluctant to commit to the idea of webcasts due to considerations concerning both logistics and exposure to criticism for collaborating with the project.

Some donors who wish to see *bitterlemons* as a media project rather than (as it was intended) an exercise in creating conditions for conflict mitigation, also tend to become discouraged. Other donors have simply developed conflict fatigue and given up on Israelis and Palestinians or on the Middle East entirely. And, of course, the global economic crisis of recent years inhibited support. Thus, during 2010, lack of funds reduced the project to 50-percent productivity. In 2011, full-scale production was renewed, with new funding obtained at least in part due to the innovation of *bitterlemons-api.org*. But 10 years is a long time for a project like *bitterlemons*, there is no guarantee how long it can be sustained, and ongoing fundraising is a serious challenge.

Case study 1: bitterlemons and the Lebanon War[1]

bitterlemons' coverage of the 2006 war in Lebanon between Israel and Hizballah illustrates the way the project interacts with and reflects events in the region and provides a sounding board for the diverse views of analysts and observers.

On the regional map that emerged in early 2006, Israel faced militant and aggressive Islamist movements on two fronts, in Lebanon and Gaza. Both Hizballah and Hamas are combinations of militia, terrorist organization, and political party, both enfranchised by democratic elections. Both are backed by Iran and its client state, Syria, reject Israel's very existence, refuse to negotiate with it, and feed on failed or weak Arab political entities.

Within a few short weeks in late June and early July 2006, both movements carried out acts of war against Israel, invading its territory to kill and abduct Israel Defense Forces soldiers. Israel responded with a prolonged air and ground counterattack. In mid-August, a ceasefire ended more than a month's fighting between Israel and Hizballah, and a United Nations force was introduced under UNSCR 1701.

One important and almost immediate Palestinian-related corollary to the fighting in Lebanon and Gaza was the shelving by recently elected Prime Minister Ehud Olmert of his plan to withdraw unilaterally from parts of the West Bank. The Israeli public felt it had been attacked unprovoked across two internationally recognized boundaries after having withdrawn unilaterally across them; this called into question at least the Gaza model of withdrawing both the settlements and the army without prior agreement with a viable Palestinian government.

In both the Israeli and Palestinian arenas, some of the ramifications of the Lebanon ceasefire appeared to be negative, both militarily and politically, while a few seemed to open prospects for possible new diplomatic departures. All these developments, and more, that took place during and after the war constituted the weekly fare of *bitterlemons.org*. It explored these issues throughout the conflict and beyond.[2]

Thus, in discussing regional ramifications of the conflict, Prof. Asher Susser of Tel Aviv University wrote on July 24, 2006, that "the weakening of the Arab state has raised the profile and relevance of primordial, sectarian and religious identities, coupled with the rise of non-state actors throughout the region. The likes of Bin Laden, Zarqawi and his successors, Hizballah and Hamas, the latter now in some mode of control of the non-state of Palestine, have created a unique brand of chaotic statelessness." Prof. George Giacaman from the Palestinian Institute for the Study of Democracy countered that the Palestinian reaction to Lebanon was "the determined attempt to reach internal [Palestinian] agreement on a package deal with the Israelis involving release of the captured soldier and an exchange of prisoners at a later date plus a ceasefire from both sides. [This] . . . seems to be the first consequence of the Lebanon escalation: first to separate the Lebanese issue from the Palestinian issue and second, to resolve the Gaza situation independently from the Lebanese situation."

Looking at the fate of the Palestinian Authority in light of the war, Prof. Mustafa Abu Sway of al-Quds University in East Jerusalem argued on August 7 that "a growing number of Palestinian voices are calling for an end to the existence of the interim PA itself in order to force Israel to assume its responsibilities as an occupier." Prof. Gerald Steinberg of Bar-Ilan University responded with a radically different formula: "Until basic changes in Palestinian self-governance take place and a more capable and pragmatic leadership emerges, de facto [international] trusteeship is likely to continue."

The applicability to the Israeli-Palestinian crisis of the international force decided on by the UN for Lebanon was also the subject of a *bitterlemons* debate. Palestinian law professor Camille Mansour asserted on September 18 that "any deployment of an international force would be largely impossible in the absence of political negotiations". Former Israeli Foreign Minister Shlomo Ben-Ami responded, to the contrary, that "the solution to the Israeli-Palestinian conflict will have to come from the international community or there will be no solution at all."

The rest of the Middle East commented on the war and its ramifications in the virtual pages of *bitterlemons-international*. Thus Egypt's Abdel Monem Said Aly, heading Al Ahram Strategic Studies Center, noted with satisfaction on September 14 that Egypt had contributed to maneuvering an "ideal conclusion to the

[Lebanon] crisis," which was to have "neither winners nor losers." Prof. Soli Ozel of Bilgi University in Turkey explained why the government in Ankara opted to contribute forces to UNIFIL II despite the public's misgivings. Nawaf Obaid of the Saudi National Security Assessment Project acknowledged that "the actual extent of the damage is now being realized, as is the fact that Hizballah will not be able to rebuild what they have promised. And the apology by Hizballah leader Hassan Nasrallah for the war was a big change in the perception that Hizballah had actually been victorious."

Lebanese think tank director Oussama Safa, writing in late August, appeared to agree, noting "Hizballah has in reality given up a major part of its ability to maneuver." A month later another Lebanese academic, Habib C. Malik, addressed the possibility of some sort of peace process emerging from the war and noted that it really depended on more distant issues: "A Syrian-Israeli peace is a function of the peaceful resolution of the current impasse with Iran over the nuclear issue," while a Lebanese-Israeli process still depended at least in part on Syria. The latter, according to Bassma Kodmani, a Syrian who serves as executive director of the Arab Reform Initiative, was preoccupied elsewhere: "The priority today for Damascus is to be rid of the pressure from the international community regarding the Hariri investigation."

That Saudis, Iranians, Lebanese and Syrians all contributed in 2006 to the *bitterlemons* project alongside Israelis and Palestinians testifies both to the growing readiness of all parties in the Middle East to debate their views openly – and to the power of the internet to break down "traditional" barriers of enmity and suspicion. Sadly, this is not always the case: the project's pool of Iranian writers dwelling in Iran has dwindled distressingly under the Ahmadinejad presidency. Lebanese dwelling in Lebanon only began to write after the Syrian military withdrawal in 2005. It remains difficult to recruit Syrian, Libyan, and even Saudi writers. Still, Alpher and Khatib have developed an extensive database of potential writers, exploiting their own far-flung contacts as well as the success of the project.

Case study 2: The short history of bitterlemons-api.org[3]

From November 2010 to June 2011, this short-lived track of the *bitterlemons* project published 64 articles in 16 editions. They featured discussions of Arab Peace Initiative-related issues, including a paragraph-by-paragraph analysis of the actual API text, among, once again, four diverse participants. *bitterlemons-api* reflected a perception on the part of Khatib and Alpher that the Arab Peace Initiative is important, but has not been analyzed and elucidated sufficiently, and that *bitterlemons* readers would welcome presentation of a broad spectrum of views on its clauses and their ramifications. At the time of its launching, it also reflected the hope that, after a year of weekly discussions, Alpher and Khatib could publish some sort of "roadmap" for actually implementing the API.

The project began auspiciously, with Arab League Chairman Amre Moussa, former Jordanian Foreign Minister Marwan Muasher, and then-foreign minister of the Palestinian Authority Nabeel Shaat recalling their hopes and plans for the API in an edition entitled, "Present at the founding: what the API framers intended". Ensuing editions asked, "How should Israel respond to the API," then went on to analyze virtually every word in this short document. By June 2011, the project was surveying Arab and Israeli public opinion on the API. This was almost certainly the most penetrating treatment of the Arab Peace Initiative by an international group of diplomats and analysts, and the one with the most exposure via *bitterlemons'* 200,000 or so readers.

But, by June 2011, the Arab world had changed. In the era of "Arab Spring," Arab and Israeli potential commentators on the API were totally preoccupied with the radical wave of change sweeping the region. The API suddenly seemed irrelevant; events were at least temporarily passing it by. Alpher and Khatib found it pointless to go on; they put the project on hold and appealed successfully to the European Union, at that point, the sole financial supporter of *bitterlemons*, to divert funds labeled for *bitterlemons-api* to two alternative projects that suggested themselves.

One was *bitterlemons* "apps" for iPad and iPhone users. This reflected a perceived need to keep pace with changes in global internet usage.

A second was an additional three new *bitterlemons* books. First, the entire API project could be wrapped up in a virtual volume that should prove useful once the Arab revolutionary phase is over. Then, too, the project's in-depth treatment of the Arab revolutionary wave itself suggested at least one virtual anthology. Finally, a second "Best of bitterlemons" book covering years five through ten of the project was planned. A fifth icon, *bitterlemons-books.org*, was added to the *bitterlemons. net* portal.

The brief life-span of *bitterlemons-api* and its metamorphosis into apps and books are illustrative of the flexibility of an internet-based project like *bitterlemons* in adapting quickly to changing circumstances and thereby staying relevant.

Conclusion

Despite a strong sense that the *bitterlemons* project has been a success, there is really no way to prove conclusively that several million dollars have been invested wisely in this project over the past decade. Just because some worldly Arabs, Israelis, Iranians, Turks, and others agree to share their disparate views on the same virtual page and many people – whose numbers and identities cannot be verified – read the end-product, does this necessarily qualify as a finite contribution to regional peace, democracy or human rights? Khatib and Alpher cannot even poll their readers for their response because, from the project's inception, they made a point of not asking readers to provide any identifying data beyond their email addresses, in the hope that this would encourage those situated in sensitive countries to subscribe to a joint Israeli-Palestinian project. Essentially, *bitterlemons* has an unusually large readership due to its pluralistic approach and informative nature. But has it "convinced" anyone?

As an Israeli, Alpher is pleased that the project has exposed a large Middle East and otherwise-interested audience to diverse and important Israeli views. Palestinian cofounder and coeditor Ghassan Khatib has viewed *bitterlemons.org* from its inception as a vital way for the Palestinian case to be delivered to a large global audience. The two have collected important testimonials from throughout the region. Abdel Monem Said Aly, long-time head of al-Ahram, told them, "You have the only serious debate I know of." Marwan Muasher, at the time foreign minister of Jordan, called *bitterlemons*, "the number one source on the web for informed debate and analysis on Middle Eastern issues," That's all well and good. But, basically, it has to be taken on faith that a web magazine so diverse and unique and so heavily read and praised contributes to a better Middle East. The coeditors have to try to maintain a healthy skepticism that keeps them seeking better ways to use the internet for doing what they do.

Afterword – Why we are closing[4]

Yossi Alpher

We are closing *bitterlemons'* two weekly e-magazines. The publications that you, our readers, have known for the past 11 years will, with this special edition, cease to exist. You deserve an explanation as to why this is happening. It is not disconnected from what is transpiring around us in the Middle East and globally.

First, for those not wholly familiar with the details of our operation, here is a brief summary of what we have produced and published. From November 2001, *bitterlemons.org* presented a weekly web magazine of Israeli and Palestinian views, including those of myself and Ghassan Khatib, on a selected topic. Beginning in July 2003, *bitterlemons-international.org* circulated a second weekly collection of analyses on a broader Middle East topic, written by commentators from throughout the Middle East and beyond. By the by, in 2010–2011 we briefly published *bitterlemons-api.org,* a series on the Arab Peace Initiative. In 2002–3, *bitterlemons.org* was published in Arabic and Hebrew.

We published two virtual books and created I-pad and I-phone apps. We attracted hundreds of thousands of readers and witnessed our articles re-circulated by hundreds of web-based and print publications. We welcomed writers from nearly every country in the region. Everything we published will remain available at *bitterlemons.net.*

All this cost money, received over the years from generous foundations, one individual, and donor countries, led first and foremost by the European Union. The donors welcomed our aspiration to involve the region's elites, along with interested parties from beyond the region, in a high-level and civilized discussion of our differences. They supported the readiness of an Israeli and a Palestinian to undertake this task.

You, the reader, were never asked to support us financially. Indeed, we never even asked you to identify yourself to us, on the assumption that reader anonymity would increase the circulation of a controversial publication produced by Israelis and Palestinians.

We never aspired to make "virtual" peace and never presented a "*bitterlemons* plan.*" Rather, we sought to debate our differences and raise the level of dialogue. Over the years, our internet and email publishing operation, based in Israel and Palestine, weathered an intifada, suicide bombings and an Israeli invasion of the Palestinian Authority. Throughout, we never missed an edition except for holidays. Until recently.

We are ceasing publication for reasons involving fatigue – on a number of fronts. First, there is donor fatigue. Why, donors ask, should we continue to support a Middle East dialogue project that not only has not made peace, but cannot "prove" to our satisfaction – especially at a time of revolution and violence throughout the region – that it has indeed raised the level of civilized discussion. Why fight the Israeli right-wing campaign against European and American state funding and the Palestinian campaign against "normalization"?

These last two negative developments also reflect local fatigue. There is no peace process and no prospect of one. Informal "track II" dialogue – *bitterlemons* might be described as a "virtual" track II – is declining. Here and there, writers from the region who used to favor us with their ideas and articles are now begging off, undoubtedly deterred by the revolutionary rise of intolerant political forces in their countries or neighborhood.

Then there is the global economic slowdown. Even countries and philanthropic institutions not suffering from donor fatigue still have to deal with declining budgets for promoting activities like ours. Obviously, the donors have every right to do with their limited funds as they see fit. But they are nearly all tightening their supervision and review procedures to a point where the weight of bureaucracy simply overwhelms efforts to maintain even a totally transparent project like *bitterlemons* and to solicit additional funds.

After more than a decade, there is also fatigue at the production end. Even weekly electronic publications that don't require old-fashioned printers and distributors nevertheless need to recruit writers, edit their articles and meet deadlines.

It's time to move on. I, personally, do so with a sense of satisfaction regarding the completely unique Arab-Israel discussion format we developed and propagated for more than a decade. I learned endlessly from this endeavor. I believe we enriched the understanding of Middle East conflicts and developments among large numbers of people in the region and beyond. I hope others will continue this pursuit of better regional understanding.

I wish to thank our readers for their consistent support. And to thank Ghassan Khatib and the highly professional staff at and around JMCC in Ramallah for making our work together such a satisfying experience for more than a decade.

Finally, we're not completely going away. We hope in the near future to keep the *bitterlemons* label alive with important alternative activities. We'll keep you posted.

Ghassan Khatib

When Yossi Alpher and I sat in my Jerusalem office in the year 2000, discussing plans for the first *bitterlemons* web magazine, we never imagined that it would grow to encompass four different publications and two books, or that it would span 12 years of the Palestinian-Israeli conflict.

That was before the second Palestinian uprising and its crushing losses, before the construction of Israel's wall and the blockade of Gaza that have physically divided us, before 9/11 that made villains of Arabs and Muslims in the West, before the population of Israeli settlers in the occupied West Bank had finished doubling despite the peace accords. And, of course, it was before the Arab uprisings that are transforming the region at this very moment.

In the beginning of this project, my hope was that *bitterlemons* would provide a venue for the Palestinian voice to be heard. And to this day, I remain proud that we seem to have achieved this – that top international policymakers were able to read the opinions of Palestinians from many walks of life and political backgrounds and engage their ideas on this forum.

(In this regard, it remains a criticism of mine and others who observe the media that Palestinians are rarely heard on their own terms. Instead, they are presented responding to Israeli concerns and answering western-derived questions, as if Palestinians have no independent dreams or visions. We must all do better).

Often in this project, we as editors have felt lucky. In the foreword to "The Best of *bitterlemons*" compilation published in 2007, I noted that we rarely had trouble recruiting writers. Despite the feeling among many in the Arab world that contact with Israelis is tantamount to accepting Israel's occupation, seldom did authors decline an invitation. Lately, we have observed that this has changed, that even once-forthcoming Palestinians are less interested in sharing ideas with Israelis just across the way. Still, we have been able to present the voices of security chiefs and political prisoners, military generals and farmers losing land, spokespersons for armed groups and peaceniks in an equal and fair manner – rather differently than the situation on the ground.

Nevertheless, this achievement is bittersweet as the scenery around us grows ever more dark and uncertain. Two decades after the signing of the Declaration of Principles that many hoped would usher in the creation of a Palestinian state and independence, freedom and security, Palestinians and Israelis are barely conversational. The structures created by those agreements have atrophied, corrupted by an increasing imbalance in the Palestinian relationship with Israel. Every day, there is new word of land confiscations, arrests, demolitions, and legislative maneuvers to solidify Israel's control. Israel's political leaders are beholden to a tide of right-wing sentiment and Palestinian leaders are made to appear ever-smaller in their shrinking spheres of control.

We are now, it appears, at the lowest point in the arc of the pendulum, one that is swinging away from the two-state solution into a known unknown: an apartheid Israel. How this new "one-state" option will be transformed into a solution that provides freedom and security for all remains to be seen. We at bitterlemons are grateful to have been able to record over time the shift in this direction and hope the archive we have created will be useful to researchers for years to come.

And so, more than anything, we want to thank our readers and contributors (often one and the same) who shared their ideas with us and were not afraid to join this conversation. I personally would like to thank my co-editor Yossi Alpher for his tireless work on this shared project. The discussion will certainly continue – I am sure of this – until Palestinians achieve their freedom and self-determination by ending the Israeli occupation that started in 1967 and establishing an independent state in the West Bank and Gaza Strip alongside Israel, thereby realizing the international consensus over the two-state solution. *bitterlemons* aspires to be a part of this, through new projects and platforms. But for now, we all wait with trepidation to see around the bend.

Notes

1 This case study is condensed, with additional alterations, from Yossi Alpher, "Bitter-lemons.org and the Lebanon War," *Foreign Service Journal,* AFSA, December 2006.
2 All quotes that follow can be accessed at www.bitterlemons.org and www.bitterlemons-international.org.
3 For background and context, see www.bitterlemons-api.org.
4 Published 27 August 2012 © bitterlemons.org and bitterlemons-international.org

6 Egypt's "Facebook Revolution"?

The role of new media in the Egyptian uprising and beyond

Sherif Mansour

Introduction

To call this chapter a "Facebook Revolution" is perhaps a bit provocative. Some Egyptians feel that new media tools such as Facebook have been given unjustified credit for what the people behind these tools achieved – namely, helping online activists in their struggle to ouster president Hosni Mubarak after 30 years of brutal rule. Nor should the focus on such tools lose sight of the "reality" of the lives overturned and lost through the course of this struggle. Still other Egyptians take issue with the term "revolution" itself, arguing that a complete dismantling of the previous Mubarak regime has yet to take place. Acknowledging both these critiques, this chapter refers to the uprisings in Egypt that began on January 25, 2011, as a "Facebook Revolution" in order to draw attention to the group of young people who were behind this movement and who are representatives of a connected, "online" generation, as well as to the actual new media tools that empowered these young people to mobilize their countrymen, online and offline, in unprecedented ways. As such, this chapter does not set out to show how new media created the Egyptian revolution. Rather, it is an attempt to analyze how a group of committed young Egyptians transformed their protests from online – from Facebook, so to speak – to the streets and, later, to the society as a whole.

In particular, the chapter will outline the evolution of young Egyptian activists' use of social and new media to mobilize Egyptians and combat the state's security apparatus. Beginning around 2003, activists began using new media technology for "low risk" campaigns, which also yielded smaller victories. However, as they gained more experience, they increasingly raised the stakes, using such tools for higher-risk political mobilizations. This process evolved over eight years and culminated in the 18 days that ushered in the removal of Mubarak in February 2011. In the later period of transition under the Security Council of Armed Forces (SCAF), young people have had to adapt their use of new media once again, this time using such tools to articulate the fundamental principles of a future democratic system and to mobilize young people around specific issues, including election voting advocacy, monitoring government, and seeking justice for their fellow activists who were killed, imprisoned, or attacked.

In order to demonstrate how young people employed various new media tools to bring about political change in their country, this chapter will review a variety of sources. including online journals, blogs, and news articles in both English and Arabic. Furthermore, the author of this essay was in close contact with many of the activists and bloggers described in this chapter and thus also draws on personal conversations and communication with these young Egyptians for further insights.

Background: Egypt before the REVOLUTION

Any discussion about the role of new media in Egypt's revolution has to examine first the underlying grievances that led to the uprising. New media tools are only relevant in this discussion because people employed them to protest, challenge, and overcome serious threats to their freedom and long-term security.

Though for some observers of Egypt (and the region more broadly), the 2011 uprisings appeared "out of nowhere," in reality, many Egyptians – from across political and religious lines – had been fighting for democratic reforms in recent years. However, since 1952, such efforts have been consistently crushed or thwarted by successive military regimes, of which Mubarak's was only the latest. As will be discussed below, the Mubarak regime used a number of "soft" and "hard" tactics to maintain its power. On the one hand, the regime tried to give the façade of openness to domestic and international critics alike through "elections," superficial gestures of opening civil society and promoting economic liberaliza- tion, while on the other, it continued to rely on brute force, torture and intimida- tion to silence opponents.

Mubarak's Egypt could thus be considered a hybrid regime where democratic practices were present but shallow.[1] Mubarak and those in leadership positions in his National Democratic Party (NDP), made an enormous effort to win legiti- macy with the population by organizing elections, elections that they alone would win handedly.[2] For example, during the parliamentary elections in 2010, the NDP claimed they had won 90 percent of the seats; yet they also noted that out of 41 million registered voters, only 27.5 percent participated.[3] Even if this were a reliable figure, it would still represent one of the lowest parliamentary election turnouts in the world.[4]

The state also maintained a powerful propaganda machine to promote further its "soft" power. State media acted as mouthpieces for the regime, and many inde- pendent journalists and newspapers were repeatedly intimidated or shutdown. The Mubarak regime also ostensibly allowed "civil society" groups to operate, but required them to register with the state; a law that effectively shut down any groups that were actively opposed to the regime.

In addition to these "softer" measures, the Egyptian government also did not hesitate to use brutal force when needed. According to the Constitution, the presi- dent is afforded tremendous powers over the government.[5] However, Mubarak extended his powers even further by ruling under special "Emergency Laws," which he maintained throughout his entire reign and which granted him unlimited powers. Specifically, he relied on a massive system of secret police and intelligence forces that enjoyed tremendous authority and legal impunity. These security forces were notorious for their merciless and widespread use of torture. The Egyptian Organization for Human Rights (EOHR) cited more than 150 torture cases, in which at least 80 resulted in death between the years 2000 and 2005 alone.[6]

However, and unlike other oppressive regimes, like China who invested heavily in making internet inside only for sharing information and thus managed, for the most part, to minimize its ability to mobilize people, Egypt did not. It went to employ limited censorship efforts, plus security forces monitoring, and media control to limit the impact of internet on public live. That worked for a while.

New media's role in Egypt's revolution and transition

Denied the political space to put forward opposition political candidates, restricted from using civil society organizations to openly demand reforms and respect for human rights, and given limited space to openly criticize the government through the formal media channels (i.e., newspapers and television), opposition figures had few spaces left to organize and express their disapproval of the regime since 2003. The internet thus became the primary venue for Egypt's disaffected youth. While progress within the formal political struggle remained quite uneven, because of the gap between those who are online and offline, the online sphere consistently expanded and moved forward. Egypt boasted the largest number of internet and cell phone users in the entire African continent. Internet exposure grew from less than 1 percent in 2000 to 20 percent in 2009.[7] The number of blogs in Egypt rose from just 40 in 2004 to an estimated 160,000 in July 2008, according to a report released by the Egyptian Cabinet's Information and Decision Support Center (IDSC).[8] Facebook penetration in Egypt jumped from less than one million in 2008[9] to 8.8 million in 2011, more than two-thirds of whom were between the ages of 18 and 34.[10] The country also now has more than 130,000 Twitter users.[11]

While the rest of the country was still offline, and 34 percent of adult Egyptians were illiterate between 2005–2010,[12] increased access to satellite channels and mobile phones were similarly important, acting as platforms to transfer online media information and challenging traditional media coverage. Between 2005 and 2010, the number of households with a television increased by a third.[13] Satellite television broadcasting from outside national borders – including Al Jazeera, provided access to increasing numbers of non-state-controlled media sources.

Access to such technology, however, in itself would not form the basis of social and political change. It is also not a guarantee that it will be successful in changing the regime. Thus, the next sections will examine how young people's use of new media technology to promote political change began to evolve. It will show how tangibly they managed in six overlapping phases to form the social capita and the critical mass necessary to start the change process.

The bloggers phase: Kefaya and young bloggers (2003–2007)

The first phase coincided with Egypt's first nonviolent uprising called the "Kefaya" movement (Kefaya means "enough" in Arabic). The Kefaya movement was built on a broad coalition of groups and individuals from varying ideological, religious, and political persuasions, all dedicated to challenging Mubarak and the possible succession of his son, Gamal. Kefaya's ability to bring together diverse groups and organizations around a common cause was unprecedented in Egyptian politics.

The movement was also significant in that it marked the first time that formal political groups in the country formed an alliance with a small cohort of youth bloggers in Egypt. Together they developed innovative ways to protest and reach out to regular Egyptians. For example, Kefaya created an online platform where people could affirm the movement's manifesto, which explicitly referred to President Mubarak as a dictator. This campaign gave interested Egyptians the opportunity to show their support for reform in an anonymous (if they chose to not use their real name) "low-risk" way without having to go out in the streets. With only 7.5 percent internet access at the time, the movement still managed to collect more than 17,000 signatures – an encouraging number for reformers at the time.

Though the Kefaya movement eventually dissolved due to internal divisions, it represented a "watershed" moment for Egyptians, demonstrating the possibility of organizing a secular opposition movement in Egypt around issues of democracy and reform and revealing how the internet could be employed to bring young people into the movement. Bloggers in particular began to craft their "trade" during this movement and continued well after the formal Kefaya protests had ended. They not only provided alternative voices and commentaries that contradicted the state controlled media, but they also began using "video blogging" as an effective tool to challenge the State's propaganda machine. In effect, they learned to "let the camera speak for itself." With his use of YouTube videos, Wael Abbas became a pioneer in this video blogging. His most famous posting, shot on a mobile phone camera, showed police brutalizing a prisoner in their custody. Abbas bravely posted the video on his blog; within days, the video had been seen by thousands, and in a few weeks, by millions of Egyptians. Egyptians were horrified and the state was forced to respond by convicting the two policemen in November 2007. This event soon inspired other bloggers, including websites such as TortureinEgypt.net, to begin documenting abuses by the state.

Despite these important gains within the opposition movements both in terms of "street" activism and the rise of bloggers and online activism, they had not yet dramatically altered the political landscape inside the country. By the end of 2007, the Egyptian regime seemed confident and opposition was seen divided and ineffective.

The Facebook phase: April 6 Facebook and labor mobilization (2007–2010)

In 2008, several young people used the internet social-networking website, Facebook, to create an online group to protest rising food prices in Egypt. Within several weeks, the group had managed to get 80,000 supporters to join. What was particularly remarkable was that many young people signed up with their real names and contact information – raising the stakes from the previously "low-risk" online petitions. When a government controlled textile factory in the city of Mahalla called for a strike on April 6, 2008, to demand better pay (in the face of increased food prices), the group called on their supporters to show their solidarity with the Mahalla strike by refusing to go to work that day.

The Egyptian government was shocked to find out that almost one-third of the population stayed at home that day, in what proved to be the first successful online mobilization on such a large scale. The government scrambled to satisfy some of the demands of the strike, by lowering some prices of essential commodities, raising the annual increase in wages at an unprecedented rate. They also detained some of the Facebook group administrators – including Ahmed Maher and Esraa Abdelfattah – for several weeks. By the time they were released, the April 6 group was now known across the country, and April 6 became the day of national protest all over the country.

The "April 6 group" thus represented an important progression in "internet organizing" for addressing political and social agendas. For many Egyptians, the group proved that Facebook – indeed social-networking tools of any kind – could impact and mobilize in the "real" world.[14] It also demonstrated the first instance of formal solidarity between young people and Egypt's worker movements, which had much more organizational capacity and experience in working on the ground and in reaching out to offline and illiterate communities. Perhaps most significantly, the group also refuted "Mubarak's self-fulfilling prophesy as the only alternative to the Muslim Brotherhood will continue to hold Egypt back from the democracy its people deserve."[15] The group soon gained support from formal political opposition parties[16] and attracted attention in the international media.[17]

While internet organizing involves mobilizing people to take action against the regime using the internet, "internet advocacy" aims to get the message out about specific issues to the broader public and to international stakeholders. The most important case of internet advocacy in the context of Egypt involved the case of Khaled Said, a relatively apolitical young Egyptian who was in an internet café when police told him to leave. When he refused, he was beaten and then taken into custody without any formal charges. By the time his family had found out what had happened to their son, they were shown his battered and broken body. These images were soon placed on Facebook by various rights groups and activists. Khaled Said instantly became a symbol for Egyptians of the Mubarak regime's brutality. Thousands of young people dressed in black all over the country to protest.[18] In the month after his death, more than a quarter million people joined the Facebook group, "We are all Khaled Said," which called for investigations in his case and putting the police officers who tortured him to trial for criminal charges.

This case in particular affected Egyptians for a number of reasons. First, Said appeared to be a seemingly "average" Egyptian youth, who was not involved in any political activity when he was tortured and killed. Second, by 2010, the Egyptian security employed around 1.5 million people.[19] The Interior Ministry's budget had increased in recent years to "face increasing protest,"[20] and the government spent more on internal security than what it spent on housing or healthcare.[21] Knowing that their government was paying police to attack their own children brutally, when they were not willing to pay more for basic goods, caused massive outrage.

The "change" phase: Signature campaign and parliamentary election (2010)

In late 2009 and early 2010, three major events took place in Egypt, which dramatically altered the political landscape. First, Mubarak became very sick, causing many inside and outside the country to rethink their alignments and positions within the country. Second, Dr. Mohamed Elbaradei, an Egyptian Nobel Prize winner and former Director General of the International Atomic Energy Agency (IAEA), declared his willingness to run for election against Mubarak – albeit with the caveat, that the process would have to be reformed to allow for credible competition. Unlike other opposition figures, Elbaradei had widespread international standing, a reputation for independence (i.e., standing up to the United States on the Iranian nuclear program), and a lack of "political baggage," since he had not been part of the political process in Egypt before. These made him both a unifying figure for the opposition, as well as a difficult target for the regime.

Elbaradei launched a national campaign to unite opposition around a collective proposal to amend the Constitution, which he called the "National Association for Change." The proposal included significant changes in the election process to allow for free and fair elections. To demonstrate the popularity of these demands, his campaign sought to collect millions of signatures from Egyptian citizens – inside Egypt and abroad. Moving even further than "Facebook" petitions and groups, this petition called for people to write down their real names and addresses, forcing people to take greater personal risks and responsibilities for change. Despite these risks, Elbaradei managed in the first three months to collect more than one million signatures (online and offline).

The third event that challenged the status quo in Egypt was the parliamentary elections in November 2010, discussed above. Although the opposition was united in calling for election reforms ahead of the elections, the Egyptian government promised free and fair elections and yet offered no legal guarantees or changes to the election framework. The opposition was divided into two camps on how best to respond to the regime. The first camp, which included Elbaradei's Association for Change, Al Ghad and Algabha (liberal) parties, chose to boycott the election. The second camp, which included the Muslim Brotherhood and Al Wafd (liberal) party, chose to participate in the elections.

As the first camp expected, the first round of the elections witnessed massive irregularities, fraud, and violence and resulted in an almost complete monopoly of the ruling NDP party. After seeing the overwhelming number of violations and the loss of almost all opposition candidates, all of the opposition forces, including Al Wafd and the Muslim Brotherhood, decided to withdraw from the runoff elections that were going to decide the remaining 10 percent of the seats. Instead, they joined other opposition parties who had boycotted the elections from the beginning.

The NDP made a strategic mistake with this election. Instead of winning what they really needed – a two-thirds majority giving them control of the legislative process while allowing some space for the opposition to exist without really having an effective voice – the government tried to take everything and leave nothing to chance, showing them to be weak and insecure. On the other side, the elections were an opportunity for the opposition to unite. The late return of Muslim Brothers and Al Wafd party to the boycott camp was a victory for Elbaradei and his quest for challenging the system.

The revolution phase (January 15–February 11, 2011)

Continuation of online and offline mobilization created a tangible success record for Egyptians in their protest against Mubarak. It also created space for increasing risk-taking spirit by the general public to gradually break down the fear barrier. What started in 2003 with 17,000 mostly anonymous online signatures on Kefaya's petition became 80,000 signatures with names and Facebook accounts on April 6, 2008. It then became one million signatures with full names, and home addresses from their national ID under the leadership of Elbaradei's National Association for Change.

Also, the formal opposition has by now almost completely united against the regime, the young people forging alliances with the labor movement, and various youth activists honing their use of new media tools effectively to a captive audience of a few million Egyptians, all they needed was an opening in the political landscape to bring people to the streets.

Fortunately, they received that opening from a wholly unexpected place: Tunisia. Brave young people and the labor movement in Tunisia joined together, utilizing a combination of new media campaigning and organizing and grassroots mobilization to ouster President Ben-Ali on January 14, 2011. Egyptian youth were not only inspired by the Arab world's first successful nonviolent revolution in their lifetime, but they also began to study their tactics and strategies more closely. As Steven Cook, Senior Fellow at the Council on Foreign Relations, noted on his way out of Cairo on January 23, 2011, the events of Tunisia "added so much momentum to pretty significant opposition that already exists."[22]

Eager to capitalize on this truly remarkable moment, leaders of the April 6 group, administrators of the Khaled Said Facebook page, and youth leaders of Elbaradei's National Association for Change came together to call for a national "day of anger" on January 25, 2011 – chosen ironically and deliberately by the young people because it was also the national day for celebrating the Egyptian police force. Selecting this day touched on the issue of police brutality, one of the most unifying issues for all Egyptians.

In the 10 days between when Ben Ali left Tunisia and the assigned "day of rage," youth groups were furiously organizing. The central platform for communication and strategic mobilization became the "We Are All Khaled Said" Facebook page,[23] which tripled its membership in those 10 days, attracting more than 200,000 new members. The group's administrator, who was later revealed to be Wael Ghonim, a Google executive, devised a brilliant marketing campaign that capitalized on Facebook's ability for interactive communication. Ghonim would use the page to repeatedly ask all members to creatively engage others and show their support for the upcoming January 25 protests in different ways. People used other Facebook groups, Twitter, text messages, mass email messages, online videos, and music videos, among others, to spread news and instructions about the protest. Members sent in their personal photos with signs expressing their support for the protest and calling upon others to join. Many of the pictures were sent by Egyptian abroad. One of them was specifically taken inside the holy mosque of Mecca, sending moral religious support for the "day of outrage." Others showed Muslim and Coptic members pledging to go out united to the protest.[24]

Members of the page produced songs with clear, defiant language and meaningful cultural symbols. Member "Rami Dunguan" made a rap song called "Against the Government,"[25] which went viral in mid-January, calling for national rebellion. Another creative example came from Asmaa Mahfouz, a young Egyptian female activist made a video saying that she was going down to the protests, but appealed to her male and female colleagues, upon every Egyptian, to go to the street to defend her honor.[26] Art groups like the Asfalt team, produced a popular song on January 23, two days before the protest, named "writing a letter for tomorrow," dramatizing the need for people to speak up and believe in their rights and freedoms.[27]

By January 24, the Facebook group had grown to almost 386,000 members with almost 10 million daily page views. The page also created an "invite" for people to protest; the invite was sent to almost one million Facebook members with more than 100,000 confirming that they would attend.[28] Reaching out in these creative ways, young people began to get their friends and close circles involved – or at the very least aware of the impending protest – and the images on Facebook helped reassure these young people that they were not going to be alone if and when they stepped out on the streets on January 25. This sense of community was vital to the uprisings' success. Soon, nearly every major youth and political group had expressed their support to this call, including Elbaradei, Ayman Nour, and the Muslim Brotherhood.

By January 25, hundreds of hardcore youth activists, many of whom were already trained and experienced in nonviolent organizing tactics, began gathering in small groups around downtown Cairo and other major cities. Within hours, thousands of workers and other young activists had joined them; gaining more supporters by the hour. It was at this point that online advocacy was becoming street advocacy. Activists used "communicators" such as taxi drivers, barber shops, and doctors, to spread the news about the day and inform and excite people who did not have internet or satellite stations.[29] Leaflets were distributed, strategically, the Friday before in front of mosques and on Sundays in front of churches to attract as much attention among ordinary Egyptians. Crucial organizing tips and a "revolution manual" was distributed around the country, printed off the internet and copied on a massive scale.[30]

Youth activists also continued to rely heavily on new media tools throughout this time. Facebook and Twitter increased the volume and the speed of communication exponentially. Activists were able to identify where and when the protests would be on an hourly basis. Organizers were able to spot where police forces were and asked their colleagues to move around, trying to get away from them. This game of "cat and mouse" was playing out in favor of the young activists, who seemed to remain a step ahead of the police force, which eventually collapsed after just three days of such protests.

New media also allowed for faster circulation of critical information about losses and casualties, and informed Egyptians and the international community about developments on the ground. It was the most "televised" revolution in history, with live broadcasts for local, regional, and international networks, feeding a massive amount of footage and other materials nearly 24 hours a day. Some have even argued that the continuous attention of satellite channels, in some ways, may have increased the impact of such protests by bringing greater international pressure on to Mubarak to step down.[31]

New media tools also helped lower the cost of engagement and participation for many Egyptians who were otherwise very afraid to go out into the streets. It provided a safe entry point for many people to express their solidarity from the safety of their home. Many people chose simply to spread the news about the protest, or Tweet news, making it available for a wider audience. These internet "bystanders" played a vital role by bringing the revolution into people's homes – forcing discussions about where people stood on the revolution on a daily basis.

Movement leaders also used new media tools very effectively to control their messaging and to maintain nonviolent behavior throughout the revolution. The ability to feed information into traditional media organizations, who were themselves blocked from covering the events directly, allowed the organizers to choose their "favorite" images and isolate bad publicity. They were able to disseminate photographs of peaceful demonstrators, including those who courageously stood against police tanks and who slept on army tanks, rather than the violent protestors who threw rocks. This strategic "framing" was important in attracting international support for the Egyptians who are protesting.

One of the best examples of this strategic "framing" involved an article by *Daily News Egypt,* the most popular English newspaper, which called January 25 "Egypt's violent day of anger" and showed a video of angry protesters intended to scare the majority away from such protests.[32] Within less than 24 hours, online advocate, Tamer Shaaban, managed to use more or less the same materials from the video and reshape it to project the peaceful dimensions of the protest in a very positive and hopeful tone.[33]

Another example occurred the day before Mubarak stepped down. Egyptian activists produced an online video declaring their "victory" and announcing that they have prevailed, calling it the "sound of freedom"[34] and showing joyful Egyptian faces from Tahrir square in a very artistic and hopeful way. The video went viral, attracting hundreds of thousands of viewers in few days and has become the national theme song of the revolution, played repeatedly on Egyptian television stations after Mubarak stepped down.

While new media tools provided many advantages it also had its limitations, as Egyptians found out when Mubarak cut the internet. Suddenly, the incessant "feed" of videos, tweets, and Facebook updates came to a sudden and dramatic stop. No one could communicate except through landlines. However, this internet blackout actually helped the protesters for several reasons. First, it angered virtually every person inside Egypt who relied on the internet, even those who did not participate in the protests. Furthermore, without the constant online "updates," many began to "fear the worse" for those still out on the streets. This inspired many Egyptians to come out simply to find out what was happening to their friends, family members, and colleagues who were participating. The internet blackout also created an unplanned "decentralization" of the movement, since people could no longer follow central instructions online, and thus began improvising and organizing themselves ad hoc – making it even more difficult for the police forces to know what the next move would be.

Furthermore, new media played a minimal role once protesters occupied Tahrir square in central Cairo. Other than spreading news about what is happening in the square, Egyptians showed their true skills in tactical innovation on the ground. Protesters created an almost fully independent state within the boundaries of the square, with its own hospital, radio stations, and food facilities. Inside Tahrir, protesters used humor to keep people's spirits high and to reinvigorate tired protesters. They bravely stood their ground when Mubarak sent in thugs on camels and horses to beat the protesters. The young activists also managed to neutralize the Army when they replaced the police on January 28 by effectively appealing to individual soldiers' sense of nationalism and humanity. People made emotional and personal pleas to their "brothers" in uniform and eventually convinced even the highest-ranking officials to not side with Mubarak. The final piece of the puzzle fit into place when the workers unions' started a nationwide strike, tipping the scale decisively in favor of the protesters. After 18 days of confrontation and more than a thousand causalities, Mubarak stepped down.

Post revolution phase (February to October 2011)

In stepping down, Mubarak gave power to the Supreme Council of Armed Forces (SCAF), who assumed control over the country to "fulfill the Egyptian people's aspirations" for democracy and justice. Deciding not to shoot on demonstrators, the military earned the respect of most Egyptians, including the leading activists and opposition political forces. Celebrating their victory, many political groups felt confident that the SCAF would stay true to their commitment to transition towards democracy and most took a break for several weeks to rest and recuperate after Mubarak stepped down.

However, this trust in the SCAF soon diminished. Having no prior experience in managing a state or maneuvering the political landscape, the army lacked the necessary leadership and vision to prioritize and address the various issues that needed to be sorted in the transition. They soon showed themselves to be slow and tepid in implementing some revolutionary demands, while blatantly ignoring others. They also failed to release a clear timetable for the transition period. SCAF then seemed reluctant to fulfill its promise to hand over power to an elected government, a promise that was supposed to take place within six months.

Revolutionary forces decided to return to calls for mass mobilization, pressure SCAF to honor its commitments, and see substantive changes in the structure of the state system. Between March and September 2011, on 10 different Fridays, youth groups and various political allies took to the streets again to protest issues ranging from the prosecution of former regime personnel to demanding the end of the "Emergency Law," and creating new election laws. They once again turned to new media tools to help bring people out to the streets, but also to voice their concerns directly to the SCAF (which now has its own Facebook page).

When the annual anniversary of Khaled Said's death came in June 12, 2011, the Khaled Said Facebook group organized yet another protest calling for a new trial on his case. Thousands of young people showed up around the country, and some of them marched to the Ministry of Interior for the first time after Mubarak stepped down, to protest police brutality. They painted graffiti of Khaled Said's face on the building's wall, as a sign of defiance against the Ministry and as a statement that they would not allow torture to happen again in Egypt.[35] During this time, the administrator of the Khaled Said Facebook page, Wael Ghonim, announced that in Egypt that year, more than 1.6 million members had posted on the page more than 16 million comments, and overall, the page had been viewed more than 1.8 billion times.

With such a mass following, the Khaled Said Facebook page began articulating other key demands for the transition, including reforming the Ministry of the Interior by adding human rights principles to the curricula of police studies; reforming the election process, particularly to allow better chances for young people to participate as candidates; putting former regime people on trial and removing them from executive posts; and releasing many of the people who were put to trial on military courts.

At the same time, other young activists have been employing new media tools to perform a variety of "watchdog" functions, keeping a close eye on the ruling military council. For example when Military Police forced protesters out of Tahrir square on March, 9, 2011, less than a month after Mubarak stepped down, young activists documented and spread the news about the arbitrary arrests, torture, and forced virginity tests conducted by army officers on young female protesters. Embarrassed by the sudden international media coverage, SCAF tried to deny these allegations. However, the sheer quantity of evidence, including images, videos, and testimonies for the victims, forced them to admit to their actions.[36] Meanwhile, the SCAF also tried to intimidate young bloggers and new media activist, such as blogger Hossam Alahamalwi, with accusations of "spreading rumors about the military." However, within hours of making the announcement, online activists began an almost nonstop campaign against the military, calling for Alahamalwi's release. The tactic worked. SCAF decided to withdraw the case against him and conduct informal questioning instead.[37]

One of the most remarkable moments after the revolution was the formal dismantling of the dreaded internal security or "Amn al Dawla," which was known for its ruthless treatment of political opponents of the Mubarak regime. Young bloggers and online activists were the first to arrive to the main headquarters in Nasr City, Cairo. They stormed into the building with their cameras and took photos and videos of everything that remained inside the building, including evidence of how the former regime used to monitor phone calls and email accounts of leading activists – as well as Mubarak regime supporters. The documents from the building caused a great deal of debate within Egypt about violations of privacy conducted by former regime personnel as well as the international companies who had helped the Egyptian authorities monitor Skype conversations between activists, for example.[38] The dissemination of this information forced the new National Security apparatus in Egypt to vow not to use such tactics against political and human rights activists. It is still too early to know if such promises are being upheld.

Young activists also used new media tools to monitor various government institutions and advocate for their reform. One major institution was the state television and radio, which had acted as mouthpieces for the previous regime. After Mubarak stepped down, the national media became the central target of people's anger. Various media officials and personalities were shamed for their role in "smearing" the activists during the uprising. Many of them were forced to resign. In September 2011, after the television showed a biased "sanitized" version of the military's assault on peaceful Coptic demonstrators, which killed more than 25 people, more officials had to resign and the new Minister of Information and Media had to publicly apologize.[39]

Forcing the Army out (October 2011 to June 2012)

When SCAF came to power, they suspended Egypt's 1979 Constitution. They announced a committee to "reform" the constitution, led by a retired judge with Muslim Brotherhood leanings. They proposed nine amendments to the constitution that would allow for free and fair elections to be put forward for referendum on March 19, 2011. The move caused the first huge split between the secular and Islamist groups, who had appeared united up until this point. The secular and "civil society" forces believed it was time for the drafting of a new constitution by an elected Constitutional Assembly. They voted against the nine amendments, and they came to be known as the "constitution first" advocacy group. On the other hand, the religious and Islamist forces wanted to elect a new Parliament first, who would elect the constitutional committee. They came to be known as the "election first" advocacy group.

While the online social media sphere and the public and private media reported that a greater number of people opposed the amendments, the election results turned out to be the exact opposite. Some 77.2 percent of Egyptians voted "yes" to constitutional amendments, while 22.8 percent voted "no."[40] The results were a big shock to the revolutionary and civic groups who overestimated the power of new media and internet technology in post-Mubarak era. They, in return, decided to broaden their advocacy by using the new mushrooming media channels and launched new political parties and movements to remain relevant. But that is not without continuing using new media and internet tools.

In November 2011, SCAF representatives and members of their cabinet started to propose a military super-constitution that would greatly increase their power. This proposal, however, was met with much resistance. Youth groups and their allies in the media launched a combination of online and offline campaigns against SCAF and eventually managed to decrease its support in the population and even within its lower ranks. A public poll by has shown that after one year of the revolution, trust in the army was at an all-time low, following Muslim Brothers, and April 6 movements. It declined from 93 percent in the beginning of 2011, when they refused to shoot demonstrators during the revolution, to around 63 percent.[41] Political parties, including the Muslim Brotherhood and Salafi groups, united to call for SCAF to announce a date to leave power. However, comments by SCAF members in the media hinted that they intended to stay in power until 2013, even after the election of a new president.

Youth groups, however, started to employ innovative tactics to disrupt SCAF's plans. They mobilized Egyptians and organized manifestations to demonstrate public refusal to the extension of military power. They showed the Egyptian people that their situation had not improved in the 10 months of military rule, and that SCAF had continued many of the same corrupt practices of the Mubarak era. Youth groups launched a "liar campaign," in which they documented photos, videos, and personal testimonies of military human rights abuses and displayed them to the public using projectors across the country. This campaign was effective because it was simple, requiring only minimal resources. Members of the liar campaign projected their videos on every surface they could find, including on the walls of government buildings, at the wall of Egyptian Television, and at every social gathering or event.

Scenes from these gatherings went viral and restored hope among young people across the country. The revolutionary youth employed many forms of visual protest, including graffiti to protest against SCAF. These moves encouraged the public and private media to join the campaign to expose SCAF's abuse of power. Moreover, political and civic groups also united in calling for ongoing protests against SCAF's intentions. Members of the Muslim Brotherhood joined the protests, although they focused mainly on the upcoming parliamentary and presidential elections. Revolutionary forces remained committed to their cause, even though they were being brutally suppressed. Protests in Tahrir broke out, but Military officers crushed them. Two people were killed and 600 wounded. Muslim Brotherhood and Salafi groups subsequently withdrew their members. The toll of victims grew to more than 35 deaths and more than 1,000 wounded. After three days, SCAF was forced to make changes to the cabinet to appease the people on December 8. 2011.

Though SCAF appointed a new cabinet, demonstrators continued to pressure them, surrounding them for three weeks to ensure that the cabinet, in conjunction with the military, would concede to the revolutionaries' demands. The army used brutal force to disperse the demonstrators. Perhaps their most striking use of violence was against women, when army officers assaulted them physically and sexually, removing their clothes and dragging them across Tahrir Square. These images made their way into not only local but also international media. The "Liars campaign" members spread the photos into poverty-stricken and marginalized areas of Cairo and Egypt. Outraged by the level of violence, on December 19, thousands of women protested in Tahrir Square, shaming SCAF for their actions. SCAF could not recover from this incident, and for the first time since the revolution, Mohamed Hussein Tantawi, the head of the Council, appeared on TV at the end of the year, promising to hand over legislative powers to the newly elected Parliament and executive powers to the newly elected president by the end of June 2012, regardless of the timeline of the Constitution drafting process. He also announced that the State of Emergency would be partially lifted.

With SCAF agreeing to relinquish power, Egyptians turned their attention on to the upcoming Parliamentary and presidential elections of 2012. During the elections, the revolutionary youth and Muslim Brothers agreed to unite in front of elements of the past regime, which they called *felol* – an Arabic word, meaning remnants of the defeated enemy. They launched campaigns to expose which candidates were *felol* and where they were running in the country. They managed to limit their seats to under 5 percent of the People's Assembly, Egypt's lower chamber of Parliament. The April 6 youth movement launched a campaign called "white and black districts" in which they conducted various civic educational activities to inform voters about the new election laws and advise them on how to make responsible choices among the candidates. They joined forces with the "catch felol" (http://www.emsekflol.com/) campaign, which made black lists of former regime candidates based on their records of corruption and abuse of power during the Mubarak era. At the same time, members of the Muslim Brotherhood coordinated with other liberal and secular groups to compete aggressively against former regime members.

When the elections were concluded in January of 2012, Islamist Parties (including the Muslim Brotherhood and Salafi groups) assumed legislative powers by winning the majority of seats in the elections. For the six months that would follow, SCAF and the Islamists would engage in a struggle for power, which largely alienated liberal revolutionary forces, until SCAF dissolved the Parliament in June 2012. But, the Muslim Brothers aligned with revolutionary forces to bring their candidates Mohamed Morsi to power and then removed SCAF leadership from office.

Revolutionaries continued to expand the anti-SCAF civil resistance movement, putting pressure on the Council to relinquish its legislative and executive powers.

They documented how SCAF had exerted its power in public life, exposing its blatant corruption, not just in the post revolution era, but also over the past 60 years. They highlighted high profile cases of corruption, including one case in which auto-industry giants used luxury cars, in particular a Mercedes Benzes, to bribe a military official to provide marketing advantages to their companies. They also published other cases in which public land had been sold at very low prices to military officers and their families. The revolutionaries, who revealed these cases of corruption, were put to trial in military court but were released soon after under the pressure of the general public. The "liar campaign" consistently documented these abuses, publishing a map online revealing the locations where ex-military officials were working and benefitting from corrupt practices (http://el3askarmap.kazeboon.com/). The map was widely circulated in the media and among the general public. In June, a Gallup poll has shown that majority of Egyptians want military out of politics.[42] Due to this diligent campaign, many former military officers were barred from entering into new government institutions, local councils, and governorships under President Morsi.

Conclusions

While it is very tempting to conclude that the Egyptian revolution was in fact a product of advances in new media technology, it would be a gross misstatement. As this chapter tried to show, new media played an important role as a tool – a tool that was used skillfully and creatively in the hands of young people who took tremendous personal risks to bring change to their country. They were crucial in overcoming restrictions on information and organizing. They were also useful in expanding the reach of opposition.

Nevertheless, these tools would have been completely useless if Egyptians had not been building their critical mass, expanding their coalition, and building unity. In other words, one cannot say that new media tools like Facebook created the Egyptian revolution; however, they helped bring the inevitable overthrow of the Mubarak regime much faster and with much less violence than would have occurred without them.

Further, it is clear that new media will continue to play a greater role in Egyptian public life, during and post the transition period, which will ultimately create more mature experience to be examined by follow up research. Particularly more application of new media technology to assess public opinion, encourage participation, and monitor government behavior could be important in the near future.

Notes

1 Larry Diamond, "Thinking about Hybrid Regimes," *Journal of Democracy 13*, no. 2 (April 2002).
2 Fareed Zakaria, *The Future of Freedom Illiberal Democracy at Home and Abroad* (WW Norton, 2003, page 13).

3 "Rights Groups Contest Egypt Official Voter Turnout," *Reuters* (November 29, 2010): http://www.khaleejtimes.com/DisplayArticleNew.asp?xfile=/data/middleeast/2010/November/middleeast_November524.xml&section=middleeast

4 "Custom Data Set," International Institute for Democracy and Electoral Assistance (accessed August 23, 2011): http://www.idea.int/vt/

5 "Egyptian Constitution," The State Information Website, Available online from: http://www.egypt.gov.eg/english/laws/Constitution/chp_five/part_one.asp

6 "Human Rights Groups Report Widespread Torture in Egypt," *The Daily News,* September 26, 2006, http://www.dailystaregypt.com/article.aspx?ArticleID=3135

7 Google Public Data, based on World Development Indicators at the World Bank: http://www.google.com/publicdata/explore?ds=d5bncppjof8f9_&ctype=l&strail=false&bcs=d&nselm=h&met_y=it_net_user_p2&scale_y=lin&ind_y=false&rdim=country&idim=country:EGY&ifdim=country&tstart=-290548800000&tend=1287288000000&hl=en&dl=en&uniSize=0.035&iconSize=0.5&icfg

8 Meghan Michael, "Blogging on the rise in Egypt despite security risks, threats, says report," *Daily Gulf News,* July 31, 2008, http://www.thedailynewsegypt.com/article.aspx?ArticleID=15427

9 David Wolman, "Cairo Activists Use Facebook to Rattle the Regime,", *Wired Magazine,* October 20, 2008, http://www.wired.com/techbiz/startups/magazine/16–11/ff_facebookegypt?currentPage=all

10 http://www.socialbakers.com/facebook-statistics/egypt

11 http://interactiveme.com/index.php/2011/06/Twitter-usage-in-the-mena-middle-east/

12 http://www.unicef.org/infobycountry/egypt_statistics.html

13 http://www.e-mediainstitute.com/en/regionsandcountries/africa/egypttvmarketmap.content

14 They organized rallies to support liberal political prisoner Ayman Nour, who is in prison on fabricated charges for challenging Mubarak in the 2005 presidential elections, and critical editor Ibrahim Eisa, who is on trial for "spreading rumors about the president's health."

15 Sherif Mansour, "Egypt Facebook Showdown," *Los Angeles Times,* June 2, 2008, http://www.latimes.com/news/opinion/la-oe-mansour2–2008jun02,0,323158.story

16 Heads of opposition parties from the right (Muslim Brothers) and the left (Altagmoa party) and from liberals (Ayman Nour from Al Ghad and Osama Ghazali Harb from Algbha) were quoted in the media in their support.

17 Read: "Cairo Activists Use Facebook to Rattle Regime," *Wired Magazine,* October 20, 2008, http://www.wired.com/print/techbiz/startups/magazine/16–11/ff_face bookegypt; "Fledgling Rebellion on Facebook is Struck Down by Force in Egypt," The Washington Post, http://www.washingtonpost.com/wp-dyn/content/article/2008/05/17/AR2008051702672_pf.html; "Crackdown on Facebook Activists" *Los Angeles Times* blog, http://latimesblogs.latimes.com/babylonbeyond/2008/07/egypt-crack down.html; and "Egypt Detains Facebook Activists—Again," The Christian Science Monitor, http://www.csmonitor.com/2008/0730/p04s04-wome.html

18 http://www.elshaheeed.co.uk/tag/silent-stand/

19 Jason Brownlee, "Egypt's Incomplete Revolution: The Challenge of Post-Mubarak Authoritarianism," *Jadaliyya,* July 5, 2011, http://www.jadaliyya.com/pages/index/2059/egypts-incomplete-revolution_the-challenge-of-post

20 In Arabic: "Ministry of Interior Request 142 Million Egyptian Pounds Increase in Its Annual Budget," *Alyoum Elsabie Egyptian Daily News Website,* April 27, 2009, http://www.youm7.com/News.asp?NewsID=93278&SecID=65&IssueID=0

21 Hossam al-Hamalawy, "The General's Budget," *Arabawy.org,* November 29, 2006, http://www.arabawy.org/2006/11/29/adlys-budget/

22 "We Are All Khaled Said": Will the Revolution Come to Egypt?" *The Daily Beast,* January 22, 2011, http://www.thedailybeast.com/articles/2011/01/22/we-are-all-khaled-said-will-the-revolution-come-to-egypt.html

23 https://www.facebook.com/ElShaheeed

24 https://www.facebook.com/media/set/?set=a.107520942631112.3988.104224996294
    040&type=1
25 http://www.youtube.com/watch?v=S7n44IHSB3w
26 http://www.youtube.com/watch?v=SgjIgMdsEuk
27 http://www.youtube.com/watch?v=6uzPQgbyfR8
28 https://www.facebook.com/event.php?eid=115372325200575
29 Interview with Ahmed Maher, leader of the April 6 group in Cairo, May 6, 2011.
30 "Egyptian Activists' Action Plan: Translated," *The Atlantic*, January 27, 2011,
    http://www.theatlantic.com/international/archive/2011/01/egyptian-activists-action-
    plan-translated/70388/
31 "Al-Jazeera's Coverage of Egypt Protests May Hasten Revolution in World News,"
    The Guardian, February 7, 2011, http://www.guardian.co.uk/media/2011/feb/07/
    al-jazeera-television-egypt-protests
32 http://www.youtube.com/watch?v=5LetPoMHcRU
33 http://www.youtube.com/watch?v=ThvBJMzmSZI
34 http://www.youtube.com/watch?v=Fgw_zfLLvh8
35 "Remembering Khaled Said's Murder," *Egyptian Chronicles Blog*, June 4, 2011, http://
    egyptianchronicles.blogspot.com/2011/06/remembering-khaled-saids-murder.html
36 "Egypt Army Admits 'Virginity Tests' on Women, *CBS News*, June 27, 2011, http://
    www.cbsnews.com/stories/2011/06/27/501364/main20074749.shtml
37 Video Coverage from Al-Ahram Website, May 31, 2011, http://english.ahram.org.eg/
    NewsContentMulti/13361/Multimedia.aspx
38 "Mideast Uses Western Tools to Battle the Skype Rebellion," *Wall Street Journal*, June
    1, 2011, http://online.wsj.com/article/SB1000142405270230452080457634597086244
    20038.html
39 "Information Minister Vows to Investigate Errors in Maspero Coverage," *Almasy
    Alyoum*, October 17, 2011, http://www.almasryalyoum.com/en/node/505891
40 http://www.nytimes.com/2011/03/21/world/middleeast/21egypt.html
41 http://www.pewglobal.org/2012/05/08/egyptians-remain-optimistic-embrace-demo
    cracy-and-religion-in-political-life/?src=prc-headline
42 http://www.gallup.com/poll/155303/majority-egyptians-military-politics.aspx

7 The democratic movement in Iran

A case study of the role of online technology

Sara Bazoobandi

Introduction

The role of online technology in the emergence of the notion of democratic reforms over the past two decades has been a matter of scholarly debate. The idea of global democratic transformation was strengthened by the collapse of the Soviet Union, and the successful transition of several former communist countries toward a democratic political system encouraged people around the world to aim for democratic reforms. While some scholars, such as Paulo Virilio, argue that technological hardware and cultural software both form our environment, and that both therefore play a crucial role in political transformation,[1] others, such as Manuel Castells, believe that politics today exist only within the framework of electronic media; therefore, reform in political systems will only succeed through the intervention of online media.[2] Whether or not online communication technology is sufficient to enable every society's democratic transformation to succeed is not the focus of this study; however, one can argue with some confidence that it has undoubtedly played a significant role in spreading the narrative of democratisation globally and in an extraordinarily rapid fashion. Democratic reforms require a shift in organisational principles, as well as in the modalities of social life. The latter has been enormously changed by the rise of widespread internet access across the globe.

The rise of techno-politics has facilitated the rapid and, to an extent, the free flow of information that provides a new platform for political communication globally. Territorial matters have begun to be eclipsed by the electronic transfer of data, and new modes of identities and community, territory and sovereignty, culture and society have started to emerge.[3] In this process, democratic discourse, which has proved to be emerging unevenly and through political struggle and which is constantly under threat from antidemocratic forces, has found a new method of communication in the cyber realm for shaping the democratic character of societies across the world. On 26 January 2011, President Barak Obama called America a nation of Google and Facebook, and on 11 February 2011, President Husni Mubarak of Egypt officially stepped down from office due to two weeks of protest, which young Egyptians were proud to call Egypt's "Facebook Revolution." Online communication has become a new form of social intercourse, creating a new channel for political participation by people in many societies. Thousands of young bloggers and online journalists across the world have been taking part in online political campaigns, which have become more and more popular for attacking undemocratic regimes.

In Iran, similar to other Middle Eastern countries, the role of online media in the development of a democratic dialogue has been considerable. The rise of electronic communication has provided Iranian society with a new platform that has expanded the country's democratic discourse. Although the state has retained a key function in controlling computer-generated channels for the flow of information, society at large has maintained an active role in utilising various electronic methods of communication (e.g., blogs, Facebook pages, websites, and online newspapers) to express the legitimate political demands of Iranian citizens for democracy. At the same time, the government has constantly been monitoring the country's online networks and has made a significant effort to keep the access to electronic communication systems in Iran at a minimum level. This chapter looks at the history of democratic movement and the development of the democratisation process in Iran and gauges the extent to which online communication methods have contributed to this process. Moreover, the study reviews the government's responses to, and the efforts against, the use of new media by the democratic movement.

Democratisation process in Iran

Iran, as one of the first countries in the region to begin the process of democratisation, replaced its long-serving monarchy with a republican system in 1979. However, the Islamist elite that came to power after the success of the revolution somehow undermined the idea of democracy in Iran. Shortly after the Islamic Republic was formed, the country was thrust into eight devastating years of war with its neighbouring country: Iraq. The end of the war coincided with the death of Ayatollah Khomeini, the leader of the Islamic Revolution and the Supreme Leader of Iran. The former president, Akbar Hashemi Rafsanjani, resumed presidential office, and Ayatollah Khamenei assumed the position of Supreme Leader. Ayatollah Khamenei inherited some of the influence of power of his predecessor and sought even more power. In 1989, the Iranian constitution was reviewed and articles 110 and 57 were amended. As a result of the amendment, the supreme leader no longer needed to be a *Marja-e-Taghlid*, which literally means "Source to Imitate" or "Religious Reference," a title which the Shia clergies achieve by higher level of studying Islamic teaching, and which Ayatollah Khamenei did not hold at the time when he became the supreme leader.[4] Moreover, a new concept was added to the constitution, called: *Velayat-Motlaghe-Faghih,* which literally means absolute rule of the supreme jurisprudent. This gives an absolute right to the supreme leader to make decisions for the state, and his authority is divinely ordained and represents the 'Hidden Imam' on earth.[5] With such authority lying in the hands of the supreme leader, the concept of democracy was clearly eradicated from the Iranian constitution.

The end of the war was perhaps the first chance for the Iranian government, since the revolution, to pay more attention to economic and social development. President Rafsanjani became the first political figure of the country to propose open-market economic policies. With oil rent and aggressive foreign borrowing, the government was able to assist the Iranian society to re-create the Iranian middle class, which was devastated during the war. At the same time, a new oligarchy was formed, which in the Iranian society was closely associated with the widespread corruption and favouritism in President Rafsanjani's administration.

President Rafsanjani's eight years in the office ended with the landslide victory of President Khatami in May 1997. The other candidate in the election, Hojatoleslam Ali Akbar Nateq-Nouri, was largely known as the candidate favoured by the conservative elite, while President Khatami represented a new reformist movement originating from within the political system. Many Iranians saw the victory of President Khatami as a major achievement in bringing back the democratic spirit of the revolution some two decades after the Islamic Revolution of 1979. Despite being re-elected for his second term, Khatami has come to symbolise the powerlessness of the reformist camp within the political system of the Islamic Republic of Iran and its inability to deliver the democratic reform that was promised to the supporters of the reform in Iran.

A few months before the end of his term in office, President Khatami proclaimed that the country was at a crossroads. The supporters of one path wanted to ignore Iran's religious and cultural identity and copy the West, while those of the second group wanted to ignore people's needs, views, and votes, under the flag of religion. The third way, he claimed, was the way of the Islamic Republic of Iran, which had resulted from Iran's revolution.[6] The country was indeed at a crossroads, and the 2005 presidential election highlighted Iran's political division. On one side were the supporters of the conservative elite, led by the Supreme Leader who opposed any democratic reforms in Iran, and on the other side were those who shared a rather moderate political view aiming for a democratic system.

The ninth presidential election was held in 2005 with 12 candidates in the first round. The reformist camp nominated only one candidate, Dr Mostafa Moein, who was widely acknowledged to lack the charismatic leadership traits of Khatami. Moein managed to attract support from a very specific group among educated Iranians and university students only. The next candidate, the former president Rafsanjani, was relatively closer to the reformists' camp than the others, but because of his poor reputation and the negative image associated with the widespread corruption and favouritism that had occurred during his presidency, he gained very little support among the majority of Iranians, particularly the underprivileged and those living in rural areas. Mahmoud Ahmadinejad, on the other hand, maintained a populist character, and with the strong support of the Supreme Leader and some of the hard-line Islamist clerics, especially Ayatollah Mesbah Yazdi, managed to win Rafsanjani's 10 million votes in the second round of the ballot, with about 17 million total votes. The result was questioned by some of the candidates, in particular Hojatoleslam Mehdi Karroubi, who speculated the possibility of fraudulent behaviour in the election. However, the matter was not discussed openly, partly due to lack of interest in the country's political events among many Iranians. Such lack of interest originated from the general disappointment for democratic reforms in Iran because of Khatami's failure to deliver his democratic promises during his time in the presidential office.

During Ahmadinejad's first period, his extremist approach on an international level led to sanctions and severe economic hardship, and caused wide-ranging dissatisfaction among ordinary Iranian citizens, who were also dissatisfied by the strongly repressive social policies of his administration on various domestic issues, including the ideologically enforced dress code in public spaces and universities, heavy control of the media, and the suppression of civil society activities (e.g., women's associations and labour movements). As a result, Ahmadinejad's popularity declined significantly by the end of his first term as president of the Islamic Republic, while a strong sense of resentment was created, particularly among those who have lost interest in the country's politics after Khatami and have not contributed in the ninth election.

By June 2009, the reformist camp had learned from its previous mistakes and this time introduced a rather more charismatic figure, Mir Hossein Mousavi. At the same time, the conservative elite, who had also gained valuable experience following the eighth presidential election that had led to the victory of Khatami, was now ready to undermine the collective effort of the Iranians to replace Ahmadinejad. He was re-elected in 2009 balloting, which was accompanied by convincing allegations of fraud, widespread repression, and severe restrictions on opposition candidates, a deterioration that extended to the media environment.

Following a period of a very modest opening for the press during the first years of Khatami administration, the period that followed the election of President Ahmadinejad was notable for the closure of publications, and the detention and imprisonment of a significant number of political and civil society activists, journalists, and student activists in Iran. The events that led up to the 2009 presidential election in Iran clearly signalled Iranians' awareness of their democratic rights, while the results of the ballots were widely viewed as a setback, if not a deathblow, to the reformist forces and their democratic agenda. The rallies and demonstrations in many Iranian cities, most of which ended in violence and brutal responses by government-led forces, sent a new message to the global community, which was different from how Iran had been perceived by the outside world during the three decades that followed the Islamic Revolution of 1979. The events that occurred in the aftermath of the presidential election of June 2009 showed that the pressure for political democracy and social reform in Iran could not be stopped, and that the population had been politicized and was actively participating in the country's political scene.

The challenges of online communication in Iran

In most of the developed countries, the cooperation of the elite in the development of democracy has been an influential factor, whereas, in the case of Iran, non-state actors have played a major role in nurturing the democratisation debate throughout the country. For example, as the government increased its pressure on the streets in Iran, a greater number of Iranians tapped into online sources of communication. With planned disruption of mobile phone lines and the government's phone tapping, the online networks became the safest environment for Iranians to exchange news, organise events, and unify their political will for democratic change.

The government has reacted strongly to eliminate the effect of online communications in the development of the political opposition movement. Since the protests that followed the disputed presidential elections in June 2009, the Iranian authorities have launched an active campaign against internet freedom by employing extensive and sophisticated methods of control that go well beyond simple content filtering, although this too has become more severe since 2009. The tactics employed include deliberately slowing internet speeds at critical times to make basic online activities difficult, and ordering blogging service providers inside Iran to remove "offensive" posts. The regime has also sought to counter critical content and online organizing efforts by extending state propaganda into the digital sphere: a significant number of news websites and blogs are supported either directly or indirectly by the state.

Since June 2009, increasing numbers of bloggers have been threatened, arrested, tortured, and kept in solitary confinement, and at least one blogger has died in custody. The Iranian authorities have taken a range of measures to monitor online communications, and a number of protesters who were put on trial after the election were indicted for their activities on Facebook, blog posts, personal emails, and news websites like Balatarin (a Persian site that allows users to share links and news).

Reports of website blocking and filtering, content manipulation, attacks on and imprisonment of bloggers, and cyber-attacks all increased sharply in Iran after 2009. The government had already shown some tendency toward politically motivated controls over the internet, and this negative trend accelerated dramatically, with the creating of new institutions specifically to carry out censorship. A group calling itself the Iranian Cyber Army, known to be associated with the Iranian authorities, also managed to hack into a number of opposition and news sites through employing a mix of technical methods and forgery.

All of the above-mentioned government actions were taken based on the country's restrictive regulations for access to the internet. In February 2005, Ayatollah Khamenei, the Supreme Leader of Iran, had published a governmental framework for the country's online networks. Within this framework, the regulations for Access Service Providers (ASPs) are defined as the following:

- The creation of ASPs must be a monopoly of the government and the Ministry of Post, Telegraph and Telephone, while various other government-owned companies will be in charge of providing internet service to users from the public and private sectors.
- All government organisations must submit their proposals for having internet access to the Ministry of Post, Telegraph and Telephone. The Ministry then will review the proposals and provide them with internet access whose

technical capacity will be decided by the Ministry, based on the needs of each relevant organisation as the Ministry sees fit.

- All the ASPs are obliged to apply various controlling measures, including filtering of the websites containing material which, for ethical and/or political reasons, is forbidden.
- All the ASPs are also required to have a strong firewall system to protect the country's networks against any potential cyber-attack.
- All the providers of services to users of internet telephone services inside the country are required to share the details of their users with the Ministry of Post, Telegraph and Telephone, which information can also be shared with the Ministry of Intelligence should it be necessary.[7]

Another method that the government has used to eradicate the role of online media in the progress of political opposition movements in Iran is widespread online censorship. Following the June 2009 elections in Iran, the country's centralized filtering system evolved to the point of being able to block a website nationwide within a few hours.[8] In order to overcome blockages in Iran, users need special skills and knowledge, since the filtering methods are now more sophisticated and the authorities devote considerable resources to limiting the effectiveness of circumvention tools. Even so, activists, with the use of necessary software, have managed to communicate with one another, discuss national events in an uncensored space, and transmit news and reports of human rights abuses abroad. A study by Freedom House examined 37 countries for their freedom on the internet in 2011. While the top three places were occupied by Estonia (10), the United States (13), and Germany (16), the bottom three countries, which represent the most controlled online networks, included Cuba (87), Burma (88), and Iran (89) (see Graph 7.1). The Freedom House study also shows that Iran's internet censorship has worsened since 2009; as such, it had a score change of −13 between 2009 and 2011.[9]

In addition to restrictions on information flows and the often-brutal attacks on online activists by the government, the government has limited internet access

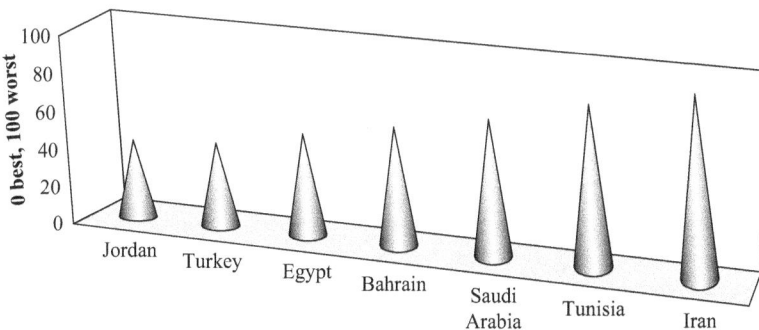

Graph 7.1 Internet censorship.

Freedom House, (2011)

in Iran. According to Freedom House, the Internet Penetration Rate (IPR) in Iran in 2011 was between 20% and 30% which is up to 10% less than the rates of Saudi Arabia, Tunisia, and Turkey (between 30% and 40%).[10] Official information published by the Iran Centre for Statistics (ICS) reports an even lower IPR (11.2%). In 2009, according to a study by the ICS, the country had, in total, 7.96 million internet users while the total population in that year was 71.84 million. The country also had 18.78 million households, of which 4.98 million (equal to 26.5 percent) had at least one member who was using the internet either at home or at work.

The majority of internet users in Iran are located in urban areas. According to the ICS, the IPR in urban areas is higher than the rural areas, with 91% of Iranian internet users located in the urban areas, while only 8.9% of them were living in rural areas. Moreover, some provinces had a significantly higher IPR than others. For example Tehran Province, in which the capital is located, had the highest IPR in the country (16.4%), followed by Isfahan Province (15.3%), and Yazd Province (14.5%). However, Sistan Balouchestan Province in the Southeast of Iran, which has a Sunni majority population, had the lowest IPR in the country (3.3%).

In addition to the widespread online censorship in Iran, the government has a specific policy for keeping the speed of internet connections very low and has obliged all the internet service providers to keep connection speeds as low as 128 kbps (85% of users in the UK have, on average, 2 mbps,[11] which is more than 15 times faster than the limit). The regime has justified these strict government-led limitations for online networks. In May 2011, in response to critical comments about the government's internet provision policies, Reza Taghipour, the Minister of Communication and Technology commented that: "the volume of information available on Farsi websites is not sufficient for it to need broadband internet services.[12] About 91.9% of the country's internet users have access to dial up internet, which is significantly slow, and only 8.9% have access to Asymmetric Digital Subscriber Lines (ADSL).[13]

All in all, the internet restrictions in Iran are partly a response to the explosion in the popularity of advanced applications like personal weblogs, Facebook, YouTube, and Twitter, through which ordinary users can easily post their own content, share information, and connect with large audiences. Since 2009, these tools have also played a significant role in political and social activism. The advocates of democracy have relied heavily on such means of online communication to mobilize supporters and organize mass rallies, and have used Twitter and YouTube to inform the outside world about the government's violent response to their protests. Videos of the demonstrations were posted on YouTube within few hours. While the government has allocated considerable resources to minimising the freedom of online networks, Iranian online network users have often been successful in bypassing these government-imposed limitations. The future of online networks is likely to remain a key challenge to the Iranian regime; hence, it is expected that more pressure will be applied by the government to control the freedom of cyberspace throughout the country.

Online journalism and blogging in Iran

Farsi bloggers have been active for some years in the cyber world, the first blog in Farsi having been created as early as September 2001 by Salman Jariri. Over the past decade, online journalism and blogging have continued to attract Iranian users, thousands of whom have created blogs in Farsi with topics that range widely from cooking and recipes to political and social analysis. The government, however, has exerted a huge effort to minimise the expansion of internet penetration and to control internet access across the country. Not only has the regime put various measures in place to control people's access to the internet, including filtering and slow internet lines, but also it has constantly controlled the activities of individual citizens, which has led to various cases of imprisonment, and physical and psychological torture.

By May 2011, nearly two years after the presidential elections of June 2009, more than 200 journalists and bloggers had been arrested, 40 of whom are still being held on charges of spying, acting against state security, or spreading false information. Around 20 news media have been banned by the regime, about 100 journalists and bloggers have been forced to flee the country, and more than 3,000 are out of work as a result of the strong measures against, or the closure of newspapers, or because the media for which they had worked have been banned from rehiring them.[14]

There are various examples of cases in which Iranian cyber journalists were attacked, arrested, and mistreated by the Iranian government. In October 2010, Hussein Ronaghi Maleki, an Iranian blogger who designed software for internet users within Iran to bypass the government's blockages, was prosecuted for his membership of the Iran Proxy network, and for insulting the president and the Supreme Leader of the Islamic Republic of Iran and received a 15-year jail sentence. On 10 May 2011, Deutsche Welle Persian Service reported that due to the unpleasant conditions in his jail cell and physical torture, the condition of Hussein's health was not good and he had been admitted to hospital.[15] The brutal attacks against Iranian bloggers have increased since June 2009; however, prior to 2009, there were also various instances of bloggers being arrested and accused of spying, insulting Islamic principles, and threatening national security. A good example was an Iranian-Canadian blogger, Hossein Derakhshan, creator of one the first Farsi blogs, who was arrested on arrival in Tehran in November 2008.

Before 2009, during the period that President Khatami was in office, there were a number of other cases of arrest, detention, torture, and eventual conviction by the Iranian regime. These cases included, for example, the arrest of three Iranian journalists, Roozbeh Mirebrahimi, Arash Sigarchi and Omid Memarian, active cyber-journalists who were living in Iran at the time of their arrests. Mirebrahimi, who was affiliated with publications such as *Etemad* and *Jomhuriyat*, was arrested in September 2004, Memarian was arrested in October 2004, and Sigarchi, the editor-in-chief of *Gilan-e Emrooz* in the northern Iranian city of Rasht was arrested on 8 January 2005. The three cyber-journalists spent time in detention facilities operated by Iran's Parallel Intelligence Apparatus and were eventually forced to make false confessions before fleeing the country upon their release.[16]

The regime's brutality and mistreatment of Iranians who are active in the online world has increased since 2009. Many social and political blogger activists have faced multiple charges and some are still imprisoned, reportedly under horrific conditions. Indeed, arresting and convicting online activists has become one of the favoured methods used by the Iranian regime to control the impact of online communication technology and to minimise the freedom of flow of information. The government has put more pressure on internet users, especially the bloggers, since 2009, and this trend is likely to be followed in the foreseeable future.

The fear of a velvet revolution

The terms 'velvet revolution,' 'colourful revolution,' and 'soft power' have become popular vocabulary items in Iran's political language since 2009. The government has duly allocated considerable resources to the strategic suppression of any democratic movement in Iran. Hundreds of political activists who were arrested in the wake of the 2009 presidential election were placed on trial. Prosecutors declared their intention of aiming for the principal leaders of the opposition, and these were eventually put under house arrest before being transferred and imprisoned in unknown locations. The regime pushed controversial cases through its deeply flawed judicial system, while the security forces continued to arrest and imprison members of the opposition and civil society activists, and launched a new round of persecution against the Baha'i religious minority.[17]

Academics, writers, and journalists have also come under massive pressure from the government, and many have been arrested or banned from travelling abroad. One of the significant tactical steps taken by the government to repress the democratisation movement in Iran was the creation of various government-sponsored think tanks, specifically the Soft Security Strategic Thank Tank. These organisations have been active in publishing a number of reports and organising various events to discuss the issue of the 'velvet/colourful revolution' in Iran, with the aim of finding solutions to tackle the perceived threats to the Islamic Republic establishment.[18] Because of such policies, Iran's freedom status has diminished significantly. Research by Freedom House in 2011 shows that the net change in aggregate score for Iran's freedom status between 2007 and 2011 declined by 5–9 points, having declined by only 1–4 points in the previous period (2003–2007) (see Table 7.1)

Writers and journalists have been under constant attack by the government of the Islamic Republic in its attempt to minimise the risk of the so-called 'velvet revolution.' The pressure, however, has increased significantly since President Ahmadinejad took office. The number of newspapers and magazines that were published with governmental permission increased three times between 1994 and 2004, but since 2005, 1.5 newspapers or magazines on average have been banned every month.[19] This has put many Iranian journalists out of work and has often

Table 7.1 Freedom status in selected countries in 2011

Country	Political rights	Civil rights	Freedom status
Switzerland	1	1	Free
Japan	1	2	Free
Turkey	3	3	Partly free
Morocco	5	4	Partly free
Jordan	6	5	Not free
Iran	6	6	Not free
Libya	7	7	Not free
Tunisia	7	5	Not free
Egypt	6	5	Not free
Saudi Arabia	7	6	Not free

Freedom House, (2011)

forced them to leave the country. Those who have not left either are in jail or suffering from financial difficulties. The government's heavy-handedness in trying to undermine a democratic transformation of Iran's political system has increased since 2009 and is likely to intensify until the end of President Ahmadinejad's term.

Iran Cyber Army (IRCA)

Political actors, whether in democratic or nondemocratic societies, have used modes of online communication to express their opinions. Nevertheless, anti-democratic forces, often driven by undemocratic regimes have become harsher in the measures that they apply to undermine the effect of online media on democratic movements. Furthermore, they have used online communication streams to promote their own views. During the mass protests that followed the June 2009 presidential election, many opposition news sites were disabled by intense cyber-attacks, and there is technical evidence confirming that government-owned IP addresses were used to launch the assaults. Security officials regularly broke into the e-mail, Facebook, and blogging accounts of opposition and human rights activists, either by changing their passwords as a signal to show them that the government was watching them closely, or simply by collecting intelligence about their plans and contacts. Moreover, a group calling itself the Iranian Cyber Army (IRCA), which is known to operate under the command of the Islamic Revolutionary Guard, has been responsible for these operations. The IRCA have managed to hack into a number of other sites with a mix of technical methods and forgery.

There is no official confirmation about who is behind the IRCA; however, it is evidently a government-led initiative. In addition to Iranian websites, there have been a number of incidents in which the IRCA has attacked certain American and Chinese websites, including the website of Voice of America, Twitter, and China's most popular search engine, Baidu.[20] In all these cases, the websites redirected the users to a site displaying a political message,[21] including slogans like "Death to

Moussavi" and "Moussavi should be executed" (in the case of Iranian websites), or "We will die if our leader orders us to fight, and if he wants, we will be patient and tolerant" and "We have proved that we can" (in the case of the others). Obviously, all the messages include a strong pro-regime element that delivers a clear message from the Islamic Republic regime.

The regime has put massive efforts into proving it has the upper hand in the so-called "cyber war" – which shows the importance of online networks in the progress the democratic opposition movements are making. The fact that the Iranian government is well prepared to fight the opposition in cyberspace again proves that online communication methods have played a strong role in nurturing the democratic demands of Iranian citizens.

Conclusions

The process of democratisation of the Iranian political system has entered a new phase since 2009, when the regime's pressure on political activists, journalists and those active in cyber space increased significantly. Following previous elections, when concerted efforts made by the Iranians to demand their democratic rights were heavy-handedly suppressed by government forces, cyberspace became a notably important channel through which the Iranian opposition could nurture the dialogue of democracy in Iran. The government therefore tapped into various measures to control this channel, from keeping the speed of internet services below the capacity of today's electronic technology to online filtering. Moreover, in order to display its technological capacity, the government created the so-called Iran Cyber Army, which specifically targets anti-regime websites. Strong government emphasis on controlling cyberspace, whether from inside or outside Iran, is clear evidence of the importance of online communication in nurturing democratic political debates in Iran. However, the power of cyberspace cannot easily be controlled by rapidly developing information technology, and the government will be unable simply to shut down all the means of communication for the dialogue of democracy in Iran.

Freedom House, (2011)

Notes

1 Virilio, Paul (1997), *Speed and Politics: An Essay on Dromology.* New York: Semiotext.
2 Castells, Manuel (1996), *The Rise of the Network Society*, Oxford: Blackwell.
3 Luke, Tim (1998), *The Politics of Cyber Space,* London: Routledge.
4 According to Shia law, a *Marja-i-Taghlid* has the authority to make legal decisions within the confines of Islamic law for followers and less-credentialed clerics. A Marja-i-Taghlid, in practice, is the highest authority on religious laws after the Qur'an and the Prophets and Imams. The Shia Islamic clergies gain this level by studying a higher level of Islamic teaching.
5 Nader Alireza, David E. Thaler, S. R. Bohandy (1997), *The Next Supreme Leader Succession in the Islamic Republic of Iran,* RAND Corporation. Available at: http://www.rand.org/pubs/monographs/MG1052.html, accessed 15 March 2013.

6 Bill Samii (2004), *Iran Report,* Radio Free Europe/Radio Liberty, Vol. 7, No. 7. Available at: http://www.rferl.org/content/article/1342675.html, accessed 15 March 2013.
7 Hoghoogh Online (2005), '*mughararat va zavabet-i shabake haie etela'a resanee-i rayane-yi*'. Available at: http://hoghoogh.online.fr/article.php3?id_article=51, accessed 16 March 2013.
8 Kelly, S. and Cook, S. (2011), *Freedom on the Net 2011: a Global Assessment of Internet and Digital Media,* Freedom House. Available at: http://www.freedomhouse.org/sites/default/files/FOTN2011.pdf, accessed 16 March 2013.
9 Puddington, Arch (2011), *Freedom in the World 2011: the Authoritarian Challenge to Democracy,* Freedom House. Available at: http://www.freedomhouse.org/report/freedom-world-2011/essay-authoritarian-challenge-democracy, accessed 16 March 2013.
10 Sanja Kelly, Sarah Cook (2011), op. cit.
11 http://www.ispreview.co.uk/story/2011/01/25/akamai-reveals-q3-2010-uk-average-broadband-internet-speed-topped-4mbps.html
12 http://www.dw-world.de/dw/article/0,,15063150,00.html
13 http://iusnews.ir/?category=konkoor&pageid=1984
14 http://en.rsf.org/iran-un-human-rights-council-votes-to-24-03-2011,39871.html
15 http://www.dw-world.de/dw/article/0,,15063047,00.html
16 Iran Human Rights Documentation Centre (2009), *Forced Confessions: Targeting Iran's Cyber-Journalists.*
17 Arch Puddington (2011), op. cit.
18 Soft Security Strategic Think Tank (2010), *The Colourful Whispers.* Available at: http://www.amniatenarm.ir/8901.aspx
19 http://www.dw-world.de/dw/article/0,,5938077,00.html
20 http://thelede.blogs.nytimes.com/2009/12/18/twitter-hacked-by-iranian-cyber-army/
21 http://news.bbc.co.uk/1/hi/technology/8453718.stm

Part III
Diaspora

8 Contemporary Kurdish Diaspora in Europe

A driving force toward peace and democracy in the Middle East

Mukhtar Hashemi

Introduction

Why Kurdish Diaspora: Rise and prominence of the diaspora concept

In recent times, and since 1980s, the use of the word 'Diaspora' has been prolif-erated, which has caused Brubaker (2005) to write in terms of the notion of 'the Diaspora,' in other words, dispersion of the meaning of the term in the "*semantic, conceptual and disciplinary space*" (ibid, p.1). Similarly, there has been a great interest in Kurdish Diaspora because its influence on the transnational politics has increased owing to two main factors. First, the establishment of a quasi-independent Kurdish State in Iraqi Kurdistan, the Kurdistan Regional Govern-ment (KRG), in 1992 increased the visibility of Kurdish Diaspora. Secondly, transnational activities of the Kurdish Diaspora from Turkey, and in particular, the supporters of Kurdistan Workers Party (PKK) in the socio-political landscapes of Europe to gain recognition of nationalist aspirations has been a catalyst for greater awareness about the influence and power of Kurdish Diaspora. For example, writ-ing for the BBC News, Dissanayake (2008) portrays Kurdish Diaspora in the UK as "*exiles wielding power from the UK.*"

There has been a flurry of research on Kurdish Diaspora, mainly in Europe (e.g., Gunter, 1991; van Bruinessen, 1995, 1999, 2000; Wahlbeck, 1998, 1999, 2002; Østergaard-Nielsen, 2002, Mino, 2004; Curtis, 2005; Glick Schiller, 2005; Khayati, 2008; Zoukui, 2008; King, 2008; Soguk, 2008; Emanuelsson, 2008; Baser, 2010; Mutlu, 2007; Askoy, 2011, KHRP, 2011 and Latif, 2012), which has greatly contributed to our understanding about the theme of this chapter.

Therefore, the main aim of this chapter is to assess the role of Kurdish Dias-poras in peace building and democracy in the turbulent region of Middle East by analysing multifaceted aspects of modern Kurdish Diaspora formations in Europe.

Geopolitics of Kurds and Kurdistan as non-state actors

In modern times, the name Kurd was used officially only in the Soviet Union (Hum-phreys and Mits, 2012). Both Tsarist and Soviet Russia acknowledged the Kurds as a separate ethnic group, though they did not support the creation of an independent

Kurdistan. Thus, 'Kurds' and their homeland 'Kurdistan' are terms that are difficult to precisely define. The Thomas Bois and Vladimir Minorsky's (1986) contribution on 'Kurds and Kurdistan' in the *'Encyclopaedia of Islam'* is perhaps one of the most comprehensive works as part of great collection of Oriental Studies. Their work was based mainly on *'Sharafnama,'* a historical masterpiece written by the Kurdish Prince *Sharaf Khan Bidlisi* (1543–1599) in 1597 (Bahraminia, 2007: 19). Bois and Minorsky (1986), and almost all the Western scholars and historians believe that Meds are the ancestral origin of the Kurds; linguist D.N. Mackenzie (1926–2001) is an exception since he dismisses the Median root of the Kurds (Khoshhali, 2000: 239). However, John Limbart (1968: 45) asserts that *"linguistic and geographic evidence"* support *"Kurd's claim of Median decent"* and *"all Kurdish dialects have maintained the basic characteristics of Kurdish* [language]."

As a geographic concept, Kurdistan does not appear on the maps, except as a marginal province named as 'Kordestan'[1] in the Iranian Kurdistan. According to many scholars, including Kurdish historians, the term Kurdistan came about in the 12th century by the Seljuks (Mirawdali, 1993; McDowall, 1997: 6). However, the term Kurdistan remains in obscurity. The geopolitical map of Kurdistan is disputed by the countries in which Kurds live, and hence the term 'Kurdistan,' which implies 'Kurdland' (similar to England, the Netherlands, and so forth) does not exist in political terms. However, in fact Kurdistan is an important segment in the political landscape of Middle East. Mirawdali (1993) quoting from Paul Rich (1991:Vii) postulates that *"Kurdistan does not exist, which is why it is so important. This anomalous structure has long been part of the Middle East conundrum."*

Based on the works of great Muslim scholar and historian *al-Masudi* (896–956) among others, there is evidence that Kurdistan consists of (i) the mountains (current Iraqi and Iranian Kurdistan between Hamadan and Arbil [Erbil or Hawlir], which was also known as *Sharaazor* as well); (ii) Hamadan, Asadabad, Dinawar and Kermanshah extending to Elam and Luristan; (iii) area between Azerbaijan and Hamadan (Takht-e Suleiman); (iv) Jazira, Mosel, Syria and Byzantine boarders with the Arabs (Pouladian, 2003: 87). *Lurs* are historically considered as Kurds (e.g., Minorsky, 1943; Pouladian, 2003) and so Kurdistan region extended to Khuzestan as well.

There are no official censuses about the population of the Kurds. Nevertheless, it is estimated that more than 35 million Kurds are living in the Middle East and Caucasian countries, which include Iran (7–9 million), Iraq (6.5 million, Turkey (20 million), Syria (1.7 million), Armenia (75,000), and Azerbaijan Republic (200,000) (Khayati, 2008; 67; Stansfield et al., 2007; KHRP, 2009; Yildis and Taysi, 2007).[2]

Methodological approach

The methodological approach, data and material

There have been many internal and external dispersions, displacements or migrations throughout the ancient, medieval and contemporary history of Kurds (e.g. Samadi, 2002; Siahpour, 2010; Pouladian, 2003; McDowall, 1997; Minorsky, 1943; Hozni, 1938; Rozhbayani, 2004; Karimian Sardashti, 2000; Tawahodi, 1980, 1985, 1988;

Hama Baqi, 2000; Faruqi, 2004; Ardalan, 2005; Asasrad, 2007; al-Fayli, 2009; Chériff Vanly, 2012; Kamandar-Fattah, 2002). Thus, historical narratives have a direct bearing on Kurdish Diaspora formations in the modern age.

The interlinked concepts of nationalism (Lyons and Mandaville, 2008, p. 2), modern state (or nation-state), transnational citizenship and politics, migration and social movements form the background setting for our understanding of Kurdish Diaspora. We have to appreciate that Europe's colonial interests in the Middle East and the breakup of Ottoman Empire had a lasting impact on both Kurdish nationalism and the Diaspora (e.g., Delir, 2004; Arikanli, 2010). For example, the rise of nationalism in the 19th century, which is linked to the rise of Sufi Sheikhs in Kurdistan, provided a platform for Kurdo-European engagements. Kurdish leaders became aware of the great European powers (see e.g., Isa; 2002; McDowall, 1997). The start of the 20th century saw the emergence of well-defined Kurdish nationalist movements (Nerwiy, 2012), which became very active in Europe from the 1960s onward. These revolutions were crushed by the regional powers, as shown in Figure 8.1, and did not gain political support in Europe (see e.g., Barezani, 2002; Taqi, 1995; Khawja, 1968, 1969 and 1970; Qazaz, 2000; Shemsher, 2002). Despite this, Kurdish Diaspora communities materialised and strengthened in size.

This chapter draws from many research works and case studies that have enriched the issue of Kurdish Diaspora. as mentioned earlier. In addition, the works of Kurdish and Middle Eastern scholars are reviewed. In 1986, the author's father, *Sheikh Sayed Muhammad Hadi Hashemi* Kurdistani (1931–1998) spiritual leader of *Solaei Qadri Order of Sufism* in Kurdistan and a Kurdish nationalist from Iranian Kurdistan (Impact, 1998)[3] and his family settled in the UK; thus, the diasporic experiences of the author can be considered as observational data. Writing as an 'insider' is advantageous, but it is paramount that ethics are maintained in writing this chapter.

Ethical aspects and discursive position

We have to bear in mind that many ethnographic analytical approaches are based on discursive biases, and thus, they are not a tool for producing impartial evidence. The discursive position of this chapter is based on the discourse of peace building and democratic role of Kurdish non-state actors in the Middle East. Thus, the discursive position of the author is shaped partly by the experience of living and working within socio-political landscapes of the UK. However, a genuine attempt has been to adhere to the scientific attitude and social research ethics (see e.g., Robson, 2011).

Conceptual constraints, issues and challenges

The creation of nation-states of Iraq, Syria, and Turkey after the fall of the Ottoman Empire divided Kurdistan into five separate entities (the other two entities are situated in the former Soviet Union and Iran). Accordingly, Kurdish Diaspora formations have been contrived by the imposed de facto boundaries. In many

Conceptual constraints, issues and challenges

1905–11	• **Kurdish Participation in Iran's Constitutional Revolution:** Anjumans or Councils were formed in major urban centres from kermanshah to Sanandaj and Mahabad.
1912–14	• **Bidlis and Barazan** uprising; lead by Mula Salim, Sheikh Shahba-Adinin Bitlis and Sheikh Abdul Salaam Barazani i; this movements was helped by Diaspiric Kurdish institution, Hiva Association (established in 1910) which was based in Istanbul, and some European cities such as Paris, Geneva and Strasburg. Sheikh Abdul Salaam was arrested near Urmia and was executed in 1914.
1918–19	• **Sheikh Mahmud Barzanji** (1882–1956) first revolution; a Kurdistan state was declared but later it was suppressed by the British. The mantle of Kurdish hope was held by Sharif Pasha in Paris Peace Conference, 1919.
1917–41	• **Sardar Rashid Ardalan revolts** against Reza Shah of Iran; he tried to revive Ardalan dynasty; Russian promised him in 1917 but non of the promises materialized. Reza Shah inflicted a heavy defeat of all the tribal leaders and in 1937 The Treaty of Saadabad was signed which provided an inter-state cooperation for border control.
1920–25	• **Sheikh Saied Piran** revolution; the Sheikh established Kurdish Independence society and attracted many educated Kurds all over Kurdistan; the revolution was brutally crushed by Mustfa Kamal and the Sheikh was executed.
1921–24	• **Ismail Simco revolution**; Simco's revolution against the Shah of Iran spanned a large area from Urmia, Mahabad, Saqez, East of Sulaimaniya and west of Arbil; he worked closely with Sheikh Mahmud in Suleimaniya.
1922–24	• **Sheikh Mahmud Barzanji** 2nd Revolution; established the Kingdom of Kurdistan and a civic administration; it was opposed by the British and he was removed and sent to exile. He died in Baghdad in 1956.
1927-30	• **Ararat (Agri) Uprising led** by Genral Ihsan Nuri Pasha; it was assisted by Khoibon Independent Party in Diaspora.
1932	• **Barzani revolt** led by Sheikh Ahmad Barazani
1941–44	• **Revolt of Hama Rashid Khan of Baneh,** Iranian Kurdistan; Hama Rashid Khan (1897–1974) tried to unite some of the Kurdish cities but was opposed by rival tribal leaders; later he joined the Kurdistan Replubci (1946–7) and the 1961–1970 Kurdish revolt in Iraqi Kurdistan
1946-47	• **Kurdistan Republic of Mahabad** led by Qazi Muhammad; the Russian withdrew support and so the two Republics of Kurdistan and Azerbaijan were defeated by Muhamad Reza Shah's forces. Mula Mustafa Barzani went to Soviet Union after the defeat.
1961–75	• **Iraqi Kurdish Revolution led by Mulla Mustafa Barzani'** in 1970 Iraqi government declared autonomy but the Kurds fall out which ended in the 1975
1975–91	• **Kurdish revolts for survival; Road to genocide:** Kurds after the defeat reorganized in Iran and used the Iran-Iraq War (1980–88) to attack Iraqi troops; the culmination of the campaign was the chemical bombardment of Halbja city. The period is characterized by internal conflicts between Kurdish parties.
1981–98	• **PKK and Abdula Ocalan;** PKK's legacy is a transformation of Kurdish society and enhancement of Kurdishness among the population; Ankara was not able to crush but Ocalan was kidnapped in 1998 and a new era has began for Kurds Under Turkish rule
1988–91	• **Anfal operation:** Road to quasi-independent Kurdish state or Kurdistan Regional Government. Saddam was weakened and so after the fall of the Saddam regime in Kurdistan, the area came under the control of iKurdish parties .
1992–now	• **Establishment of Kurdish Regional Government;** in 1992 a free election was held and a dual administration based on part-line was created. In mid 1990s onward much internal conflicts were registered but an armistice was reached with the help of Americans which led to new election in 2005 with an office for Presidency. The administration is still evolving.

Figure 8.1 Timeline of major Kurdish nationalist uprisings in the 20th century leading to the establishment of the Kurdistan Regional Government in Iraq.

research works, Kurdish Diasporas are referred to the boundary of the country of the origin, and so the danger is that Kurdish Diasporas are segregated according to the boundaries. As asserted by Brubaker (2005), this concept should not be treated as 'bounded entity'; instead, Diaspora should be treated like "*idiom, project stance and claim.*" In addition, we have to note that the influence of nation-states on Kurdish Diaspora is bidirectional as Alinia (2004) asserts that Kurdish Diaspora has strengthened and spread Kurdish nationalism and identity in those states.

The contextual setting of a Diaspora, including socio-political and institutional spaces of both 'home' and 'host' countries, needs to be considered. The homogeneity and 'unidimensional' nature of Kurdish Diaspora are questionable because they are site-specific. Khayati (2008) has illustrated the differences that exist in the formation of *Sarhadi* Kurdish Diaspora in France (Kurds from Turkey) and Kurds from Iraq and Iran in Sweden. France's exclusionary political environment, which is described as "*republican, assimilationist, universalist, secular and egalitarian*" (ibid: 50) entrenched with anti-immigrant or hostile policies toward foreigners, have imposed a different mode of action among *Sarhadi* Kurds. They have maintained their victim Diaspora discourse, whereas a favourable Swedish policy toward Kurds has created an environment for the Kurdish Diaspora to attain a developed practice of transborder citizenship (ibid: 256). Khayati (2008) illustrates that the Kurdish Diaspora community faces a varying degree of discrimination and social exclusion in Western Europe because the multicultural model of Sweden has been noted and criticised for its "*paradoxical and discriminatory (Ålund & Schierup 1991), segregationist (Magnusson 2001), racialized and exclusionary (Dahlstedt 2005; Dahlstedt & Hertzberg 2005; Kamali 2006)*"attributes (ibid: 50). However, Kurds have attained a high level of "*minority rights*" that created an enabling environment for socio-political (institutional) capacity development among the Kurdish Diaspora (ibid: 257). However, despite the heterogeneous nature of Kurdish Diaspora (i.e., different political affiliations, religious beliefs, dialects, cultural, educational backgrounds, and so forth), Kurdish Diasporas have a common attribute of having "*transnational social relation*" (Wahlbeck, 2002: 225). Since, Kurdish Diaspora stems from 'long-distance nationalism,' "*transnationalism is a subject that can no longer be ignored*" (Curtis, 2005). Thus, Wahlbeck (2002: 232) asserts that Kurdish Diaspora must be considered with the Weberian notion of *ideal type.*[4]

Khayati (2008) postulates the application of the term *asabiyya* (social cohesion, solidarity), which was coined by the Muslim sociologist Ibn Khaldoon (1332–1406). The *asabiyya* theory describes the rise and fall of civilisations. However, under the influence of the French political scientist Olivier Roy, Khayati emphasise the negative role of Kurdish *asabiyya* or *asabiyya* networks that exists among Kurdish Diaspora in Europe. Roy (1996) considers *asabiyya* to be exclusively formed among family and tribes or religious sects; however, *asabiyya* "*can also extend to clients and allies when mutual interest is involved*" (Weiss, 1995). Unlike Roy (1996) and Khayati (2008) who take a negative perspective on *asabiyya* theory and its application in a political context of loyalty affiliation, Weiss

(1995) and Chapra (2008) have appreciated the positive aspects of social cohesion theory in sustainable development envisioned by Ibn Khaldun, which is based on the concept of *asabiyya.*

Ibn Khaldun[5] used the word development '*umran*' with eight subcomponents (Ra'ad, 1993: 22): general, historical heritage, geographical, social governance and governmental (political), economical (exploitation & consumption), and cultural (thought) developments. Therefore, the problem of labelling Kurdish transnational networks as *asabiyya* networks makes Kurdish Diaspora vulnerable to unfavourable immigration and national security polices, racism, prejudice, and stereotyping, as well as generalization and oversimplification of complex social formations and integrations of a heterogeneous community. In addition, the diversity of the Diasporas that is usually ignored is seen from the prism of social fabric characteristics such as disunity, factionalism, and group (family, tribe) loyalty. This sort of label creates an atmosphere of fear and adversely affects the development and welfare of the Diasporas and restrains them to act as transnational citizens. There is a need to invigorate the role of Diasporas in community building and democratic transformations in both the host country and the homeland by acknowledging the diversity within a multicultural framework. Hence, the concept of transborder (transnational) citizenship is manifested in depicting positive aspects of Diaspora involving in the political processes, that is, political participation in "*system of norms, values and customs within a single polity*" (Glick Schiller 2005: 28). We need to avoid the situation in which Diasporas consider themselves as second-class citizens.

Therefore, one of the pitfalls of using the concept of Diaspora is disengaging the impact and the role of local political structures and the power relationship between minority-majority in the host countries (e.g. Wahlbeck, 2002). Wahlbeck (2002) asserts that local realities of diasporic experiences should not be ignored.

Contextual setting

'Virtual home' (countries of origin) of Kurdish diasporas

There is a degree of romanticism with the 'Lands of Kurds' or Kurdistan by Kurdish writers because, for instance, Kurdistan is described as "*forth paradise on Earth*" with abundant natural resources and immense natural beauty (e.g., Shafei Kurd; 1999: 20). Geopolitical setting of Kurdistan is characterised by engulfment between great neighbouring powers, which have created devastation to both Kurdish population and homeland. There is a historic hallmark that Kurds suffered both at the time of peace and war and have been subjected to inhumane treatments (e.g., Sharfkandi, 2002; 282). Generally, Kurds from the Iran, Iraq, Syria, Turkey, and Caucasus have suffered with varying degrees from internal colonialism (Gunter, 2004).

Despite suffering from one of the worst acts of carnage in the modern history, culminating in the chemical attacks on *Halabja* city (Iraqi Kurdistan) killing more than 5,000 people in 1988 and the *Anfal* military operation that claimed the lives of more than 180,000 people, Kurds from Iraq have been more successful in their nationalist aspiration. Kurdish language was recognized and Kurdish educational system started in the 1920s. In 1970, Iraqi regime declared an autonomy for the Kurdish region (without Kirkuk and Mosel) and in 1992, after the defeat of Saddam Hussein in Kuwait, a de facto Kurdish state was created, which continues to date.

Iran, which is a multi-ethnic society with 49 languages (Moqimi, 2006:21), has an integrationist policy, but the constitution states that all citizens are equal, irrespective of their ethnic background. However, full implementation of the constitution is lagging in many areas, including cultural and educational needs of the ethnic minorities. Kurds enjoy limited cultural freedoms, and there are Kurdish media and printing industry. Since late 1980s, armed conflicts have almost stopped; some of Kurdish leaders were assassinated in Europe. Since then, they have had a hard time because their activities have been restrained by not only Iran but also the Kurdish state of KRG. KRG is under immense and continuous pressure to safeguard the borderlines. For instance, Bazaz (1997: 184) documented PUK's pact[6] with Iranian Secret Services '*Etila'at*' with regard to border controls. Now, Iranian Kurdish groups are active in the Diaspora with limited success in international recognition and maintain a policy of political solution to Kurdish issue within a democratic Iran.

Kurds in Syria have been subjected to systematic assimilation policy (see e.g., Bilal, 1993; Mella, 2004) and *Arabisation* campaign since the 1960s, and many have been denied citizenship and considered as stateless refugees; in 1962, some 120,000 Kurds were removed from the population censuses (e.g., Khayati, 2008: 79). Kurds in Syria are forgotten, and they have been denied basic cultural rights.

Successive Turkish governments implemented a zero policy toward assimilating Kurds and even denying their existence after the fall of the Ottoman Empire and the creation of modern Turkey, which casts doubts on Turkey's claims about its secular democracy (see e.g., Sagnic, 2010). Turkey's brutal suppression of Kurdish identity has accompanied by savage act of genocide and mass displacement of Kurds since 1915; the massacre of Dersim in 1937–1938 amounts to an act of genocide (see e.g., van Bruinessen, 1994). Lately, state TV satellite in Kurdish was established, and Kurdish identity is stronger than few decades ago.

Based on a personal account of leading Kurdish historian and geographer, Karim Zand (b. 1925) in 1958, Kurds in former Soviet Union suffered from the communist rule; the Soviet Kurds were ethnically cleansed as they were dispersed and subjected to utmost oppression (Sadiq, 2003: 125). After the fall of the Red Empire, many Kurds left and some ended up in Europe. It is worth mentioning that both Tsarist and Soviet Russia were instrumental in setting up Kurdological studies and advanced Kurdish language and literature to some degree. The strong tradition of Russian Tsar Kurdology was continued during the Soviet era, which further revived Kurdish language. Haji Maref (1974) and Leezenberg (2011) provide a thorough review on the Orientalism and Kurdological work in Tsarist (Czarist) and Soviet Russia. As pointed out by Leezenberg

(2011), scholars working in Soviet institutions involved in *"state-supported anti-Islamic agitation,"* as well as reconstruction of the history of the region according to Marxist dogma.[7] However, perhaps, one of the important features has been the *"strong integration of "Orientals" into the scientific institutions."* There were a number of Soviet Kurds (such as *Amine Avdal* [1906–1964]; *Haji Jundi, Qanate Kurdo* [or *Kanat Kurdoev*] [1909–1985]) as well as students from Iranian and Iraqi Kurdistan (e.g., Piri, 2005) that were involved in the work of the Soviet academies in promoting Kurdology both in Kurdistan and Diaspora.

Kurdish identity and Diaspora: Issues of concern

Kurds have been criticised for (i) lacking essential characteristics of nationhood, (ii) not having an established Kurdish literature, and (iii) absence of nationalism or 'Kurdishness' among Kurdish dynasties. Some scholars such as McDowall (1997) have questioned the "nationhood" of Kurds and whether they have attained *"essential characteristics of nationhood."* According to McDowall, Kurds were disadvantaged because they *"lacked civic culture and established literature."* This refers to the fact that nomadic life was a feature of Kurdish tribes, and they maintained a strong oral tradition since much of the written literature has been lost because of chronic turbulent socio-political life in Kurdistan. There are some records of a well-developed Kurdish literature: for example, a great *Sufi* poet, *Baba Tahir* (937–1010) composed poetry in *Laki* dialect (Khaznadar, 2001: 184), as well as the *Yarisan* religious literature (901–1600) in Hawrami dialect. Driver (1922: 508) mentions some of Kurdish Scholars who composed in their mother tongue in the 11th to 15thcenturies, such as *Ali Hariri* (1009–1081), *Malai Jaziri* (1079–1161), and *Faqi Teiran* (1303–1476). *Abdul Samad Toodari,* in his book that was completed in 1687, narrates Kurdish poetry in *Hawarmi* dialect that dates back to nearly 500 years ago (Toodari, 1970: 4). Many Kurdish scholars wrote in Arabic, Farsi, and Turkish and greatly contributed to Islamic civilisation and played an important role after the dawn of Islam (see e.g., Pouladian, 2003).

However, McDowall (1997: 1) considers that *Ahamd-e-Khani* (1650–1707) was the first Kurd to think *"in terms of whole Kurdish people."Khani* tried to use different Kurdish dialects in his masterpiece *Mem wa Zin* as an attempt to present a unified language and integrate different dialects (Khani, 2008: 36). In addition, he influenced many Kurdish scholars to write in Kurdish, including the flagbearer of modern Kurdish nationalism, poet *Haji Qader Koei* (1817–1897).

Professor Q. Kurdo (1970) provides a comprehensive account of the contribution of Linguist Peter Lerch (1824–1874) to the Kurdish language. Lerch believes that Kurdish is an independent Iranian language and Kurdish grammar has a unique internal structure and asks for collecting more historical records as well as ethnographic, literary, linguistic materials to enrich the Kurdish language (Kurdo, 1970: 159).

Khoshhali (2000) asserts that the survival of a language depends on six effective factors:

- Nationalism: which strengthens national identity
- Religion: sacred texts are written in some languages that has been a source of its invigoration; e.g., Arabic language being the language of Qu'ran
- Government: that sponsors a language as its official language
- Geography: the members of a nation have easy access to each other within the homeland
- Common economic ties: with other nations, which can increase the importance of a language in trading, etc.
- Science and technology: which have a profound impact on the evolution of linguistic attributes

Given that almost none of the factors mentioned have materialised for Kurdish language, it can be argued that Kurdish language has survived despite the turmoil and trials of Kurdish history. Today, contemporary Kurdish language is able to exhibit versatility and richness to takes its place among the progressive and dynamic languages of the world.

McDowall (1997: 23) expresses cautiousness about the "Kurdishness" of dynasties that appeared in the 10th century, such as Shaddadids (951–1075), which ruled a huge area in East Transcaucasia between the Kur and Araxes rivers; Marwanids (984–1083),whose rule covered an area from Diyarbakir to Jazira, and Hassanwayhids (959–1095), which ruled an area from Shahrizur to Khuzestan (Zagros). This sentiment is resisted strongly by majority of Kurdish scholars and historians. This anthropological analytical approach used by McDowall seems to be flawed since it applies the criteria of nationalism of contemporary era (essentially a European concept) to a different socio-political setting in the past. Similarly, Edmonds (1971) casts doubt about the 'Kurdishness' of uprisings in 19th and early 20th centuries as religious, feudal, or tribal revolts with some nationalistic claims. He was off course one of the pillars of British Mandate in Iraq and later become special advisor to the newly Iraqi state that undermined the nationalist movement in Iraqi Kurdistan (al-Fayli, 2009).

According to Elphinston (1946: 91) Kurdish nationalist demands "*are not unreasonable*" but the ethnic discourse is not favoured by some scholars such as Eric Davis (2005),[8] who criticise this narrative as politically motivated and "*all possess a hidden text*" (Bengio, 2012: 8). In defence of Iraqi state, Davis completely ignores ethno-nationalism of Iraqi Kurds. Thus, the creation of nation-states in the 20th century had a profound impact on Kurdish nationalism as it came to collision with state nationalism.

Let us consider the Kurdish-Syrian conflicts as an example. The integration-ist doctrine of Syrian state is based on the concept of Syrian *Umma,* which has been described by Syrian journalist and political commentator Mazen *Bilal* (1993). Bilal postulates that the Kurdish migration in Syria inward (i.e., displacement of Kurds in Syria) is natural since *Umma* is a social unit of natural society of [multi-ethnic] people (ibid: 19). Similar to Davis, Bilal dismisses Kurdish nationalism as essentially political and cultural demands (ibid: 16) and claims that tracing down the linguistic and ancestral origin and homeland of Kurds is unable to frame the nationalistic aspiration of Kurds. According to Bilal, relating Kurds to their historic homeland 'Kurdistan' ignores the interaction, integration, and intermingling (mixing) aspects of any ethnic group with other groups both in time and place (ibid: 55). On this basis, he concludes, *"Kurds are not just descendants of Meds but they are descendants of all the other nations in the region"* (ibid: 57). Based on this analogy, Kurdish disaporic movement within Syrian *Umma* boundary is natural; the Kurdish Emirates of Ayobites, for example, prospered as they moved inward and toward Egypt, whereas as emirates were stopped and did not flourish as they tried to go northbound (ibid: 76).

In Turkey, Mustafa Kamal's strategy to deviate the imperialist forces (Britain and France) from Kurdish aspirations was based on a discourse that maintained a notion of *"sameness"*: Kurds are the same as Turks, and there is need for an independent Kurdistan (İçduygu and Kaygusuz, 2004).

The clash between nation states versus Diasporas has caused Brubaker (2005) to propose a question whether we have *"moved from the age of nation-state to the age of Diaspora."* According to Gunter (2004), a Kurdish state that is aspired by Kurdish Diaspora cannot be attained unless there is a total collapse of the four states. Therefore, Kurdish Diaspora maintains a high level of cultural activities to combat zealous state-nationalist practices endorsed by their supports in the international community.

As noted by Mino (2004: 331), Diaspora communities have a great affinity to the nationalist ideology as *"there is a dialectic relationship between exile, homesickness and nationalism."* On this basis, these feelings are entrenched once the Diasporas face discrimination and exclusions from the receiving societies. Based on many case studies, Mino asserts that Marxist and feminist inclinations have been weakened by the nationalist tides as Diasporas embraced nationalism (ibid: 332).

Wahlbeck (1998) asserts that *"the Kurds did not regard themselves as an ethnic minority within the context of the country of exile; instead their ethnicity was defined within social relations in the country of origin."* Mino (2004: 333) makes an important observation about the construction of Kurdish identify in her Swedish case study. Kurdish identity does not run against the Swedish identity or Swedish society but it is constructed *"in opposition to the dominant national identities in the countries of origin."* In this case, Kurdish identity centres on nationalism to resist the domination of nationalities imposed by the nation-states controlling Kurdistan. However, the Kurdish identity in Sweden is mobilised as a point of difference to resist the negative image of being a non-Swede or a non-state actor having a stigma of an immigrant. The Kurdish identity is seen within an ethno-cultural context or minorities that are living outside the mainstream society; thus, Kurdish identity is positional with reference of being migrants or minorities in the periphery. Thus, with respect to Swedish Society, Kurdish identity is *"more open, reflexive and positional."* This is certainly true for younger (second, third, etc.) generations, as well as the old Diaspora communities.

Formation of Kurdish Diaspora in Europe: toward 'transnational' citizenship

Geopolitical attributes

According to van Bruinessen (1995, 1999, 2000) and McDowall (1997), Kurdish Diaspora can be found in metropolitan urban centres of the Middle East, such as Damascus, Istanbul, Baghdad, Tehran, Izmir, and Ankara, as well as Western Europe (mainly in Germany, France, Sweden, and UK), Australia, and North America (Canada and USA).

The formation of Kurdish Diaspora in Europe has gone through four distinct phases: (i) *toward the end of the Ottoman rule*: the emergence of Kurdish media and presence of Kurdish students in the European urban centres such as Zurich, Geneva, London, and Leipzig; (ii) *1950s onwards*: the economic boom of western Europe demanded to recruit a large number of "guest workers" especially in Germany; and (iii) armed conflicts and coercive assimilationist polices of the states covering Kurdish homeland resulted in Diaspora movements outside Kurdistan and uprooted Kurds from their homeland; and (iv) political developments from 1980s onward, such as 1979 Iranian Islamic Revolution; 1980 Turkish coup d'état, and the emergence of the Kurdish Workers Party, PKK, and Iran-Iraq War (1980–1988). Since 1915, Kurdish wars have been one of the main reasons for refugee and migratory movements among Kurds (Hamdi, 1998; Hassanpour & Mojab 2004; Emanuelsson, 2005; Khayati, 2008).

Estimating the size of Kurdish Diasporas is not an easy task. Many researchers such as Gunter (1991) and Khayati (2008) have tried to establish an estimate the populations of Kurdish Diasporas. In highlighting the cultural dimension of Kurdish Diaspora, Johnston (2006) postulates that one-third of Kurds are living outside Kurdistan. According to this report, some 3 million Kurds live in Istanbul alone. Now, the Kurds in Khorasan (eastern Iran) are almost 700,000 strong. Johnston (2006) places Kurds in the Caucasus as Diaspora as follows: Turkmenistan (40,000), Azerbaijan (150,000), Armenia (45,000), and Georgia (60,000). This shows that Kurds in former Soviet Union have lost territorial claims in these former republics. Kurdish Diaspora in the Middle East concentrates in Afghanistan (200,000) and Lebanon (80,000). Notably, there are many Kurds living in Izmir, Adana, and Mersin, in Turkey; Baghdad, in Iraq; Tehran and Tabriz, in Iran. A small population of Kurdish Diaspora lives in the USA (20,000) and Canada (6,000). Johnston (2006) estimates that 85% of the 1.3 million Kurds in Europe are from Turkey, and up to 800,000 of the total number live in Germany. Kurdish Diasporas are found in France (150,000), UK (100,000), Sweden (100,000), Netherlands (100,000), and Switzerland and Austria (60,000)

Emergence of Kurdish state in Iraq and end of cold war

The Halabja chemical attack in 1988 and the mass exodus of hundreds of thousands of Iraqi Kurds in 1991 fleeing from Saddam Hussein's assault, which was played on small screens all over the world, gave Kurdish Diaspora a reason to provide financial and legal movements. The creation of a *Safe Haven* by the Allies to protect Kurds as an interventionist migration policy (see e.g., Weiner, 1993) was unprecedented. The tide of freedom in Eastern Europe gave new hopes for the Kurds in Diaspora and Kurdistan.

Therefore, there are two common features of Kurdish nationalist politics during all the revolutions (Figure 8.1): (i) formation of transnational networks; and (ii) cross-border alliances with states that have denied Kurdish self-determination (Denise, 2004). However, since 1991, there has been a marked difference in the transnational activities of Kurdish Diasporas. These communities have been providing financial and legal support thorough NGO and human rights campaigners in Europe's transnational spaces (Denise, 2004). Kurdish culture and language have flourished (McDowall, 1997: 547), and most Kurdish Diaspora identifies as Kurds in the first place (Denise, 2004).

A new generation of Kurdish Diaspora has surfaced according to Denise (2004); the pattern of dispersion and the way the Kurds scattered in Europe has created diversification and differentiation of Kurdish nationalist projects in Europe. According to Denise, "the *idea of Kurdish statehood is limited to cyberspace*" and the idea of Greater Kurdistan *Kurdistani-e-Yakparcha* (i.e., integrated Kurdistan) "*is not salient among Kurdish Diaspora*" (ibid: 112). From his experience and knowledge as a member of Kurdish Diaspora in Europe, the author argues that Kurdish statehood is a prominent idea in the community, but most of the attention has gone to the success of the KRG and most of the Kurds relate to Iraqi Kurdistan, irrespective of their country of origin. For example, in the aftermath of Syrian Arab Spring revolt against the Syrian regime, Mansour (2012: 3) describes how Syrian Kurds are looking up to KRG and Masod Barzani, its president as "*'margieya' 'authority' that Syrian Kurds look to.*" Nevertheless, pan-Kurdish nationalism is not well supported due to their realistic outlook. In addition, the process of refugee dispersion and uprooting is gradual and may lead to the creation of multiple refugee Diaspora *as stated by Bose* (2006: 66).

According the Bengio (2012: 15), adopting autonomy option in Iraqi Kurdistan "*seemed less threatening to the central government*" and so it could be realized more easily than independence. For many Kurds autonomy is a pathway to full independence. Mikesell and Murphy (1991) have introduced a formula to represent the minority aspirations, including Kurds in Kurdistan, which is given as below:

$$\frac{RAP}{SAI}\, formula = \frac{Objectives\,to\,stay\,within\,a\,nation-state}{Objectives\,to\,withdraw\,from\,larger\,society}$$

$$= \frac{\textbf{Recognition, Access, Participation}}{\textbf{Separation, Autonomy, Independence}}$$

The persistent aspiration of $\frac{R}{AI}$ has moved to an evolving aspiration of $\frac{\Box}{I}$, which indicates that the tensions has increased in the last few decades and the evolving aspiration is toward independence.

Since the 9/11 attacks, terrorism has been linked to Diaspora communities. Migration is a matter of national security, and this concept has been intensified after 9/11 September attacks in New York. Thus, Diaspora communities are affected by migration polices of host nations. Sweden and Britain have changed their policy toward Iraqi Kurds, and they have deported many asylum seekers back to Iraqi Kurdistan (e.g., Khayati, 2008: 85). Additionally, KHRP (2011: 15) notes that Kurdish asylum seekers being Muslims have been adversely affected by the media discourse on national security stemmed from '*Islamophobia*'[9] and immigration policy.

Therefore, this alarmist attitude toward non-state migrant actors as a source of terrorist attacked is echoed by many policy-making think tanks. For example, Simmons (2007) asserts that "*every country in the world today is facing 'stateless' terrorist attacks and the problems coming from 'global migration'*" [emphasis by the author]. Accordingly migrants affect the quality both social and profession life of citizens of the host countries and prove to have an impact on national security. However, the notion of 'self-determination,' which is entrenched in democratic theory, is bound to have an impact on the migration movements (Philpot, 1995) and so migration is a fact of democratic process all over the world, and much of Kurdish Diaspora formation has been due to the struggle for self-determination.

Refugees have been described as the "'*disquieting element*' *in the order of the nation-state in so far as s/he violates the basic principles of the nation-state and questions what is perceived as a mandatory link between state-nation-territory*" (Toninato, 2009).

King (2008) carried out an interesting study on Iraqi Kurdish returnees and their influence on the Kurdistan society's values and norms and the formation of an imaginary Diaspora in Iraqi Kurdistan. King concludes that many Kurds are "*becoming a diasporic people even though most have never left 'home'*" (ibid: 221).

As will be described in the next section, a new transnational space has been created for Kurdish Diaspora to involve in the process of peace building and democratisation in the Iraqi Kurdistan and subsequently in the rest of Kurdistan. For example, with the help of Kurdish Diaspora, National Conference for Fayli Kurds were established in 2009 and Iraqi Prime Minster attended their second anniversary in 2010 (Aswat-al Iraq, 2011). Fayli Kurds have strong ties with the Arab and Shiite Iraqi community, and many have invested in Jordan and have claimed their Iraqi national identity. Iraqi government have issued citizenship to 120,000 Fayli Kurds (Shafaq, 2012) since more than 400,000 were forced out of Iraq (i.e., Baghdad and parts of Diyala province, e.g., Khanaqin, Mandali, etc.) during the 1970s and 1980s.

By inspecting Figure 8.1, we can notice that Kurds experienced short periods of quasi-independence including Shiekh Mahmud Barzanji's Kurdish states in 1918–1919 and 1922–1924 and the *Mahabad* Republic in1945–1946. Therefore, the emergence of quasi-independent Kurdish state in Iraqi Kurdistan in 1992 is one of the biggest achievements of Kurdish nationalist movements cherished by all segments of the Kurdish society and has had a great influence on the formation of Kurdish Diaspora activities in Europe (Khayati, 2008: 257).

Stansfield et al (2007) asserts the importance of KRG's evolvement, which can influence Kurds in the region. They note that Kurdish political demands are limited (although Kirkuk, Mosel, Khaneqin, and others parts of Kurdistan are unresolved), but there is a movement of masses toward strengthening national awareness and aspirations.

Kurdish Diaspora as a driving force toward peace and democracy at 'virtual home and real home'

Challenges and opportunities: Peace and democracy starts at real home

As shown in previous sections, it is argued that peace and democracy for Kurdish Diaspora start at 'real home,'or, in other words, the host country. There are two main issues: reform of Kurdish politics (e.g., Khayati, 2008) and redefinition of the scope of transnational political field to include local politics (e.g., Mino, 2004). Ethnonationalism of the 1960s–1980s are no longer appealing to many in the Kurdish Diaspora, especially the younger generations. There are some examples of innovative projects, such as the creation of a Kurdish customary justice system consisting of the Kurdish Peace Committee (KPC) to resolve diverse array of cases, including family disputes to minor criminal cases (Latif, 2012).

One of the most vulnerable groups is refugees and asylum seekers. The role of community centres within European transnational spaces needs to be strengthened to provide assistance to this disadvantaged segment of Kurdish Diaspora. The Kurdish Cultural Centre (KCC) in London, which is one of the first community centres in the UK, was established in May 1985 as a voluntary refugee organisation providing advice, information, and assistance to members of the Kurdish Community in the area of immigration, welfare rights, housing, health, integration, employment, and training. In 1986, the author had its first contact with KCC and, together with other members of the family, became a member of KCC. KCC is largely a refugee-oriented group and does not play a visible role in the Diaspora or transnational social fields. Thus, since 2005, KCC is dealing with voluntary and compulsory returnees, which has been hallmark of British immigration policy. The 2008 Immigration and Citizenship Bill introduce the idea of "*earned citizenship*" for foreigners who want to become British (Dissanayake, 2008).

One of the disheartening aspects of participating in the affairs of such centres is the issue of power struggle within these organisations. KCC was (and is) the hub for Iraqi Kurds whom dominated the politics of running the organization. There was a great deal of power struggle to control KCC. Kurdish leftist elite such as *Kamal Mirawdali* lost control from 1991 onward, PUK and KDI supporters gained control after the changes that occurred in Iraqi Kurdistan, and the KRG was created in 1992.

Kurdish Diaspora in Europe has been effective in getting support for the Kurdish cultural aspiration and not the political aspiration; for example, French's socialist government has helped to establish and fund the Kurdish Institute in Paris headed by Kendal Nezan (Khayati, 2008: 12). Sweden is the hub for Kurdish Diaspora cultural activity in Europe (Khayati, 2008: 49). Swedish government has *"given official recognition to the Kurdish National Union and helped to finance the publication of over twenty books in Kurdish for adults and children."* Sweden has allowed the creation of various Kurdish professional associations for teachers, doctors, and so forth. Kurdish Institute in Paris has been close to the EU and has worked toward the recognition of Kurdish identity and cultural needs of the Diasporic community (Johnston, 2006).

Kurds as Non-State Actors have received little attention compared to other issues, such as those affecting Palestinians. However, this trend has recently changed, but not necessarily to the advantage of Kurdish transnationalism. Much of the attention has been on the role of PKK in galvanising Kurdish identity in Europe. For example, Gunter (1991: 13) highlights the *"underground conflicts"* among Kurds from Turkey and the 'gang culture,' which has been the hallmark of PKK movements in Europe. Gunter speculates that these activities may be aimed at *"eliminating defectors, attacking ideological foes, extorting money, and striking at collaborators."* Without presenting any evidence, Gunter hints at implicating PKK in the assassination of the Olof Palme (1927–1986), Swedish Prime Minister (Gunter, 1991: 13). According to Philips (2007: 11) Kurdish Diaspora in Europe (i.e., Switzerland, Britain, Sweden, Belgium, Denmark, and Cyprus) has been funding PKK through *"cultural associations and information centres such as the Kurdish Employers Association, the Kurdish Islamic Movement, and the Kurdish Red Crescent."* PKK's annual income estimated at 500 million US Dollars in 1998 and still had an income of 150 million US Dollars in 2005, mainly through the sale of heroin in Europe.

Phillips (2007) believes that the process of democratisation in Turkey will help the Kurdish cause as human rights and cultural and political reforms *"would effectively address Kurdish grievances."* He argues that dealing with the PKK requires carrot-stick policy; the financial revenues of the PKK to be targeted and limited and licenses of Kurdish TV media enterprises to be revoked (Philips, 2007: 6).

A landmark in the history of Kurdish media as a nation-building exercise by the Kurdish Diaspora was the establishment of the first satellite TV station, namely MED-TV in 1995 (McDowall, 1997; Hassanpour, 1998; van Bruinessen, 1999; Khayati, 2008); later, in 1999, the Independent Television Commission in the UK revoked its license. This is in line with recommendation made by Philips (2007) eight years later. However, Kurdish media has been resilient: a few months later MEDYA TV was on air, and since then, a flurry of other satellite stations started to broadcast in Kurdish as listed by Khayati (2008: 92). Many radio stations have also been established, and some have been specifically intended for the Kurdish Diaspora in Europe. Mutlu asserts that Kurdish Diasporic institutions from Turkey have been able to use internet as a tool to achieve their goals (Mutlu, 2007: 27).

In order to have a viable role in peace-building and democratic process in the Middle East, it is vital that political organisations in Diaspora are remoulded and reformed to embrace openness and increase their representativeness. Khayati

(2008) uses a power-centred approach to reconstruct the current nationalist discourse in terms of power relations and human rights. He attempts to convey the "*voice of those diasporan Kurds who want to see democratic change in Kurdish politics*" (ibid: 255). In the process, Khayati (2008) unpacks the contemporary Kurdish Diaspora as a victimized community experiencing "oppression and trauma" in the "homeland of origin" to include the socio-political attributes of the Diaspora community, or, in other words,"*concrete and tangible network formations and institutional activities that take place in both time and space.*"

European transnational spaces offer contradictory and paradoxical condition for Kurdish Diaspora activities, as was evident in the Öcalan refusal to stay in Europe (Rogers, 2004: 180). According to Stansfield et al (2007),"*rights of self-determination, for example, rarely trump the necessity of maintaining stability in regions of geopolitical importance.*" Thus, non-state actors do not fit easily to the jigsaw of nation-state setup. Therefore, according to Soguk (2008), one of the challenges that faces Kurdish Diaspora movements in Europe is going against the diplomatic tide, which aims to imprison the community in "*spatially Cartesian and politically state orientated*" landscape (space), which ignores transnational and transversal social formations. Soguk (2008) describes Kurdish Diaspora formations in Europe as "*transversal practices that communicate against the disciplinary boundaries imposed upon the political imagination through traditional International Relations.*"

Kurdish Diaspora from different countries of origin has had a varying degree of success in working in European transnational spaces. According to Denise (2004), Iraqi Kurds have benefited from the European political spaces and have gained recognition internationally, whereas Kurds from Turkey and Iran are much less fortunate. For example, Kurds from Turkey have been "*delegitimised at 'home and criminalised' 'abroad*'" (ibid: 113). Iranian Kurds have had not much success in attracting recognition, and they have mainly worked with Iraqi transnational networks. Similarly, Syrian Kurds have been ignored, and their concerns have been taken within the human right and reform of the Syrian regime framework. It is worth mentioning that in the late 1980s, the Syrian Kurds led a pan-Kurdish organisation, Kurdistan National Congress, KNC, in London, in established Western Kurdistan Government in Exile in 2006 (Mella, 2007). KNC has no legal status and had little sympathy from the UK government. Generally, Kurdish Diaspora is restrained by relationship between home and host governments.

Europeanisation of Kurdish Diaspora: Lobbying and advocacy

Kurdish Diaspora formation has been influenced by local experiences of long-distance nationalism within transnational social fields as well as multiculturalism of the Diaspora space. Based on a Kurdish migrants case study in Halle, Germany, Glick Schiller (2005: 38) states that "*the overarching Kurdish experience and identity some of these migrants come to share are being produced by the local public culture in Halle.*" Baser (2010) has noted that the many Kurds from Turkey enhanced their *Kurdishness* (or *Kurdayati*) when they arrived in the Diaspora.

According to Mutlu (2007), Kurdish Diaspora in Europe has been Europeanized as it has established powerful organizations working at different governance level on the political landscapes of Europe. Mutlu (2007) has examined the role of three Kurdish Diaspora organizations working at European and nation-state levels namely Kon-Kurd (*Konfederasyona Komelen Kurd li Ewrupa*), a pan-European Confederation of Kurdish Associations in Europe stationed in Brussels; Yek-Kom (Association of Kurdish Organizations in Germany) with about 50 members and Kom-Kar (*Yetkiya Komelen Kurdli Elmanya*) with about 40 members.

Although Kon-Kurd's constitution draws on the role of the organization in Europe, it goes beyond the European border, lobbies the EU on the Kurdish struggle in Turkey, and thus represents a classic case of using Diasporic space to engage in the politics of the homeland (Mutlu, 2007: 27). Yek-Kom has been involved at nation-state level and entered German political space to "*to pressure the German government to get involved in the Turkish government's practices against the Kurds and to give the Kurdish Diaspora a political space from which to operate*" (Mutlu, 2007: 27). As noted by Khayati (2008: 87), German policy-makers think of political activism of PKK related Diaspora as illegal and so face many challenges with regard to its internal policies on immigration and citizenship. Banning PKK in EU, including France and Germany, has had a psychological impact on some segments of Kurdish Diaspora in Europe; a worker in Marseille felt that "*in Europe we obtain neither political freedom nor residence permits for starting a decent life*" (Khayati, 2008: 87). Marlies (2010) states that naming PKK as a terrorist group was a blow to Kurdish nationalism. Kidnapping Abdula Öcalan created resentments among Kurdish Diaspora irrespective of political affiliation and Europe witnessed huge protests by thousands of Kurds demanding justice for Kurdistan and Öcalan (e.g., Khayati, 2008; Newland, 2010: 13; Wahlbeck, 2002)

Yek-Kom is a perfect example of a Diasporic organization that deals with helping the Kurdish community to interstate into the German economy, as well as associate with PKK and Kurdish struggle in Turkey. In addition, it has created think-tanks "with intellectual objectives" such as The Kurdish Human Rights Project (KHRP) located in London (Mutlu, 2007: 28). KHRP as a registered charity have gained a great deal of support from wide range of governments, private trusts and foundations, and other grant-making bodies. Spearheaded by Kerim Yildiz and Feeney, Cardinal Hume's advisor on refugees, KHRP began to use EU, European Commission on Human Rights, Organisation for Security and Co-operation in Europe (OSCE), and several UN governance mechanisms to submit urgent action appeals with a commitment to protect the human rights of all persons within the Kurdish regions irrespective of race, religion, sex, political persuasion, or other belief or opinion.

The new generation of Kurds has a different outlook from first and second generations: contemporary issues in the Diaspora space, including racism, equal opportunity, and employment; social welfare and youth alienations influence them. From the author's experiences in the UK, a Kurdish youth in London relates to 'Black and Asian' or 'Muslim' Diaspora issues as well. Those writing only about Kurdish Diaspora in terms of nationalist and ethic terms had ignored this issue. Thus, Kurdish Diasporic landscape's mosaic nature sometimes is over-looked. Many Kurds in the UK are proud of their British heritage and education, and belong to their local niches. Kurdish Diaspora in the UK is participating in the local British politics: many Kurdish councillors in London lobby about politics back at home. Some members of the Diaspora use financial muscles to invest in Kurdistan (Dissanayake, 2008). Similarly, *Alevi* Diaspora in Istanbul, for exam-ple, have started investing millions of dollars to improve the living conditions of their ancestral villages (Askoy, 2011: 99).

In Sweden, many Kurdish organizations are affiliated with political forma-tions in Kurdistan, which are lobbying at national level such as Federation of Kurdish Associations in Sweden (*Kurdiska Riksförbundet i Sverige*), the Council of Kurdish Associations in Sweden (*Kurdiska Rådet i Sverige*), and the Kurdish Union (*Kurdiska Unionen*) (ibid: 56).

Similar to European Kurdish Diaspora, Joseph (2008:5) states that Kurdish Mus-lim Diaspora in the United States consider engagement in the process of lobbying as their American identity: "*we are Kurds, yes – but we are also Kurdish Americans.*" In order to enhance the Kurdish identity, Kurdish Diaspora in Europe has prac-ticed long-distance nationalism together with outreached activities including public relations and awareness campaigns. Karadaghi (2012) calls upon the newly estab-lished Kurdish Diaspora in the United States to use varied methods to try to achieve the aim of Kurdish National Congress – North America KNC-NA – of indepen-dence including lobbying and advocacy, media campaigns, publicity stunts, polls, and research and policy briefings. Since the Kurdish community is new, there is a need for enhancement of socio-economic structures and community building in the United States and Canada. Therefore, business initiatives are encouraged by KNC.

Based on a case study about Kurdish migrants from Turkey, Nell (2008) con-cludes that:

- Kurdish Diaspora can be mobilised quickly and effectively due to the exis-tence of Diasporic institutional and socio-political networks in Netherlands;
- These networks encourage the community to integrate in the socio-political landscapes of the host country;
- Contrary to the widely held view that transnational activities are violent, vio-lent transnationalism is rarely practiced and limited;
- Elite transnational actors who return to their homeland are rarely given politi-cal position due to lack of trust and doubtless about their loyalty; and
- "*[I]f the first generation migrants realise that their residence is permanent, their political transnational involvements on the whole decreases*" (ibid: 203).

Nell thus introduces a time factor into the political transnational activities, as sec-ond generations are not bound to get involved, that is, it is not a matter of fact but a matter for their conscience.

Zoukui (2008) argues that the EU's governance system encourages the role of civil society and lobbying groups. PKK has cleverly used the governance model of EU and well understood the tripartite relationship between EU member-states and lobby/pressure groups by using Turkey accession application as an entry point to voice Kurdish legal rights and force Turkey to make a choice about its actions. On the other hand, EU's governance structure and model was instrumental in transforming "PKK Diaspora" from a violent group to a social-movement organization. Not only PKK has changed. There is a tide of transformation in Turkey which has to be welcomed; Prime Minister *Recep Tayyip Erdogan* on behalf of the state has apologised for the death of thousands of Kurds in Dersim in 1937 (van Bruinessen, 1994; Ahmad, 2012). This apology came 75 years late but indicates a change of policy toward the Kurdish issue and the influence of Kurdish Diaspora to bring about this transformation.

Dissanayake (2008 a) expresses the sentiments of the Kurdish Diaspora in the UK. What is now uniting the community is an increasing feeling that a key priority has to be those Kurds who live here and not just those back home. Many Kurds in north London perceive themselves as "*second class citizens*" and they worry about education and underperformance of Kurdish youth and want to change that situation. '*Charity begins at home.*'

Rethinking 'Kurdayati'nationalism: A proactive approach for peace and democracy

Kurdish nationalism or '*Kurdayati*' is hooked on the principle of self-determination (e.g., KNC, 1998 for KNC Charter). According to Stansfield et al. (2007), among others, no Kurdish politicians are asking for an independent Kurdistan state except "*some rather noisy if powerless leaders of Diaspora groups.*" One of these voices is Jewat Mella, President of the Western Kurdistan Government in Exile and KNC, London even complains about the treatment of the semi-independent Kurdish state of KRG toward their activities (Cemawar Newspaper, 2007: 9).

KNC is perhaps a lone voice in Kurdish politics but has a wide appeal, especially among younger generations in Diaspora and those who want a change in Kurdish politics. In modern time, Kurdish political activists in the Diaspora were mainly from leftist, Marxist, or secular organisations. These blamed the failure of Kurdish liberation movements on the backwardness of the Sheikhs and the Kurdish aristocracy who lead the movements from 1880 to late 1950s, that is, before the establishment of political parties. Therefore, there has been a clear conflict between the old 'religious' and new 'secular and Marxist' nationalisms. KNC brought a fresh thinking by calling for unity to achieve the ultimate goal of Greater 'United' Kurdistan. In comparison, Mella (1985: 21; 2005: 33) praises the positive and immense role that Kurdish Sufi leaders have had in the uprising liberation movements in Kurdistan:

> *Sufi ways have played an important role in the Kurdish liberation movement since most of the Sufi Sheikhs were leaders of the people whereby they defended the rights of their followers and dependents from their cells and helped them against the injustice caused by the colonising countries.*

Without any doubt, Kurdish identity and nationalism in Europe and Kurdistan have been bolstered, and Kurdish Diaspora has improved its place in the international affairs. They have played a major role in the accession application of Turkey to EU, which can be translated into establishment of fundamental rights, justice, cultural freedom, and political representation for Kurds in Turkey. However, Kurdish-EU/US interests are complicated by the process of self-determination that involves the breakup of existing states in the Middle East, which is seen as a destabilising factor threatening peace and democracy in the region.

Since Kurdistan is perceived as an anomaly in the Middle East, it is vital that its pivotal role in peace building is reinforced. Some Kurdish media has led this strategy by acknowledging the requirement for a balancing act between Kurdish nationalism and regional peace and security, which is promoted by US/EU. For example, in 1998, KurdishMedia.com[10] United Kurdish Voice was co-founded by Dr *Rebwar Fatah*, *Peshraw Namo* and *Welat Lezgin*. In the 1990s, Fatah was working with refugee charities such as British Refugee Council and created a lobby group called "*Hawkarani* Kurdistan" and founded Kurdish media enterprises in the UK and Australia. Fatah is also affiliated with Kurdish Democratic Alliance and Kurdistan Centre for Democracy in the Middle East (KCDME), which are transnational networks working in Kurdistan and Diaspora. Kurdish-Media.com "defines a state of *"United Kurdistan "as an isle of peace at the heart of the Middle East"* and attempts to portray Kurdistan as a *"civilised nation in the international arena."*

Kurdistan Democratic Alliance (KDA) and KCDME were co-founded by Ayob Barezani, cousin of KRG's President. Both organisations are registered in the UK as a non-profit, community-based organization working in Kurdistan and Diaspora promoting the culture of democracy and tolerance in the Middle East. In 2009, KDA produced a draft election manifesto that outlines its vision for good governance in the Kurdistan regional area. Despite its inaccurate and rather obscure statements about religious and ethical attributes of Kurdish community, the manifesto is an attempt to entrench democratic principles and good governance system in Kurdistan, highlights the role of the Kurdish Diaspora, and facilitates their return.

KDA, KCDME, and KurdishMedia.com are very critical of the current KRG set up and would like to put in place a more civilised democratic system. KRG is known for its corruption and family monopolies of power. These voices in Diaspora have supported the Movement of Change '*Bzutinewey Gorran*' that has shaken the political order in Kurdistan asking for the end of monopoly of power and uproot of corruption.[11]

Emanuelsson (2008) explores the merits of involving Kurdish Diaspora in the development process of the Kurdistan region by implementing peace building and democratisation initiatives. Kurdish Diaspora has been mobile and active in Iraqi Kurdistan helping in the area of capacity development (KRG, 2008). For example, UK's Kurdish Medical Association organised training and scientific conferences and tried to establish a robust healthcare system (KuMA – UK2008). On the other hand, KRG has tried to attract Kurds in Diaspora to invest in the region. Kurdish Diaspora community can provide a link between East and West and bridge the gaps in the heterogeneous society to create social cohesion and a drive for sustainable development.

Emanuelsson (2008) highlights both structural and nonstructural measures that have to be taken in order to help the region to attain a better life. Nonstructural measures include social justice, rights, equality, good governance, and institutional capacity development. However, structural infrastructures are vital to keep the process of development. Kurdish Diaspora have to be encouraged to build transnational bridges for investments, humanitarian assistance, and professional exchange and seeking partners among government officials and activists in the countries of settlement. For this to happen, transnationality (dual citizenship) of Diaspora has to be respected.

Kurdayati concept need to be reoriented by creating a culture of tolerance and coexistence, and moving away from imported concepts such as Marxist dialectic interpretations of ethnicity, nationalism of the nation-state, and historical myths of the 'homeland.' As mentioned before, almost all historians agree that the presence of oil reserves in Kirkuk, Mosel, and *Khanaqin* was a prime reason for splitting up Kurdistan. Paradoxically, Kurdish nationalist projects in Diaspora have tried to do a deal with global forces such as USA without any regard for Kurdish national sovereignty or sustainable energy policy. Therefore, the reorientation of *Kurdayati* should encompass regional cooperation, shared responsibility based on common goods, values, and comanagement of natural resources by envisaging supranational governance mechanisms to deal with fragmentations and disparity in terms of political, economic, and social aspects within nation-states in the Middle East region.

Conclusions

Kurdish Diaspora in Europe has grown in size and stature strengthening Kurdish cultural, education, and nationalism aspects. Kurdish language and culture have been enriched in Diaspora. According to Aktar (2012), Kurdish language teaching experiences in Sweden and Netherlands provide an opportunity to start Kurdish education in Turkey. The Turkish state asked *Sivan Perwer*, a famous Kurdish singer who immigrated to Germany in 1976, to come back to Turkey for the opening of the state Kurdish satellite (Aksoy, 2011), despite a ban on his album records in Turkey. This indicates cultural influences of Kurdish Diaspora in Kurdistan.

The diversity of Kurdish Diaspora poses a stern challenge to Kurdish statehood concept, despite strengthen nationalism home and abroad (Denise, 2004). Therefore, *Kurdiayati* movements need to be reoriented in order to deal with the changing attitudes and circumstances. Kurds have gained international recognition and visibility with vibrant culture and language, but politically, they are trapped in the wider Middle Eastern politics, which are influenced by global policies toward energy, food, and water security. Kurds must understand very well the energy-food – water nexus and position themselves accordingly.

Early Kurdish Diaspora was mainly involved in Kurdistan politics through transnational networks, but since the 1990s, there has been a change of emphasis concerning the nationalist aspiration described by Eminent Kurdish Scholar Ala-Adin Sajadi (1907–1984) as Kurdish struggle for peace and freedom (Sajadi, 1996: 24). Kurdish Diaspora has chosen to take a 'human rights' and secular route, which was a plausible strategy to avoid humanitarian disasters and atrocities against Kurds in future. The Halabja holocaust had a remarkable impact on Kurdish Diaspora politics. Therefore, as noted by Enteesar (1992), there was a need to reconstruct Kurdish ethno-nationalism from the perspective of human rights and international laws with the hope of preventing genocidal policies like those that have persecuted the Kurds in both Turkey and Iraq. However, without political support of EU and member states, Kurdish transnational networks will be frustrated and disappointed with paradoxical and contradictory state of affairs in European transnational spaces, which was evident in the case of preventing PKK leader, *Öcalan* to stay in the European space.

Kurdish Diaspora has been active in all levels of governance at local, state, regional (e.g., EU), and global (e.g., UN) and has been 'Europeanised' in the sense that they have taken advantage of transnational spaces to advance the Kurdish question. However, as pointed out by Soguk (2008), transversal practices of Kurdish Diaspora are ignored as they proceed beyond diplomatic boundaries of the EU, the United States, and other global and regional powers. However, there is consensus that Kurdish issue must be recognized and addressed within the nation-states framework (see e.g., Robins, 1993). Kurdish Diaspora in Europe can play a pivotal role in ethnic reconciliation in the Middle East by supporting the creation of supranational governance mechanisms for peace and reconciliation in the Middle East. European Union is a good example of supranational governance system that has maintained peace in Europe for more than six decades. That is why it deserves the *Nobel Peace Prize* in 2012.

Notes

1 It is noted that the spelling of the term *Kordestan* is kept different in all Iranian official documents to avoid any cross references to the term *Kurdistan,* which is the homeland of all the Kurds in the region.
2 The figures in brackets are estimated by KHRP (2009), except the population of Kurds from Iran which is estimated by Yildis and Taysi (2007).
3 See Impact (1998); *Sheikh Sayed Muhammed Hadi Hashemi Kurdistani* was based in Dolab, which is 45km outside Sanandaj. He was a prominent Kurdish dissident supporting the idea of Kurdish independence within a supranational federation of Middle Eastern states, which exhibits strong cultural, ethical, and religious ties. The family of the late Sheikh belongs to the *Barzanji Sayyeds* (or House of Prophet Muhammad). In

1998, he died in London and was buried in *Dolab*. In Kurdistan, there are two main Orders of Sufism, namely Qadri and Naqeshbandi. There are many branches of each order. One of the main branches of the Qadri Order is the Solaei branch, which operates in both Iraqi and Iranian Kurdistan, including Sulaymani, Sirwan (Diyala), Kermanshah, Kordestan, West Azerbaijan, and Kermanshah provinces, as well as the Arab-populated area in mid Iraq around Baghdad and Anbar province, namely the cities of Faloja and Rumadiya.

4 The concept of *ideal type* was envisaged by Max Weber (1864–1920); it is "a conceptual tool to approach reality" and so, in this sense, it can be considered as a "*conceptual construct*" (see, e.g., Swedberg, 2005: p.120).

5 English translation of Ibn Khaldun's Al-Muqaddimah is available at: http://www.muslimphilosophy.com/ik/Muqaddimah/

6 Letter from Jalal Talabani to Mr Jabbari, written in Tehran dated 28 September 1995; this letter was allegedly left in the Patriotic Union of Kurdistan (PUK)'s offices in Erbil (Hawlir).

7 There are some sweeping criticism of the Soviet Kurdology works; see, for example, Asatrian (2009), who argues that Kurdology has been politicized and marred with "*industry of amateurs*" and "during recent decades many ideological elements of non-academic provenance have found their way into the academic milieu and created constant stereotypes and a set of clichés, which, in fact, have nothing to do with reality." For obvious reasons, politicising Kurdology is not surprising.

8 Davis, E. (2005). *Memories of State: Politics, History, and Collective Identity in Modern Iraq*. Berkeley: University of California Press.

9 The term Islamophobia was formally coined by the Runnymede Trust in 1997 (e.g., Tamdgidi 2012). Runnymede Trust was established in 1968 to challenge racial discrimination, influence legislation and to promote multi-ethnicity in the UK (Tamdgidi 2012). According to Wikipedia (Islamophobia, http://en.wikipedia.org/wiki/Islamophobia, last accessed 6 October 2013), Islamophobia is prejudice against, hatred towards, irrational fear of, or racism towards Muslims. The Runnymede report defined Islamophobia and "closed views of Islam" as follows (Runnymede Trust 1997: 2, as cited by Tamdgidi 2012: 57): '(i) Islam [is] seen as a single monolithic bloc, static and unresponsive to new realities; (ii) Islam [is] seen as separate and other—(a) not having any aims or values in common with other cultures (b) not affected by them (c) not influencing them; (iii) Islam [is] seen as inferior to the West—barbaric, irrational, primitive, sexist; (iv) Islam [is] seen as violent, aggressive, threatening, supportive of terrorism, engaged in 'a clash of civilisations'; (v) Islam [is] seen as a political ideology, used for political or military advantage; (vi) Criticisms made by Islam of 'the West' [are] rejected out of hand; (vii) Hostility towards Islam [is] used to justify discriminatory practices towards Muslims and exclusion of Muslims from mainstream society; and (viii) Anti-Muslim hostility [is] accepted as natural and 'normal. (see Runnymede Trust (1997). Islamophobia: a challenge for us all. Report of Runnymede Trust Commission on British Muslims and Islamophobia, London, Runnymede Trust.)

10 See http://www.Kurdishmedia.com

11 This movement is led by *Nawshirwan Mustafa*, ex-PUK member.

References

Ahmad. A. (2012). *Erdogan's Kurdish Challenge*. Huff Post Religion, Social Reading, Religion section, Blogs, posted 3 March 2012.

Aksoy, O. (2009). Sivan Perwer and Kurdish Music: I Would Return to Turkey to Contribute to Peace. *Kurdish Herald*, 1(2): 9–10.

Aksoy, O. (2011). Music of the Kurdish Alevi Diaspora in Germany: Struggling '*with*' and '*for*' Multiple Identities. *Perspectives on Europe, Council of Europe Studies*, 2(41): 96–99.

Aktar, C. (2012). Inclusion of Kurdish language in education system. *Today's Zaman*, June 27, 2010 edition.

Ardalan, M. (2005). History of Kurds. Iraq, Arbil: Aras Publishing [in Kurdish].

Arikanli, Z. (2010). Kurdish Nationalism in Iraq (1918–1926): What Significance the 'Mosul Question'?, *Alternatives: Turkish Journal of International Relations*, 9(4): 91–131.

Asatrian, G. (2009). Prolegomena to the Study of the Kurds. Iran and the Caucasus, 13: 1–58.

Asasrad, F. (2007). *The Kurdish Issue after enactment of Iraqi State Management Act*. Egypt, Cairo: Madbouli Bookshop [in Arabic].

Aswat-al Iraq (2011). Over 22,000 Iraq's Faili Kurds deported by former regime, Maliki says. Available from: http://en.aswataliraq.info/(S(zktzbk45w1tg3vicldinio55))/Default1.aspx?page=article_page&id=145102 (last accessed 11 October 2012).

Bahraminia, O. (2007). History of Kurds of Jazira region from year 447 til 656 after Hijra. Iran, Tehran: Ihsan Publications [in Farsi].

Barezani, M. (2002). *Struggles of Kurdish people for Freedom and liberation and Movement of Mula Mustafa Barzani*. Trans by Muhammdi, M., Iran, Saqez: Muhammadi Publications [in Farsi].

Baser, B. (2010). Stateless Diasporas and Their Long Distance Nationalist Activism in Host Countries. *Paper presented at the 5th ECPR Conference, 23rd–26th June 2010* hosted by University of Oporto (Faculty of Economics) and University Fernando Pessoa.

Bazaz, S. (1997). Kurds in Iraqi question. Jordan/Amman: Ahliya Publishing [in Arabic].

Bilal, M. (1993) Kurdish question: myth or truth. Lebanon/Beirut: Bisan Publishing [in Arabic].

Bois, T. and Minorsky, V. (1986). Kurds, Kurdistan. In: Bosworth, C.E. (ed.). The Encyclopedia of Islam. Vol. 5 (pp. 438–486), The Netherlands/ Leiden: Brill.

Bose, P. (2006). Dilemmas of Diaspora: Partition, Refugees, and the Politics of "Home." *Refuge*, 23(1): 58–68.

van Bruinessen, M. (1994). Genocide in Kurdistan? The suppression of the Dersim rebellion in Turkey (1937–38) and the chemical war against the Iraqi Kurds (1988) In: Andreopoulos, G. J.(ed.)., *Conceptual and historical dimensions of genocide* (pp. 141–170). Philadelphia: University of Pennsylvania Press.

van Bruinessen, M. (1995). The impact of the dissolution of the Soviet Union on the Kurds. *Paper presented at the International Conference on Islam and Ethnicity in Central Asia*, St Petersburg, 14–18 October, Utrecht University.

van Bruinessen, M. (1999). *Migrations, mobilizations, communications and the globalization of the Kurdish question*. Working Paper No. 14, Islamic Area Studies Project, Tokyo.

van Bruinessen, M. (2000). Transnational aspects of the Kurdish question. Working Paper, Robert Schuman Centre for Advanced Studies, European University Institute, Florence.

Cemawar Newspaper (2007). Interview with Jewat Mella President of Western Kurdistan Government in Exile: PUK and KDI are worse than Kurdistan occupiers in terms of their hostility towards our work, 2(218), pp. 9 [in Kurdish].

Chapra, M. Umer (2008) Ibn Khaldun's theory of development: Does it help explain the low performance of the present-day Muslim world? *The Journal of Socio-Economics*, 37: 836–863.

Chériff Vanly, I. (2012). The Deportation of the Faili Kurds From Iraq; available from: http://www.faylee.org/english/articles/doc5.php; (last accessed, October 11, 2012).

Clifford, J. (1994). Diasporas. *Cultural Anthropology*, 9(3): 302–338.

Cohen, R. (1997). *Global Diasporas: An Introduction*. UK/London: University College London Press.

Curtis, A. (2005) "Nationalism in the Diaspora: A Study of the Kurdish Movement. Nationalism, Ethnicity and Conflict, Canada/Waterloo: University of Utrecht.

Delir, K. (2004). How southern Kurdistan was incorporated into Iraqi State. Kurdistan Regional Government, Suleimani: Ministry of Culture [in Kurdish].

Denise, N. (2004). Transnational networks: new opportunities and constraints. *Middle East Policy*, 11(1): 111–114.

Dissanayake, S. (2008). Exiles wielding power from the UK. BBC News website, 4 December 2008.

Dissanayake, S. (2008 a) UK Kurds fight separate battles. BBC News, 9 December 2008.

Driver, G. R. (1922). Studies in Kurdish History. *Bulletin of the School of Oriental Studies, University of London*, 2(3): 491–511.

Durham, W. D. (2010). The 1920 Treaty of Sévres and the Struggle for a Kurdish Homeland in Iraq and Turkey between World Wars. Doctoral Dissertation, Oklahoma State University.

Edmonds, C. J. (1971) Kurdish Nationalism. *Journal of Contemporary History*, 6(1): 87–107.

Elphinston, W. G. (1946). The Kurdish Question. *International Affairs*, 22(1): 91–103.

Emanuelsson, A. (2005). *Diaspora Global Politics: Kurdish Transnational Networks and Accommodation of Nationalism*. Doctoral dissertation, Department of Peace and Development Research, Gothenburg University, Sweden.

Emanuelsson, A. C. (2008). Transnational Dynamics of Return and the Potential Role of the Kurdish Diaspora in Developing the Kurdistan Region. Advanced Research and Assessment Group, Defence Academy of the United Kingdom.

Enteesar, N. (1992). *Kurdish Ethnonationalism*. Boulder: Lynn Rienner Publishers.

Faruqi, O. (2004). *Kurdistan on a historic path according to documents and records*. Tehran: Ana Publishing [in Farsi].

al-Fayli, N. S. M. (2009). *Faylis: History, tribes, folklore, ethnic heritage*. Kurdistan Region/Erbil: Aras Publishing.

Ghafor, A. (2002). *Kurdistan's petroleum: Economic-geographic characteristics*. 2nd edition. Iraq: Kurdistan Regional Government, Ministry of Culture Press [in Kurdish].

Glick Schiller, N. (2005). Transborder citizenship: an outcome of legal pluralism within transnational social fields. In: von-Benda Beckman, Franz and von-Benda Beckman, Keebit (eds.), Mobile People, Mobile Law: Expanding Legal Relations in a Contracting World (pp. 27–50), UK/ London: Ashgate.

Gunter, M. M. (1991). Transnational Sources of Support for the Kurdish Insurgency in Turkey. *Conflict Quarterly*, 11 (2): 7–29.

Gunter, M. M. (2004). Why Kurdish Statehood is Unlikely. Middle East Policy, 11(1): 106–110.

Haji Maref, A. (1970). Kurdology in Russia and Soviet Union. In Muhammad, M. (ed.). *Sieving the harvest of Kurdontology in Europe* (pp. 74–132), Iraq, Baghdad: Kurdish Scientific Council Publications [in Kurdish].

Hama Baqi, M. (2000). Shaikh Obaidolah's Revolution 1880 in Qajarian documents. Arbil (hawlir): Education Ministry Publishing [in Kurdish].

Hamdi, W. (1998). Kurds and Kurdistan in British Documents. A documentary study published in Arabic in London, 1992; Trans. by Khoshhali, B., Iran, Hamadan: Nur-e Elm Publications [in Farsi].

Hassanpour, A. and Mojab, S. (2004). Kurdish diaspora. In: Ember, M., Ember, C. R. and Skoggard, I. (eds.). *Immigrant and Refugee Cultures Around the World*, *Encyclopedia of Diasporas: Volume II: DiasporaCommunities*, Canada/ Toronto: Kluwer Academics/ Plenum Publishers.

Hozni, H. (1938). Mukrian Kurdistan or Atropatene. Iraq, Rawandoz: Zari Kermangi Publishing [in Kurdish].

Humphreys A. and Mits, K., (eds.). (2012). *Kurds: The Red Book of the Peoples of the Russian Empire*. Institute of the Estonian Language, NGO Red Book. http://www.eki.ee/books/redbook/kurds.shtml (last accessed 11 October. 2012).

İçduygu, A. and Kaygusuz, Ö. (2004) and The Politics of Citizenship by Drawing Borders: Foreign Policy and the Construction of National Citizenship Identity in Turkey, Middle Eastern Studies, 40(6): 26–50.

Impact (1998). Obituaries: Sheikh Muhammad Hadi Hashemi Kurdistani.

Isa, H.M. (2002). The Kurdish Issue in Turkey. Egypt, Cairo: Madbouly Bookshop [in Arabic].

Johnston, R. (2006). *The cultural situation of the Kurds*. Parliamentary Assembly Report on 7 July 2006, Committee on Culture, Science and Education, Council of Europe.

Joseph, E. (2008). The Open Society and Its Critics: Minorities and Political Lobbying in the United States. Z Word Online Journal, American Jewish Committee.

Kamandar-Fatta, I. (2002). The deportations of the Fayli Kurds. Paper presented at International Conference on Iraqi Refugees and Internally Displaced Persons (pp. 18–20), 4 July 2002, France, Paris: Alliance Internationale pour la Justice.

Karadaghi, P. (2012). Kurdish Diaspora and Advocacy-Lobbying Efforts. Paper presented at the 24th Kurdistan National Congress of North America, 13 May 2012.

Karimian Sardashti, N. (2000). Turkmens in Kurdistan. *Awina Journal,* 53–54: 80–84.

Kendal, N. (1993). The Kurds under the Ottoman Empire. In Chaliand, G. (ed.). *A People Without a Country* (pp. 11–37), New York: Olive Branch Press.

Khani, A. (2008). Mem wa Zin. Tras. by Jan Dost. Syria, Damascus: Zeman Publishing House [in Arabic].

Khawja, A. (1968). What I witnessed. Volume 1, Iraq, Baghdad: Shafiq Printing [in Kurdish].

Khawja, A. (1969). What I witnessed. Volume 2, Iraq, Sulamaniya: Kamaran Printing [in Kurdish].

Khawja, A. (1970). What I witnessed. Volume 3, Iraq, Sulamaniya: Raparin Printing [in Kurdish].

Khayati, K. (2008). From Victim Diaspora to Transborder Citizenship? Diaspora Formation and Transnational Relations among Kurds in France and Sweden. Linköping studies in arts and science, No. 435, Department of Social and Welfare Studies, Linköping University, Sweden.

Khaznadar, M. (2001). The History of Kurdish Literature. Volume I, Hawlir (Arbil): Aras Publishing and Distribution [in Kurdish].

Khoshhali, B. (2000). Kurdish linguistics and History of Kurdistan. Iran: Hamadan: Fan-Avaran Publishing [in Farsi].

KHRP (2009). Impact Report. UK/London: Kurdish Human Rights Project, KHRP.

KHRP (2011). What Impact does UK Government Legislation and Policy have on the Kurdish Diaspora? Diaspora Dialogues for Development and Peace Project, Berlin: Berghof Peace Support/Luzern: Centre for Just Peace and Democracy.

King, D.E. (2008). Back from the "Outside": Returnees and Diasporic Imagining in Iraqi Kurdistan. *International Journal on Multicultural Societies,* 10(2): 208–222.

KNC (1998). *Charter of the Kurdistan National Congress. 4th Kurdistan National Congress, held in London on 10–11 October 1998.* UK/London: KNC Media & Communication Committee.

KRG (2008). *The Kurdistan Region: Invest in the Future.* USA/ Washington DC: Newsdesk Media Inc.

KuMA – UK (2008). Report on the First Scientific Conference of Hawler Medical University. Conference held in Erbil, 26–28 April 2008, UK/London: Kurdish Medical Association in the UK (KuMA – UK).

Kurdo, Q. (1970).Writings of Lerch about Kurds. In Muhammad, M. (ed.). *Sieving the harvest of Kurdontology in Europe* (pp. 133–160), Iraq, Baghdad: Kurdish Scientific Council Publications [in Kurdish].

Latif, T. (2012). Kurdish Customary Law in Practice. Paper presented at the Second International Conference on Kurdish Studies."The Kurds and Kurdistan: Considering Continuity and Change," at University of Exeter, 6–8 September 2012.

Leezenberg, M. (2011). Soviet Kurdology and Kurdish Orientalism. In: Kemper, M. and Conermann, C. (eds.). The Heritage of Soviet Oriental Studies (Routledge Contemporary Russia and Eastern Europe Series) (pp. 86–102), UK, Abingdon: Routledge.

Limbert, J. (1968). The Origins and Appearance of the Kurds in Pre-Islamic Iran Author. *Iranian Studies*, 1(2): 41–51.

Lyons, T and Mandaville, P. (2008). Global Migration and Transnational Politics: A Conceptual Framework. Working paper 1, Project on Global Migration and Transnational Politics, Center for Global Studies, George Mason University.

Mansour, R. (2012). The Role of Iraqi Kurdistan in the Syrian-Kurd Pursuit of Autonomy. Qatar/ Doha: Report for Al Jazeera Centre for Studies.

Marlies, C. (2010). Designated Terrorists: The Kurdistan Workers' Party and its Struggle to (Re)Gain Political Legitimacy. *Mediterranean Politics,* 15(3): 393–413.

McDowall, D. (1997). A Modern History of Kurds. UK, London: I B Tauris.

Mella, J. (1985). Kurdistan: Land and People without Homeland. UK, London: Kurdologia [in Arabic].

Mella, J. (2004). Colonial Polices of Syrian Baath Party in Western Kurdistan. UK/London: Kurdistan National Congress, KNC [in Kurdish].

Mella, J. (2005). Kurdistan and the Kurds: A Divided Homeland and a Nation without State. UK/London: Western Kurdistan Association Publications.

Mella, J. (2007). Western Kurdistan which Is Occupied by Syria. UK/London: Western Kurdistan Association.

Mikesell, M. W. and Murphy, A. B. (1991). A Framework for Comparative Study of Minority-group Aspiration. *Annals of the Association of American Geographers*, 81(4): 581–604.

Minorsky, V. (1943). The Guran. Bulletin of the School of Oriental and African Studies, University of London, 11(1): 75–103.

Mirawdali, K. (1993). Kurdistan and Kurds: towards a cultural definition. Paper presented at the International Conference; The Kurds Political Status and Human Rights. Georgetown, Washington, D.C., March 17–19–1993, UK/London: The Kurdish Information Centre.

Moqimi, (2006). Report on Cultural Engineering Forum by H. Damchi. *Biweekly Gazette of Cultural Engineering*, 1(3): 20–22 [in Farsi].

Mutlu, C. (2007). Kurds in Cyberspace: The Kurdish Diaspora, the Internet and its Impact on the Kurdish Question. On Politics (online), 119–137.

Nell, L. M., (2008). Transnational Migrant Politics in the Netherlands: Historical Structures and Current Events. Doctoral Dissertation at the Faculty of Social and Behavioural Sciences, FMG: Amsterdam Institute for Social Science Research (AISSR).

Neibuhr, V. C. (2006). Travels of von Carsten Neibuhr in Iraq in the 18th Century. Trans. By: Amin, M. H. from German, Beirut, Lebanon: Arab Encyclopaedia House [in Arabic].

Nerwiy, H. K.T. (2012). The Republic of Kurdistan, 1946. Doctoral dissertation, Faculty of the Humanities, Leiden University, Netherlands.

Newland, K. (2010). *Voice after Exit: Diaspora Advocacy.* Washington, DC: Migration Policy Institute.

Østergaard-Nielsen, E. (2002). Working for a solution through Europe: Kurdish political lobbying in Germany. In: Al-Ali, N. S. and Koser, K. (eds.), *New approaches to migration?: transnational communities and the transformation of home* (pp. 186–201), London; New York: Routledge.

Phillips, D. L. (2007). *Disarming, demobilizing, and reintegrating the Kurdish Worker's Party.* USA/ NY: The National Committee on American Foreign Policy.

Philpot, D. (1995). In defence of self-determination. *Ethics,* 105(2), 352–358.

Pouladian, A. (2003). Kurds under the Rule of Islamic Caliphate. Iraqi Kurdish Regional Government, Sulaymani: Ministry of Culture Publication [in Kurdish].

Piri, F. (2005). Narratives from Kurdish arts and politics. *Sirvan Weekly,* dated 20 Oct 2005.

Qazaz, R. (2000). Political and intellectual struggles of Kurds in early 19th Century til mid-20th century. Trans. By Muhammadi, A, Iran, Tehran: Muhammadi [in Kurdish].

Ra'ad, S. M. (1993). Development in the '*Al-Muqqadema* of Ibn Khaldun. Third edition. Syria/Damascus: Talas Publications [in Arabic].

Robins, P. (1993). The Overload State: Turkish Policy and the Kurdish Issue. *International Affairs,* 69(4): 657–676.

Robson, C. (2011) *Real world research.* Third edition, Chichester: John Wiley.

Rogers, A. (2004). A European Space for Transnationalism? In: P. Jackson, P., Crang, P. and Dwyer, C. (eds.). *Transnational Spaces* (164–182). London: Routledge.

Roy, O. (1996). Groupes de solidarité au Moyen-Orient et en Asie centrale, Etats, territoires et réseaux. Les Cahiers du CERI N 16 [in French].

Rozhbayani, M. J. B. (2004). Daqoq in History. Book Series 223, Sulaymani: Ministry of Culture, Regional Government of Kurdistan [in Arabic].

Sadiq, T. S. (2003). A brief history of Kurdistan. Kurdistan Regional Government, Sulaymani: Ministry of Culture Publishing.

Sagnic, C. (2010). Mountain Turks: State ideology and the Kurds in Turkey. Information, Society and Justice, 3(2):127–134.

Sajadi, A. (1996). The history of the Kurdish revolt. Second edition, Iran, Saqez: Muhammadi Publications [in Kurdish].

Samadi, S. M. (2002). Kurdish Tribes and Nomads. Mahabad, Iran: Rahro Publishing [in Kurdish].

Shafaq News (2012). Iraq announces citizenship for 120 thousand Faili Kurds. Available from: http://www.shafaaq.com/en/news/2721-iraq-announces-citizenship-for-120-thousand-faili-kurds-.html (last accessed 11 October 2012).

Shafei Kurd, J. (1999). Historical Geography of Kurdistan. Iran, Tehran: Non-wal Qalam Publications [in Farsi].

Sharfkandi, A. (2002) History of Ardalan. Iran, Tehran: Tazenegah Press [in Kurdish].

Shemsher, B. N. (2002). (ed.). British declassified documents on the issue of Kurds in Turkey (1924–1938): Sheikh Saied Piran, Agri and Dersim revolutions. Trans. By Ali. S., Kurdish Regional Government, Sulaymani: Translation House, Ministry of Culture [in Kurdish].

Siahpour, K. (2010). The Political-Military Role of Fars and Khuzestan Kurds during the Islamic Conquests Era (Text in Persian) Journal of Iran History, 3(66): 97–116.

Simmons, A. D. (2007). Globalization and its Effect on National Security. Forum on Public Policy Online, Volume 3.

Soguk, N. (2008). Diaspora, Transversal Communication and the Euro–Kurds. *Review of International Studies,* 34(1):173–192.

Stansfield, G., Lowe, R. and Ahmadzadeh, H. (2007). *The Kurdish Policy Imperative*. MEP BP 07/04. UK/London: The Royal Institute of International Affairs, Chatham House.

Swedberg, R. (2005). *The Max Weber Dictionary: Key Words and Central Concepts.* Stanford, CA: Stanford University Press.

Tamdgidi, M.H., (2012). Beyond Islamophobia and Islamophilia as Western Epistemic Racisms: Revisiting Runnymede Trust's Definition in a World-History Context. *Islamophobia Studies Journal,* 1:1, p. 54–81.

Taqi, A. (1995). Kurdish struggle against British Colonial rule in Ahmad Taqi's memoirs. Tran. By Muhammadi, A. Iran/Tehran: Ahmad Muhammadi [in Farsi].

Tawahodi, C. (1980). A Historical account of Kurdish Diaspora to Khorasan in defence of Independence of Iran. Volume 1, Iran, Mashhad: Koshesh Printing [in Farsi].

Tawahodi, C. (1985). A Historical account of Kurdish Diaspora to Khorasan. Volume 2, Iran, Mashhad: Mashhad Publishing Organisation [in Farsi].

Tawahodi, C. (1988). A Historical account of Kurdish Diaspora to Khorasan. Volume 3, Iran, Mashhad: Ferdosi University Publishing [in Farsi].

Toodari, S.A. (1970). A summary of the History of Awraman and Mariwan. Trans. By Muhammad Mala Karim, Iraq, Baghdad: Salam Al-azami Printing [in Kurdish].

Toninato, P. (2009). The Making of Gypsy Diasporas. Translocations: Migration and Social Change, An Inter-Disciplinary Open Access E-Journal, 5(1).

Wahlbeck, Ö. (1998) Transnationalism and Diasporas: The Kurdish Example. Paper presented at the International Sociological Association XIV World Congress of Sociology, July 26—August 1, 1998, Montreal, Canada.

Wahlbeck, Ö. (1999). *Kurdish Diasporas: A Comparative Study of Kurdish Refugee Communities*. London: Macmillan.

Wahlbeck, Ö. (2002). The concept of diaspora as an analytical tool in the study of refugee communities, *Journal of Ethnic and Migration Studies,* 28(2): 221–238.

Weiner, M. (1993). Security, Stability and International Migration. *International Security,* 17(3): 91–126.

Weiss, D. (1995). Ibn Khaldun on Economic Transformation. *International Journal of Middle East Studies*, 27(1): 29–37.

Yildis, K. and Taysi, T.B. (2007). *The Kurds in Iran: The Past, Present and Future*. London: Pluto Press.

Zoukui, L. (2008). *The Europeanization of the Turkish Kurdish Worker Party and Its Enlightenment to China*. Working paper series on European Studies, *Vol. 2, No. 2,* China/Beijing: Institute of European Studies, Chinese Academy of Social Sciences.

9 The Jewish American peace camp

New expressions of the Jewish diaspora

Yehuda Magid

Introduction

Since its modern-day inception in the early 1970s, the Jewish American Peace Camp (JAPC) has metamorphosed from an anathema within mainstream Jewish American society into a community speaking for a significant segment of the Jewish American population. This change did not happen instantaneously; rather, it required decades of effort by a plethora of Jewish American peace groups in the United States. AIPAC, once considered the monolithic voice of Jewish America on issues pertaining to Israel, now faces its first considerable challenge from the left, in the form of the new organization: J Street. While still reviled and assailed by the right, the JAPC has gained widespread legitimacy within the Jewish-American community. With such legitimacy, today, the peace groups in the American-Jewish diaspora pose a real challenge to traditionally powerful Jewish-American organizations such as AIPAC and the Council of Presidents of Major Jewish Organizations (Presidents' Conference). Whereas these organizations were once able to claim unified support from the entire Jewish-American community,[1] powerful venues now exist for members of the JAPC to both express themselves openly and influence US policy.

In this chapter, I shall discuss the history of the JAPC, contextualizing its current standing and activities, the rise of J Street and its challenge to AIPAC and the Presidents Conference, and the variety of methods utilized by groups within the JAPC.

Terms and concepts

The distinction between right and left in the context of Israeli politics centers largely around one issue: the Israeli-Palestinian conflict. The basic tenet of the right is that Israel is morally, historically, or legally justified in maintaining control over the West Bank and Gaza Strip. The left, conversely, is defined by its belief that Israel is not justified in occupying the Palestinian territories, in some cases, for purely practical reasons and, in other cases, for moral reasons. It is important to note that this definition is not predicated on the policies that one supports but rather the core beliefs that drive one's thinking. In other words, simply supporting a two-state solution today does not place an individual or organization on the left side of the Israeli political spectrum, just as Prime Minister Netanyahu's support of a two-state solution in his 2009 Bar Ilan speech did not redefine him as a leftist. The issue of support for a two-state solution, while once providing a convenient method of delineating right from left, has become so widely accepted within the public discourse, both in Israel and in the American diaspora, that it no longer serves to distinguish between the two sides of the political spectrum. Therefore, supporting a two-state solution is not, by itself, enough to determine whether a position is left or right.

Similarly, what once defined individuals and organizations as members of the JAPC no longer holds true. Supporting a two-state solution is no longer a determining factor in characterizing one as a member of the JAPC. Instead, the defining factor would seem to be a belief that Israel is not justified in maintaining the occupation of the West Bank and Gaza Strip, and an interest in working to achieve a peaceful resolution of the Israeli-Palestinian conflict in a way that respects the dignity and aspirations of all parties. Therefore, an organization that advocates a two-state solution but argues that Israel is not *obligated* to end its occupation of the Palestinian territories, legally or morally, would not be considered a member of the JAPC today.[2]

History of the JAPC

A brief examination of the history of the JAPC illuminates just how far American thinking has shifted regarding the Israeli-Palestinian conflict.

Breira and New Jewish agenda – A forerunner

Beginning with early Zionist thinkers in the 19th century, intense internal debate/criticism existed regarding Jewish communities in Palestine, especially on issues concerning Jewish-Arab relations. In the 1950s, intellectuals coming primarily from the left-wing Israeli political party Mapam published a dovish magazine called "New Outlook" in order to connect Zionists in the peace camp worldwide. This provided a foundation for the founding of an American diaspora group called Breira in 1973. Breira was founded by veterans of the Vietnam War protest movement and counter-culture Jews in 1973 in order to legitimize public dissent within the American-Jewish community. While some organized dissent had existed within the Jewish community before this time, the 1973 Yom Kippur War shocked many American Jews and created a sense that the absence of a solution to the Arab-Israeli conflict was an untenable situation.[3]

Breira marked a stark shift in the Jewish-American community's attitude toward Israeli policy. As we shall discuss below, the established Jewish-American organizations such as AIPAC and the Council of President of Major Jewish Organizations believed their duty was to defend Israeli government policy without question. Breira, however, sought to focus on what it perceived as injustice within Jewish-Israeli society, as well as the injustice suffered by Palestinians under Israeli occupation. It is important to note here that members of Breira were not individuals emerging from outside of the political establishment, rather many members were people deeply involved in Jewish organizations who had long felt sidelined and unable to express themselves freely for fear of retribution.[4]

The dynamic within the American-Jewish community in the early 1970s would prove too difficult for an organization advocating positions that while today would be perceived as moderate views, at the time were considered almost blasphemous. Most contentious of all was Breira's support for a two-state solution, a notion so outside the mainstream in the Jewish-American discourse that Breira members came to be labeled self-hating Jews, anti-Zionists, and even traitors.[5] Evidence suggests that the Israeli government led by Yizhak Rabin (first term, 1974–1977) was directly involved in stoking animosity toward Breira within the Jewish-American community.[6] This came despite, or possibly because, of the initially positive attention the group received within the Jewish-American community, as well as within broader American political circles.[7] The crescendo of enmity toward Breira reached its climax during the organization's first, and only, policy conference. Individuals affiliated with right-wing Zionist groups broke into the conference, physically assaulting Breira participants.[8] Though this event ultimately marked the end of Breira organizationally, its pro-Israel and pro-peace message did not disappear from the Jewish community.

In these early days of the JAPC, the strategic focus was on educating American Jews about the reality and injustice of the situation facing Palestinians both in Israel and in the occupied territories, as well as alternative visions of peaceful coexistence. Breira published a newsletter, a small magazine called "Interchange," translated Israeli media and government sources, and sent liberal individuals from within the Israeli authority structure to speak to American Jews around the country.[9] This would set the foundation for the work of a number of smaller groups that formed following the collapse of Breira, and would ultimately help to shift opinions within the Jewish-American community and the US population as a whole.

In 1980, shortly after the collapse of Breira, the New Jewish Agenda (NJA) was formed by former Breira members to carry on the organization's work. The focus, as with Breira, was to continue to educate the American-Jewish community about alternative views and approaches to the conflict, as well as to advocate for a more nuanced approach.[10] Two issues particularly important to the NJA were the role of women and inter-ethnic dialogue to alleviating social inequality and injustice. NJA set up a number of dialogue groups made up of African Americans and American Jews, as well as groups comprised of women from these communities. NJA took its women's dialogue to the 1985 UN Women's Conference in Nairobi, where they added Israeli and Palestinian women to their dialogue initiative. By bringing together women from both sides of the conflict, NJA was able to avoid divisions stemming from a "Zionism equals racism" resolution, which marred the two previous UN women's forums.[11] NJA's interracial dialogue groups eventually culminated in NJA's conference on Anti-Semitism and Racism, held in Philadelphia on November 8–10, 1991.[12]

Also important was the founding in 1980 of the New Israel Fund, a joint effort by primarily North American Jews and Israelis (later extended to Europe) to create an alternative to the mainstream Jewish philanthropies for Israel. Thus, they began providing money and technical assistance specifically for Israeli nonprofits working to "protect human rights, improve the status of women, bridge social gaps, further Jewish-Arab coexistence, and foster pluralism and tolerance" both within Israeli society and between Israelis and their Arab neighbors.

Americans for Peace Now (APN) and more

The period following the 1983 war between Israel and Lebanon marked another turning point for the JAPC. The war, largely perceived as Israel's first war of choice, so mobilized the Israeli public that the pro-peace organization Shalom Achshav (Peace Now), which had been founded in 1978, was able to garner major support in Israel. Initially called American Friends of Peace Now, APN was formed in 1981 locally and 1982 nationally, as a support group in the United States for the work of Shalom Achshav. Interestingly, while Shalom Achshav had benefited from widespread support in Israel, APN remained largely marginalized during the 1980s.[13] However, this period was to mark a fundamental shift in the way the Jewish-American community thought about the notion of "pro-Israel."

Whereas the prevailing notion of whether one was to be considered pro-Israel was long predicated on an either/or (either you are for unquestionably or you are against Israeli) conception, new thinking allowed for a far greater degree of nuance. Many American Jews who considered themselves pro-Israel began to challenge positions held by the Israeli government and supported by AIPAC and other establishment Zionist organizations. In fact, a majority of American Jews purported to support "active US involvement" in the conflict, and even supported the notion of "territorial compromise," at a time in the 1980s when this position was explicitly rejected by Likud-led governments in Israel.[14] APN introduced the slogan "to be pro-peace is to be pro-Israel," and became the major (maybe the only) national Jewish organization challenging the traditional Jewish diaspora positions of AIPAC and the Conference of Presidents. Gradually, it became a very strong organization, attracting thousands of contributors and supporters, not only providing Shalom Achshav with funds and exposure but also producing increasingly valued analyses and reports for lobbying as well as educational purposes. As part of the latter, APN brought (and still brings) Israeli and Palestinian figures to the United States while also organizing public discussions and dialogue. The organization also assiduously cultivates relations with Jewish communities in various parts of the United States but also with administration figures and elected officials in Washington. Through these connections, by means of lobbying and public advocacy, APN played a significant role in drawing American attention to such issues as settlement building in the occupied territories and the danger to the security and future of Israel from continued Israeli-Palestinian conflict. The organization enthusiastically supported the Oslo Accords in the 1990s, when AIPAC and other conservative Zionist groups were little better than lukewarm or outright opposed.

As APN increasingly concentrated its efforts in Washington, grassroots groups began to emerge in the JAPC, most notably Brit Tzedek. Advocating basically the same message, this organization created chapters throughout the country, often organized alongside Reform synagogue public action committees. Brit Tzedek cooperated with APN locally and with various Israel peace groups as the latter began setting up support groups in the United States in the 1990s.

Another group to appear was the Israel Policy Forum, founded by a previous director of APN in 1993 and designed to promote analyses and advocacy for peace to mainstream American Jews, as well as to influence the American administration. Like Brit Tzedek, it did not identify with any one group in Israel, but unlike Brit Tzedek, and APN, it was not an activist but rather a policy-oriented group. IPF's focus is on three primary elements of the conflict: the need to maintain the United States' image as an honest broker; the importance of US security assistance to Israel; and the need for a two-state solution. IPF works to "mobilize mainstream policy, community and business leaders to advocate for responsible U.S. engagement that advances the shared interests of the United States and the State of Israel. [The organization] conducts targeted advocacy meetings in Washington, private and public educational briefings for leaders across the country, and delegations to link American leaders with their counterparts in the region. [In addition] IPF also produces insightful commentary, analysis and policy recommendations backed by IPF's expansive network of influential analysts, former government officials, and community and business leaders."[15] If IPF saw itself as more mainstream (or more centrist) than APN or Brit Tzedek, the Jewish Peace Lobby, founded in 2002, was decidedly to the left of these groups. A very small and little known group, it could probably be characterized as the radical wing of the JAPC; it was the first of these to call for an independent Palestinian state (as early as 1988).

Since the early 1990s, attempts to silence and delegitimize individuals and organizations within the JAPC have continued. However, they have proven far less effective than in years past. There are two primary reasons for this. First, the decades long education campaigns carried out by the JAPC have made a substantial impact on US Jews' understanding of the conflict. By providing a more accurate depiction of the conflict and introducing alternative visions for its peaceful resolution, the JAPC was able to garner support for a more nuanced approach to the conflict. Secondly, the positions of both the Israeli public and government have slowly shifted. Whereas support for a two-state solution and negotiations with the PLO were once considered "heretical," such positions were slowly becoming established government policy in Israel. No longer hindered by a sense of disloyalty to Israel engendered by publicly apposing Israeli policy, the American-Jewish community could openly support policies once considered anathema within the community.

The rise of J Street and the challenge posed to AIPAC

The founding of J Street in 2008 fundamentally changed the landscape of the JAPC. J Street, a self-proclaimed "pro-peace – pro-Israel" advocacy group, has emerged as a liberal counterweight to the traditionally right leaning AIPAC and the Conference of Presidents of Major Jewish Organizations (President's Conference). Founded in April 2008 by former Deputy Domestic Policy Advisor to President Clinton Jeremy Ben-Ami, who now serves as J Street's executive director, the organization sought to unify the Jewish left wing in America. J Street is a nonprofit corporation consisting of three legally independent organizations. J street represents the lobbying arm of the organization; J Street PAC raises money for candidates who support J Street's agenda; and J Street Education Fund, Inc., works to educate the public in the wisdom and necessity of a more nuanced and liberal approach to the Israeli-Palestinian Conflict.[16]

J street is not, however, an organization that was created from the ground up. It may be understood as an amalgam of large number of small peace groups, including Brit Tzedek into one umbrella organization.[17] Despite years of hard work and dedication, the power and influence yielded by AIPAC and the President's Conference in the United States has long eluded the pro-peace community in America. J Street's founding was a direct response to this ongoing dynamic, the materialization of the notion that to challenge the established right in America, the pro-peace community would have to challenge them at their own game. As of 2011, J Street claimed support from more than 177,000 online supporters, 500 students, and 650 Rabbinic cabinet leaders. Further, J Street's second annual national conference, held in February 2011, was attended by more than 2,000 supporters, including 500 students, making the event the third largest gathering of Jews in North America.

The most significant contribution by J Street to the JAPC is its lobbying strategy. Lobbying may be understood as "a form of advocacy with the intention of influencing decisions made by legislators and officials in the government by individuals, other legislators, constituents, or advocacy groups."[18] While the JAPC continues to function as a fairly nebulous entity, it has established an organization led by Washington beltway insiders capable of raising significant sums of money to be directed toward the support of friendly US politicians. In this way, the JAPC can directly challenge AIPAC where it wields its greatest power, in its ability to help supportive politicians win elections. During the 2010 elections, J Street launched J Street local, setting up local branches in 40 US cities; doubled the amount of funds raised by JStreet PAC in 2008, distributing more than $1.5 million to congressional candidates; endorsed 61 federal candidates from 28 states, 45 of whom won their races; accounted for 30 percent of all pro-Israel PAC funds distributed during the election; and remained the single largest pro-Israel PAC in America.[19]

AIPAC and the President's Conference

AIPAC and the President's Conference represent the right-leaning Jewish lobbying groups in the United States. The term "right leaning" denotes tacit, rather than

explicit, support for right-wing policies. It is inherently more difficult to characterize individuals or organizations that implicitly support a right-wing agenda as
being "right wing." This is understood quite well by AIPAC and the President's
Conference, and is why both organizations go to great lengths to avoid any public
positions that might characterize them as such. This does not mean, however, that
these organizations are neutral; a more thorough examination illuminates particular political leanings.

Founded in the 1950s AIPAC is an organization devoted to Israel advocacy.
It has grown to more than 100,000 members in the United States and has been
described by the *New York Times* as "the most important organization affecting
America's relationship with Israel."[20] AIPAC considers political advocacy as the
core of its mission, and therefore, each year is involved in more than "100 legislative and policy initiatives involving Middle East policy or aimed at broadening
and deepening the U.S.-Israel bond."[21] However, because AIPAC is a domestic
lobby group and not a political-action committee (PAC), it cannot directly contribute to political candidates. This does not mean, however, that AIPAC is not
an important source of political funding for politicians in America. Instead of
directly contributing to politicians, AIPAC directs its members to donate to candidates deemed sympathetic to, and supportive of, AIPAC positions.[22] AIPAC
focuses on the US legislative branch, while the President's Conference focuses on
the executive branch of the US government.

The President's Conference was created in 1956 at the behest of Secretary of
State John Foster Dulles as a response to the overabundance of Jewish groups
approaching the executive branch about issues relevant to the Jewish-American
community. The organization today represents 52 Jewish-American groups,
and therefore possesses a large amount of influence while also suffering from a
large degree of diversity and disagreement within its ranks on specific issues and
policies.[23]

Within the organization, each member group possesses one vote, regardless
of the size of its membership. The result is that the largest groups, the Union for
Reform Judaism (URJ)[24] and the United Synagogue of Conservative Judaism,
each receive one vote, even though their members far outnumber those in groups
such as the Orthodox Union or American Friends of Likud. The result is that
the Reform and Conservative communities, which represent the largest groups
in the President's Conference and tend to fall on the liberal side of the political
spectrum, are limited – indeed outvoted – by the large number of small conservative groups, which each possess one vote within the conference.[25] The outcome is
an imbalanced representation of the American-Jewish community, with an advantage to its more conservative constituency.

In order to assess J Street's strategy and to understand how it directly challenges the influence of right-leaning traditionally powerful Jewish organizations,
it is necessary to first examine how such groups may be defined as "leaning right."
A useful exercise here is to examine the positions and attitudes toward Israeli
settlement expansion of the two most influential Jewish-American lobby organizations – AIPAC and the President's Conference. Working under my assumption that the left side of the Israeli political spectrum is defined by its refusal to

accept as legitimate Israel's occupation of the Palestinian territories, support for such policies by definition exclude an individual or organization from the JAPC, and the political left more generally. Further, support for Israel's continued settlement expansion in the Palestinian territories would denote a political leaning right of enter.

AIPAC does not hold any formal position regarding Israeli settlements, though the organization's behavior indicates a definite attitude toward the issue. Acutely aware of the negative attitudes held by a significant portion of the American people and US administrations toward Israeli settlement expansion, AIPAC refrains from overtly expressing its opinion on this issue. However, following the Israeli government's announcement of the expansion of an existing East Jerusalem settlement during Vice President Joe Biden's visit on March 9, 2010, AIPAC took a strong stance against the resulting tension generated between the Israeli government and the Obama administration. On the eve of its annual conference, AIPAC put out a press release urging President Barak Obama to "take immediate steps to defuse the tension with the Jewish State" and "make a conscious effort to move away from public demands and unilateral deadlines directed at Israel."[26] Conspicuously absent here was any mention of the announced settlement expansion that lay at the heart of tension between the two governments.

While conspicuous absence of any criticism of Israeli policies regarding settlement expansion on its own, does not establish the conservative leanings of the organization, the nature of its relationships with varying Israeli governments helps to solidify the argument. Whereas AIPAC has traditionally been quit close with the right-leaning Likud party in Israel, acting as its representative arm in Washington, AIPAC has struggled to maintain the appearance of unity with left-leaning Labor governments. In his article titled "Deal Breakers," published in *The American Prospect*, Michael Massing points to three events that help to illuminate AIPAC's political leanings; its cozy relationship with the Shamir government in the late eighties and early nineties; its silence and lack of support for the Rabin government's peace initiative; its pressure on congress to pass a bill that would make mandatory the transfer of the US embassy in Israel from Tel Aviv to Jerusalem (a move believed to have been designed as an effort to scuttle the Oslo talks between the Israelis and Palestinians – a move directly challenging the efforts of Israel's Labor government); and its efforts to prevent the US government from leaning on Prime Ministers Ariel Sharon and Benyamin Netanyahu on the issue of settlement expansion, despite large-scale support for active US government involvement on the issue among the Jewish-American population.[27]

The President's Conference acts, theoretically, as a conduit for opinions from the whole spectrum of political leanings of Jews in America. For this reason, no one attitude toward settlements exists within the organization. However, due to Conference's structural design, a disproportionate amount of power lies in the hands of a small number of influential members of the organization. Beginning in 1986, the most influential member of the President's Conference has been Malcolm Hoenlein. Hoenlein served as the Conference's Chairman from 1986 until 2008, and has served as the Vice Chairman from 2008 to present. Hoenlein has maintained vigorously that he is "not an ideologue,"[28] though an exploration of his past reveals a definite right-wing attitude in favor of and support for the Israeli settlement enterprise. For example, Hoenlein has been quoted positing that "Jews have a right to live in Judea and Samaria, part of the ancient Jewish-homeland – just as they have the right to live in Paris and Washington."[29] Moreover, he has contributed directly to the Israeli settlement enterprise. For a number of years in the 1990s, Hoenlein served as an associate chairman for the annual fundraising dinners held in New York for the settlement of Beit El one of the oldest settlements located just outside Ramallah (in the West Bank).[30] While one could argue that attending such an event would not on its own make one an ideologue, actively leading fundraising efforts to promote and finance Israel's settlement expansion would seem to strengthen such a characterization.

Following the election of President Obama in 2008, the President's Conference elected Alan Solow, a long-time Obama supporter, as chairman of the President's Conference. The choice was most likely made in an effort to maintain a positive relationship with the executive branch since the more liberal Obama administration replaced the outgoing neoconservative Bush administration. The Jewish community voted for President Obama by a 78 percent margin, and Solow's appointment was a clear message to the president that one of his close supporters would be speaking to him on behalf of the Jewish community.[31] As Steve Grossman, president of AIPAC during the early Clinton administration, explained, "The ability to have good chemistry with the administration and the president is a significant asset."[32]

Despite his long-time support of Barak Obama, however, Solow has proved an adversary on the issue of Israeli settlements. In response to the Obama administration's insistence that Israel cease all settlement construction in East Jerusalem, Solow attacked the position in a statement co-signed by Vice Chairman Hoenlein. In the statement, Solow defended the notion of a unified Jerusalem under Israeli sovereignty, as well as settlement expansion in the eastern sections of the city.[33] The attitude regarding Israeli settlements, which emerges from an examination of statements by the Conference's most influential members, seems to be quite supportive of Israel's settlement enterprise.[34]

J Street – A challenge?

Unlike AIPAC and the President's Conference, J Street openly addresses the issue of Israeli settlements. On their web page, J Street candidly proclaims that "J Street supports President Obama's continuation of nine previous U.S. administrations' policy against settlement construction, including in East Jerusalem." Further, in Fall 2010, the organization said "J Street shares the Obama administration's view that the expired ten-month period of restrictions on settlement construction should be renewed to allow direct negotiations to continue toward comprehensive Israeli-Arab peace."[35] On October 14, 2011, J Street President Jeremy Ben-Ami released a statement decrying Israel's plans to construct the new settlement of Givat Hamatos in east Jerusalem, the first such project since the founding of Har Homa in 1997.[36] In his statement, Ben-Ami reiterated J Street's position that such actions constituted "unilateral actions" on the part of the Israeli government, a veiled reference to the Israeli government's contention that Palestinian attempts to attain statehood through the UN were unilateral and therefore unjustified and counterproductive.

However, though J Street has grown dramatically in its first two years, its ability to raise funds is still dwarfed by that of AIPAC.[37] Despite this disadvantage, however, J Street has cemented itself as a substantive challenge to the monopoly on Jewish-American public opinion long held by AIPAC and the President's Conference.

Traditionally, as discussed above, established right-leaning Jewish organizations have been successful in branding groups within the JAPC as illegitimate and insignificant. As long as these groups remained fractured, preventing them from raising significant sums of money and thus influencing members of the US government through campaign funding, groups such as AIPAC and the President's Conference could convincingly argue that they represented the unified voice of the Jewish-American public. Utilizing a grassroots strategy focused on education, the JAPC was able to shift opinions within the Jewish-American community, chipping away at the hegemonic view established by groups such as AIPAC and the President's Conference. This decades-long process was critical, since the formation of J Street and its swift rise to prominence would have been an anachronism in the seventies, eighties, or nineties. The organization could not have achieved the level of success it has thus far, given the either/or understanding of the notion of "pro-Israel" and refusal to recognize the legitimate rights of the Palestinian people to self-determination so prevalent in the Jewish-American community in those decades. J Street appears not only to have established the legitimacy of the JAPC within both the Jewish-American community and the American political establishment, but it has organized in such a way as to capitalize on the shift in Jewish-American attitudes that earlier groups had helped to foster.

Variety of efforts for peace

While education, and, more recently, lobbying, have dominated the activities within the JAPC, a variety of alternative strategies and tactics have been utilized to help American Jews become more intimately involved in the resolution of the Arab-Israeli conflict. Here I explore four categories: (1) alternative trips to Israel for young adults, (2) utilizing the center of Jewish-American community, the synagogue, to promote the left-wing agenda, (3) inter-cultural activities, and (4) the most controversial, the promotion of boycotts, divestments, and sanctions (BDS) against Israel's occupation.

Alternative trips to Israel

Since its inception in 1994, the Birthright program has attempted, rather successfully, "to strengthen participants' personal Jewish identity and connection to the Jewish people."[38] By providing a free trip to Israel for young adults, many of whom have had little or no connection to Judaism in their youth, the program utilizes experiential learning to promote a positive attitude toward Israel in young diaspora Jews. The aim of the program is not to provide an accurate depiction of Israeli society, nor to immerse participants in Israeli culture, nor to promote sustainable relationships between participants and their Israeli counterparts. Rather, Birthright trips are highly structured to minimize, to the degree possible, spontaneous interactions between participants and their environment, criticism of Israeli policies, or difficult questions regarding activities carried out by the Israeli military. In other words, Birthright aspires to instill in participants a positive attitude toward Israel in hopes that in returning to their diaspora communities, they will actively support Israeli policies.

The success of the Birthright program has spurred JAPC affiliated groups to utilize the effectiveness of experiential learning in promoting a nuanced approach to the Israeli-Palestinian conflict. The Olive Tree Initiative (OTI) is one such group. Founded in 2007 by a "diverse group of [University of California – Irvine] students from Jewish, Christian, Muslim, Druze and non-religious backgrounds with varying perspectives on the Israeli-Palestinian conflict," the Olive Tree Initiative is "modeled after [notions of] empiricism – gaining knowledge through experience. [the program enables] students to travel to the region and learn about the conflict from a personal perspective, independent of the media."[39] It is important to note here that the aim of the initiative is not to advocate specific policies; in fact, the Olive Tree initiative strictly prohibits any political advocacy by any of its chapters – both within the United States and during trips to Israel-Palestine. The strategy of the organization – to educate young Americans by providing a broader, more nuanced view of the conflict – is founded in the general strategy utilized by the JAPC since the inception of Breira. However, OTI's tactic of utilizing experiential learning in a multicultural group represents a tactical shift.

Notable here as well is J Street's ultimately unsuccessful attempt in 2010–2011 to organize and fund a Birthright trip to Israel that would cater to a "progressive Zionist" audience and focus on issues of "social Justice."[40] Though the trip was closely coordinated with Birthright's subsidiary, Israel Experience, the trip was ultimately rejected by Birthright. In defending its decision, Birthright insisted approval of such a trip would breach its commitment to political neutrality.[41] This argument is undermined, however, by Birthright's support for Israel trips organized by AIPAC that explicitly focused on the political reality in the state of Israel.[42] J Street's attempt to organize such a trip under the auspices of Birthright represents a slightly different tactic than that utilized by OTI. While both aim to utilize experiential learning to promote a nuanced approach to the Israeli-Palestinian conflict, J Street aimed to do so within the framework of the traditional Jewish-American establishment, while OTI has rejected acting within the confines of the establishment. It will be interesting to see whether J Street continues this tactical approach, abandons its desire to utilize experiential learning in this manner, or shifts toward a more independent approach, such as the one exemplified by OTI.

The left wing and the American synagogue

While the percentage of Jews who classify themselves as observant and/ or affiliated with a specific branch of Judaism has steadily declined in past decades, especially among the younger generation of American Jews, the synagogue still plays a central role within the Jewish-American community. For this reason, Jewish spiritual and religious leaders still demand a great deal of respect in the United States and play a crucial role in the political attitudes of their congregations and communities. J Street, APN, and others have attempted to utilize the influence held by religious figures to strengthen their base of support, creating rabbinical groups. J Street boasts over 600 rabbis and cantors as members of its "Rabbinic Cabinet."[43] Increasingly, Jewish religious leaders affiliated with the JACP have pursued creative avenues for raising awareness of, and lending credence to, alternative positions regarding the Israeli-Palestinian conflict.

One example of such a group is Rabbis for Human Rights – North America (RHR-NA). Founded in 2002 to support the work of Rabbis for Human Rights in Israel, RHR-NA "is an organization of rabbis from all streams of Judaism that acts on the Jewish imperative to respect and protect the human rights of all people. Grounded in Torah and [their] Jewish historical experience and guided by the Universal Declaration of Human Rights . . . [RHR aims] to protect the human rights of Jews, Palestinians, and all others living in Israel and the Palestinian Territories."[44] RHR-NA, like many other JAPC groups, aims to change perceptions regarding the Israeli-Palestinian conflict through education techniques. RHR-NA does so in a number of ways, including the release of its annual report regarding issues of human rights in Israel-Palestine, trips to Israel-Palestine where individuals interact in a number of intimate ways with populations on both sides of the conflict, and its biennial North-American Rabbinic Conference on Judaism and Human Rights, which it claims has educated more than 1,000 rabbis, cantors, rabbinical and cantoral students, and other Jews about Jewish human-rights values, and about ways to engage in contemporary human-rights struggles.[45] Important here is the organizations focus on educating and organizing religious leaders within the Jewish-American community. RHR-NA understands the elevated status still maintained by religious leaders within the community and, therefore, aims to utilize that status by disseminating its views through a top-down approach. Whereas efforts to educate the public directly are important, RHR-NA maintains that it is more efficient to organize community leaders than to focus only on the population as a whole. These community leaders are instrumental in the formation of political attitudes among their constituencies and communities, and provide a far more compelling voice than would any national organization. By fusing issues relating to human rights and religious doctrine, RHR-NA seeks to provide a theological basis for American Jews to be receptive to, and supportive of, a more nuanced and objective perception of the Israeli-Palestinian conflict.

Intercultural activities

The tactic of intercultural activities provides a unique dilemma for the JAPC. While it is difficult to overstate the benefits inherent in activities that work to humanize the "other" through constructive individual contact, many in the Jewish-American community view such activities with suspicion and distrust. Right-wing groups exploit these feelings to strengthen their characterization of the JAPC as disloyal, traitorous, anti-Zionist, and even anti-Semitic. This phenomenon is not a recent development; Breira received a similar response when its members met with members of the PLO in an attempt to advocate for negotiations between Israel and the PLO. As one of Breira's biggest detractors, political scientist Rael Jean Issac posited, "If a Breira member was not malevolent, he was simply a sucker."[46] It would therefore stand to reason that as a reeducation strategy was necessary for the JAPC to gain legitimacy within the Jewish-American community, a similar campaign is necessary to legitimize activities between Arabs in general and Palestinians in particular and Jews. Efforts in this direction have been conducted on an informal basis at the grassroots level for many years in the form of "cousins" groups, such as a very long-standing one in Southern California and others in Milwaukee, Chicago, New York, and elsewhere.

Of a more organized nature, APN has led an effort to increase cooperation between Jews and Arabs in the United States. Working together with the Arab American Institute (AAI), APN has developed an innovative set of surveys that seek to illuminate the similarities between Jews and Arabs in the United States. Founded in 1985 by James Zogby as a nonprofit, nonpartisan national leadership organization with the stated mission of nurture and encourage the direct participation of Arab Americans in political and civic life in the United States, AAI has been designated by the Census Bureau as its only Census Information Center dedicated to analyzing data on the Arab-American community.[47]

In 2002, and again in 2007, AAI and APN commissioned Zogby International (ZI) to conduct the first-ever side-by-side poll of Jewish- and Arab-American public opinion to gauge support within both communities for Arab-Israeli peace. The surveys "confirmed that strong majorities in both the Jewish and Arab American communities remain committed to the right of both Israelis and Palestinians to live in secure and independent states; support a negotiated settlement to final status issues such as Jerusalem, refugees, and borders; and consider a resolution to the conflict in the US national interest. Accordingly, Arab and Jewish-American public opinion supports an end to the occupation and a freeze in West Bank settlement construction . . . In addition, both communities believe it is important for Arab Americans and Jewish Americans to work together to achieve peace."[48] However, the survey also found that both communities remain largely unaware of these common views and underestimate each other's support for the security and independence of both Israel and Palestine. By providing empirical data to support the argument that the Jewish and Arab communities in the United States agree fundamentally about their visions for a peaceful conclusion to the conflict, APN and AAI are able to debunk the claim that the "other" is hostile and uncooperative. Similar to the negative Jewish-American attitudes regarding a two-state solution in the 1970s, such notions cannot be eradicated overnight. However, just as a sustained educational effort succeeded in shifting the Jewish-American attitudes in the 1970s, 1980s, and 1990s, a similar effort apparently is needed to change attitudes among American Jews and Arabs about the "other." In providing such an effort, APN is at the forefront of providing alternative viewpoints to the American-Jewish community in order to foster a more nuanced and balanced approach to the Arab-Israeli conflict.

BDS – A controversy

Currently, the most controversial tactic employed by some in the JAPC is support for boycotts, divestments, and sanctions (BDS) against Israel. While there is much internal discussion and disagreement within the JAPC about whether to support or even address such tactics, and what the framework of such tactics should look like, BDS is seen by many left-wing Jews as a viable and powerful nonviolent tool for resisting and combating the Israeli occupation from the diaspora. While methods and tactics discussed until this point have centered on changing attitudes on the conflict through education, BDS represents a wholly different approach. A group called the Jewish Voice for Peace (JVP) argues that BDS provides an avenue for individuals within the diaspora to affect change halfway around the world without so much as leaving their living rooms. Whereas it is often hard for individuals to conceptualize how their "meager" contributions, whether monetary or through nonmonetary support of the JAPC, will result in real change on the ground, JVP maintains that BDS would provide an avenue for direct action. This approach rests on the central tenant of business, namely that decisions are made based on their impact on profits. Therefore, the best way to prevent businesses from cooperating with and helping to sustain the Israeli occupation is to threaten their profits directly by way of boycotts, divestment, and sanctions.

According to JVP's 2010 public statement on BDS, the organization "support[s] divestment from and boycotts of companies that profit from Israel's occupation of the West Bank, Gaza, and East Jerusalem. This includes companies operating in or from occupied Palestinian territory, exploiting Palestinian labor and scarce environmental resources, providing materials or labor for settlements, or producing military or other equipment or materials used to violate human rights or to profit from the Occupation."[49] JVP has suffered intense criticism regarding its BDS position, often referred to as anti-Semitic and traitorous by right-wing Jews, and it has been shunned by Hillel's on college campuses.[50] The main, if not all, the larger JAPC groups, notably J Street, APN, the Reform Movement, and others, reject BDS on the grounds both that sanctions are liable to have the opposite effect; that is, they would lead to a "rally round the flag" reaction in the Israeli public and assist the government in its dismissal of outside criticism on the grounds that an organized international delegitimization campaign is being waged against the country. There does appear to be some support in the JAPC, however, for selective sanctions, namely, boycott of products made in the settlements.

Conclusions

Jewish-American attitudes about the Israeli-Palestinian conflict have undergone a fundamental change in the last four decades; whereas support for a two-state solution and negotiations with the PLO were enough to destroy Breira in the 1970s, these views are now the established position of the Israeli government and supported by more than 80 percent of American Jews.[51] Young secular American Jews feel less attached to Israel than their parents' generation and reserve the right to challenge Israel and its policies.[52] While the shift cannot be attributed to the efforts of the JAPC alone, there is little doubt that efforts by the JAPC in the form of educational initiatives and grassroots organization around an alternative vision helped to foster a more nuanced view of the conflict by the Jewish-American community. Jewish-American peace groups have employed a wide variety of direct and indirect strategies and tactics for encouraging a peaceful and just solution to the Israeli-Palestinian conflict. With the emergence of J Street, the JAPC has ostensibly emerged a more organized force capable of challenging the near hegemony of public influence held by AIPAC and the President's Conference.

Despite J Street's rapid rise to prominence and the potential challenge it represents to AIPAC and the President's Conference, the organization currently finds itself in a precarious position. Due to the emphasis J Street puts on growing its base of supporters, it runs the risk of alienating its more dedicated and energized liberal base. J Street's inability or unwillingness to engage actively the issue of BDS ultimately resulted in a raucous breakaway session at their 2011 national conference in which arguments broke out at the entrance when J Street staffers attempted to prevent conference goers from entering the overflowing area. Further, J Street has supported America's veto of both the United Nations Security Council (UNSC) draft resolution condemning Israeli settlements and the UNSC resolution for the creation of a Palestinian state. In doing so, J Street has begun to alienate members of its progressive base as its positions have become more difficult to differentiate from those of AIPAC. The barometer by which J Street's success will be measured is whether it can garner greater influence within the US government while remaining true to the ideals on which it was founded. Despite these concerns, the JAPC maintains its greatest-ever level of support within the United States, and for the first time, by way of J Street, the JAPC poses a substantial challenge to the right-leaning Jewish-American establishment.

Notes

1 There were few ways to prove this claim, but they were able to (1) procure wide support in the Jewish American population and (2) successfully portray the Jewish-American peace camp as illegitimate.

2 There are some who believe that an organization advocating one state solution cannot be considered part of the JAPC because it does not respect the overwhelming support for self-determination of both sides, by way of a two-state solution. At best, one might say such advocates are on the fringes of the JAPC. (Ephraim Yaar and Tamar Hermann. "War and Peace Index—March 2009." Tel Aviv University. August 23, 2011: http://www.israelpolicyforum.org/files/peaceindex2009_3_3–1.pdf)

3 Brettschneider, Marla. *Cornerstones of Peace: Jewish Identity and Democratic Theory.* New Brunswick, NJ: Rutgers, 1996. pp. 41–42

4 Brettschneider (1996); p. 43.

5 Brettschneider (1996); p. 44.

6 Thomas, Michael. *American Policy towards Israel: the Power and Limits of Belief.* New York: Rutledge. 2007. p. 36, and Brettschneider (1996), p. 44. This was the time of the 1975 UN resolution equating Zionism with racism—a time when Israel was particularly sensitive to outside criticism, even from diaspora groups.

7 Brettschneider (1996), p. 43.

8 Thomas (2007), p. 36.

9 Brettschneider (1996), p. 43.

10 Brettschneider, p. 117.

11 This led eventually to the creation of the Jerusalem Link, composed of leading Israeli and Palestinian women organized in West Jerusalem—Bat Shalom and the East Jerusalem—the Jerusalem Women's Center. Nepon, Emily. "Jewish Feminism." *The History of an Organization 1980–1992.* November 20, 2011: http://www.newjewishagenda.net/feminism.php

12 More than 500 people attended the conference, of which 300 (60 percent) were women. Nepon, Emily. "Economic and Social Justice Task Force." *The History of an Organization 1980–1992.* Web, November 20, 2011: http://www.newjewishagenda.net/econSJ.php

13 Brettschneider (1996); p. 49.

14 Brettschneider (1996); pp. 50–51.

15 "About IPF." *Israel Policy Forum.* November 20, 2011: http://www.israelpolicyforum.org/page/about-ipf

16 "About." *J Street.* August 11, 2011. http://jstreet.org/about/about-us

17 APN, while involved in the creation, remained outside because of its link to a specific Israeli movement, Shalom Achshav. The purpose of J Street was to unify the JAPC without preference for one organization or another in Israel.

18 "Lobbying." *Wikipedia, the Free Encyclopedia.* August 20, 2011: http://en.wikipedia.org/wiki/Lobbying

19 "About." *J Street.* November 20, 2011: http://jstreet.org/about/

20 "What is AIPAC?" *AIPAC.* October 2010: http://www.aipac.org/about_AIPAC/26.asp

21 "What is AIPAC?" *AIPAC.* October 2010: http://www.aipac.org/about_AIPAC/26.asp

22 Massing, Michael. "Deal Breakers." *The American Prospect.* March 11, 2002. September 1, 2011: http://www.prospect.org/cs/articles?articleId=6166

23. "About the Conference." Conference of Presidents of Major American Jewish Organizations. October 2010: http://www.conferenceofpresidents.org/content.asp?id=52

24 The URJ was known as the Union of American Hebrew Congregations until 2003.

25 Massing (2002).

26 "Press Release." *AIPAC.* March 2010: http://www.aipac.org/Publications/AIPAC_CALLS_ON_OBAMA_ADMIN_TO_DEFUSE_TENSION.pdf

27 Massing (2002).
28 Malcolm Hoenlein in Massing (2002).
29 Malcolm Hoenlein in Massing (2002). The terms *Judea* and *Samaria* are the biblical names for areas comprising the West Bank. When the right wing came to power in Israel in 1977, it adopted these names for all official references. Generally, these terms are used primarily by the government and the right wing—almost as a recognized code of support for Jewish claims to the West Bank.
30 Massing also notes that Be El is a highly ideological settlement whose members have been known to work actively to provoke Palestinians in their attempts to scuttle the peace process: Massing (2002).
31 Rennert, Leo. "National Jewish Leader Turns against Obama." *American Thinker.* July 24, 2009. September 3, 2011: http://www.americanthinker.com/2009/07/national_jewish_leader_turns_a.html
32 Guttman, Nathan. "Obama's Jewish Backers May Be in the Middle as U.S.– Israel Tensions Rise." *The Jewish Daily Forward.* 22 May 2009. http://www.forward.com/articles/105954/
33 Solow, Alan; Hoenlein, Malcom. "Statements on Construction in Jerusalem." Conference of Presidents of Major Jewish Organizations Press Release. July 21, 2009. http://www.conferenceofpresidents.org/pressrelease.asp?ArtCat=1&ArtId=165
34 Rabbi Eric Yoffie, President of the Union for Reform Judaism, has argued that the conference is dominated by small groups far to the right that work to silence liberal and moderate voices from within the organization: Massing (2002).
35 J Street. "Settlements." *J Street* website. August 28, 2011: http://www.jstreet.org/page/settlements
36 "J Street calls Givat Hamatos plans 'Not Just Bad Faith, but Bad Policy'."*J Street.* November 10, 2011: http://jstreet.org/blog/j-street-calls-givat-hamatos-plans-bad-policy/
37 In 2010, J Street PAC raised $1.5 million, which was distributing among 61 candidates. *J Street PAC Tops $1.5 Million in 2010 Making it Largest Pro-Israel PAC. J Street.* September 4, 2011: http://jstreet.org/blog/post/jstreetpac-tops-15-million-in-2010-making-it-largest-proisrael-pac_1

While AIPAC's total contributions are impossible to gauge due to the fact the organization directs funds toward candidates, rather than directly contributing to them, estimates far outnumber those of J Street. Since 1998, AIPAC has spent more than $20 million on congressional lobbying and $5 million in the past decade on trips to Israel for US politicians. Since 1990, the whole of the Pro-Israel PAC gave $96 million in congressional campaign contributions, and it is estimated that AIPAC has been involved in directing a majority of these funds through local political-action committees. "AIPAC: America's Pro-Israel Lobby." *News 21*. University of Southern California Annenberg School of Communication and Journalism. Web, August 27, 2011: http://usc.news21.com/madeline-story/aipac-money-0
38 Magid, Shaul. "Which Birthright? Why Choosing Home over Homeland May Not Be So Bad." *JEWCY.* May 13, 2008. August 28, 2011: http://www.jewcy.com/arts-and-culture/which_birthright_why_choosing_home_over_homeland_may_not_be_so_bad. An outstanding study of birthright is Shaul Kelner, *Tours that Bind: Pilgrimage, and Israeli Birthright Tourism,* NYU Press, 2010.
39 *Olive Tree Initiative Website*. Olive Tree Initiative. August 14, 2011: http://www.olive treeinitiative.org/
40 According to the J Street's website, the trip was named "Explore Israel: progressive Zionism and Social Justice."
41. "Clarification Regarding J Street." Birthright. February 1, 2011. September 1, 2011: http://www.birthrightisrael.com/site/News2?page=NewsArticle&id=12339. The exact same thing occurred when APN tried to organize a Birthright trip some years earlier.

42 Birthright argues that the AIPAC trip focuses on the Israeli political system, "with an approach similar to a political science class," and that they have, and will continue to conduct, trips focusing on Issues of social justice. As is general policy for AIPAC, the organization vehemently denies any political leanings are vehemently.
43 "J Street Rabbinic Cabinet." *J Street.* September 1, 2011: http://jstreet.org/rabbis-and-cantors/
44 "Mission Statement." Rabbis for Human Rights—North America. August 28, 2011: http://rhrna.org/who-we-are/mission-statement.html
45 "History and Accomplishments." Rabbis for Human Rights—North America. November 12, 2011: http://rhrna.org/who-we-are/history.html
46 Steven T. Rosenthal. *Irreconcilable Differences? The Waning of the Jewish Love Affair With Israel.* Brandeis University Press. 2001. p. 38.
47 American Arab Institute website. AAI. September 1, 2011: http://www.aaiusa.org/pages/census-2010/
48 American Arab Institute, Americans for Peace Now. "Seeing Eye to Eye: A Survey of Jewish American and Arab American Public Opinion." 2007. September 1, 2011. http://aai.3cdn.net/70392c6c9708b2d5f1_0dm6bh9x6.pdf
49 "Jewish Voice for Peace Statement on BDS." Jewish Voice for Peace. August 20, 2011. August 28, 2011: http://jewishvoiceforpeace.org/content/jvp-issues#1
50 The latest example was the rejection of JVP by the Hillel at Brandeis University in March 2011, explicitly due to their support of targeted boycotts against goods produced in Israeli settlements. This decision was in line with Hillel's recently issued guidelines rejecting the legitimacy of any BDS tactics against the state of Israel. Bacon, Jesse. "Brandeis Hillel Rejects Jewish Voice for Peace Campus chapter." *Jewish Voice for Peace.* March 9, 2011. Accessed August 12, 2011: http://jewishvoiceforpeace.org/blog/brandeis-hillel-rejects-jewish-voice-for-peace-campus-chapter
51 American Arab Institute, Americans for Peace Now: p. 10.
52 Beinart, Peter. "The Failure of the American Jewish Establishment." *New York Review of Books.* June 10, 2010. Accessed August 12, 2011: http://www.nybooks.com/articles/archives/2010/jun/10/failure-american-jewish-pestablishment/?page=1

References

"About IPF." Israel Policy Forum Website. November 20, 2011. http://www.israelpolicy forum.org/page/about-ipf

"About." J Street Website. August 11, 2011. http://jstreet.org/about/about-us

"About the Conference." Conference of Presidents of Major American Jewish Organizations Website. October 2010. http://www.conferenceofpresidents.org/content.asp?id=52

"AIPAC: America's Pro-Israel Lobby." *News 21.* University of Southern California Annenberg School of Communication and Journalism Website. August 27, 2011. http://usc.news21.com/madeline-story/aipac-money-0

American Arab Institute, Americans for Peace Now Website. "Seeing Eye to Eye: A Survey of Jewish American and Arab American Public Opinion." 2007. Accessed September 1, 2011. http://aai.3cdn.net/70392c6c9708b2d5f1_0dm6bh9x6.pdf

American Arab Institute (AAI) Website. Accessed September 1, 2011. http://www.aaiusa.org/pages/census-2010/

Bacon, Jesse. "Brandeis Hillel Rejects Jewish Voice for Peace Campus Chapter." Jewish Voice for Peace Website, March 9, 2011. Accessed August 12, 2011. http://jewishvoice forpeace.org/blog/brandeis-hillel-rejects-jewish-voice-for-peace-campus-chapter

Beinart, Peter. "The Failure of the American Jewish Establishment." *New York Review of Books,* June 10, 2010. Accessed August 12, 2011. http://www.nybooks.com/articles/archives/2010/jun/10/failure-american-jewish-pestablishment/?page=1

Brettschneider, Marla. *Cornerstones of Peace: Jewish Identity and Democratic Theory.* New Brunswick, NJ: Rutgers, 1996.

"Clarification regarding J Street." Birthright website. February 1, 2011. Accessed September 1, 2011. http://www.birthrightisrael.com/site/News2?page=NewsArticle&id=12339

Ephraim Yaar and Tamar Hermann. "War and Peace Index – March 2009." Tel Aviv University. Accessed August 23, 2011. http://www.israelpolicyforum.org/files/peaceindex 2009_3_3–1.pdf

Guttman, Nathan. "Obama's Jewish Backers May Be in the Middle as U.S.-Israel Tensions Rise." *The Jewish Daily Forward,* May 22, 2009. Accessed August 28, 2010. http://www.forward.com/articles/105954/

"J Street PAC Tops $1.5 Million in 2010 Making it Largest Pro-Israel PAC." Accessed September 4, 2011. http://jstreet.org/blog/post/jstreetpac-tops-15-million-in-2010-making-it-largest-proisrael-pac_1

"J Street Rabbinic Cabinet." J Street Website. Accessed September 1, 2011. http://jstreet.org/rabbis-and-cantors/

"Jewish Voice for Peace Statement on BDS." *Jewish Voice for Peace.* August 20, 2011. Accessed August 28, 2011. http://jewishvoiceforpeace.org/content/jvp-issues#1

Kelner, Shaul. *Tours that Bind: Pilgrimage, and Israeli Birthright Tours.* New York: New York University Press, 2010.

"Lobbying." Wikipedia. Accessed August 2011. http://en.wikipedia.org/wiki/Lobbying

Magid, Shaul. "Which Birthright? Why Choosing Home over Homeland May Not Be So Bad." *JEWCY,* May 13, 2008. Accessed August 28, 2011. http://www.jewcy.com/arts-and-culture/which_birthright_why_choosing_home_over_homeland_may_not_be_so_bad

Massing, Michael. "Deal Breakers." *The American Prospect.* March 11, 2002. Accessed September 1, 2011. http://www.prospect.org/cs/articles?articleId=6166

"Mission Statement." Rabbis for Human Rights – North America website. August 28, 2011. http://rhrna.org/who-we-are/mission-statement.html

Nepon, Emily. "Economic and Social Justice Task Force." The History of an Organization 1980–1992. Accessed November 20, 2011. http://www.newjewishagenda.net/econSJ.php

Nepon, Emily. "Jewish Feminism." The History of an Organization 1980–1992. Accessed November 20, 2011. http://www.newjewishagenda.net/feminism.php

Olive Tree Initiative Website. Olive Tree Initiative website. Accessed August 14, 2011. http://www.olivetreeinitiative.org/

"Press Release." AIPAC website. Accessed March 2010. http://www.aipac.org/Public ations/AIPAC_CALLS_ON_OBAMA_ADMIN_TO_DEFUSE_TENSION.pdf

Rennert, Leo. "National Jewish Leader Turns against Obama." *American Thinker,* July 24, 2009. Accessed September 3, 2011. http://www.americanthinker.com/2009/07/national_jewish_leader_turns_a.html

Rosenthal, Steven T. *Irreconcilable Differences? The Waning of the Jewish Love Affair with Israel.* Waltham, MA: Brandeis University Press, 2001.

"Settlements." J Street website. Accessed August 28, 2011. http://www.jstreet.org/page/settlements

Solow, Alan; Hoenlein, Malcom. "Statements on Construction in Jerusalem." Conference of Presidents of Major Jewish Organizations Press Release, July 21, 2009. Accessed

August 15, 2009. http://www.conferenceofpresidents.org/pressrelease.asp?ArtCat=1&ArtId=165

Thomas, Michael. *American Policy towards Israel: the Power and Limits of Belief.* New York: Rutledge, 2007.

"What is AIPAC?" AIPAC website. Accessed October 2010. http://www.aipac.org/about_AIPAC/26.asp

10 The role of the Maronite diaspora

Charlotte Karouby

Introduction

The peculiarity of Lebanon lies in the pluri-confessional nature of its society, among which various threatened minorities strive for survival in an environment that has not always been prone to laicity and peaceful coexistence. This multi-ethnic patchwork has earned for Lebanon the name of a "mosaic," a term that became the first to define the Lebanese societal feature. It consists of 17 recognized religious denominations and cultural groups living together, including 12 Christian denominations that are considered as Oriental churches. Among these 12 groups, the Christian Maronites represent the most important Christian community, followed by others such as the Greek, the Armenian, the Syrian, or Chaldean Catholics. The Muslim population accounts for four other religious denominations and is much larger than the Christian one since the Palestinian settling. It is divided into the Sunnis and Shi'ites, to which are added the Alawi and Druze communities. In the last place, the Jewish minority accounts for a very small part of the overall population.[1]

According to data from vital registration systems published by the daily *Al-Nahar* on November 13, 2006, and encompassing all the Lebanese population (about 4,855 million inhabitants), the ratio is clearly balancing out in favour of the Muslim Population (65 percent compared to 35 percent of Christians), due to more fertile demographic behavior and, flowing from it, a more numerous young opulation.[2]

Nevertheless, Lebanon is not reduced to its small territory and to its multicultural particularisms. What makes the study of Lebanon so interesting is that, in contrast to other self-sufficient countries, it cannot be understood without taking into account the dependent relationship it maintains with its neighbours and with the world.

As the favored penetrating point of Occidental capitalism within the Arab world, as a bridge toward the other Arab countries, and as a pivotal financial centre, Lebanon had to undergo the cumulated effects of its marginalization during the civil war of 1975, which opposed mainly the Christian Maronites to the Palestinians' defenders and Muslim Nationalists, also called "Arabists." Mostly fuelled from the outside, violent rivalries lasted 15 years and were allayed, to some degree, with a *pax Syriana* in 1990.

The peculiar international nature of the conflict, together with the growing impact of global politics within the state's political affairs, let the Lebanese conflict be at the reach of many external influences, including the Lebanese diaspora.[3]

In this complex civil war, the Christian Maronite diaspora played a major role both during the conflict, by providing its support to the Christian Lebanese, and in its aftermaths, by taking part in the country's reconstruction work. Numerous peace-building efforts also stemmed from the Maronite diaspora community, which both felt the responsibility to help, having fled from the conflict, and knew to what extent political cohabitation under the rules of laicity was necessary for long-standing peace to be successful.

The civil war was a turning point in Lebanon's history, which more than ever made the intervention of external help necessary. During this emergency situation, Lebanon has seen most of its resources mobilized for the sake of its survival.

Migratory movements, democratized communication means, and the new media also played their parts in shaping new solidarity ties and networks bonding the homeland with the hosting one.[4] Lebanese migrants, who were forced to go abroad in the throes of the 1975 civil war, share common traumatic memories and developed networks to maintain their former identity and sense of belonging to Lebanon. The Maronite diaspora played a crucial part in the strife by supplying resources to the sides involved in the rivalry. As many diasporas committed to provide help back home, it had a critical role in framing the conflict outcome. Was the Christian Maronite diaspora exacerbating the conflict's violence and hindering its resolution by supplying resources? Or, on the contrary, was the diaspora's involvement a means to interfere positively in the conflict toward its resolution?

Our central area of interest throughout this study is to understand the role played by the Lebanese diaspora within the civil armed conflict from 1975 to date.

When mentioning the Lebanese diaspora, we will refer more particularly to the Christian Maronite diasporic community, whose presence and power abroad largely outweigh the other Lebanese diasporic groups and whose transnational political activism was significant enough to be an agent of change within the conflict. Other diasporic groups, such as the Lebanese Sunni Muslims or the Catholic Greek orthodox, will also be mentioned as part of the Lebanese migratory movements and as part of the analysis of the conflict itself.

Seeking to understand the impact of the Maronite diaspora on the conflict, the focus of our attention will be divided in two parts.

We first will elaborate on the conflict as the ground for the diaspora's identity and as the underlying reasons for its transnational activism. We will examine the Christian Maronites migratory movements before and during the civil war to better grasp in which socio-economical context they provided their help to the side in conflict.

Then, we will look at the Maronite diasporic transnational politics and activism. To measure the diaspora's impact on the conflict, we will examine the remittances, the transfers of skills and knowledge, as well as the diaspora's political activism in its hosting countries to finally review all the means the diaspora used to influence the conflict, whether it was positively or negatively in terms of peaceful resolution.

The foundations of the Maronite diaspora: Conflicts and migration flows

Located at the crossroads of commercial routes and constituting for centuries the Occidental point of entrance to Middle Eastern and Asian routes, the land which did not bear the name of Lebanon yet has always been the theater of many migration trends and emigratory waves. This geographical feature, together with the region's history, has shaped much of the Lebanese ancestral nomadic and commercial culture.[5]

The Lebanese emigrated mainly to Europe during the Industrial Revolution and to North and South America, during the First and Second World Wars. Aside from the American continents, other secondary destinations, such as Egypt, have been lands of refuge in the past for many Christians after the various deathly slaughters that have affected Lebanon until the Nasserian revolution rose in 1952.

From 1975, the civil war created a third migratory wave. For lack of having comparable data to the precedent sources, it is possible to rely on the results of a study led by the USJ (University of Saint Joseph of Beyruth) in 2001 to understand the geographical distribution of this last emigratory wave. This study examined the emigrated population from 1975, estimated to be about 600,000 people, who still possesses family and relatives in Lebanon. In opposition with the previous waves, the Lebanese do not settle as much as they used to in South America due to a serious decline in the region's economic situation. North America, on the other hand, and especially Canada, constitutes a more attractive destination.

The numerous migration waves to the Persian Gulf comprise the new feature of this third emigration period. The Lebanese people, benefiting both from their opened education to the Occident and from their good command of the Arab language, can settle in the Persian Gulf as managers and as technical or commercial intermediaries contributing to the economical development to the oil monarchies.

Occidental Europe is another destination of the Christian Lebanese diaspora and mainly attracts wealthy families who usually settle in France due to its old colonial ties with Lebanon. Africa and North America are also preferred hosting countries but usually welcome lower socio-economical layers of the Lebanese diaspora.

Between 1975 and 2001, of all the Lebanese population that left the country to flee from the civil armed conflict, about 30 percent settled in North America, mainly in Canada, about 26 percent settled in Europe, about 19 percent settled in Arab countries in the Gulf and in Maghreb, while about 14 percent settled in Australia and New Zealand.[6]

This overview of emigration waves of the Lebanese diaspora allows us to understand the high adaptability of the Lebanese people stemming from a centuries-old nomadic culture and the socio-economical context in which they provided their help to the sides in conflict.

The diaspora's role in the turmoil of the 1975 armed conflict up to date

The Lebanese civil war involved various actors who all added their terms to the conflict; it also constituted the ground for much of the diaspora's identity and represented the underlying reasons for its transnational activism.

Various parameters explained the rising tensions: the Christian executive power's relationships with Syria, the Palestinian issue, and the internal political crisis.

In Lebanon, the Muslim population had risen more rapidly than the Christian one had and imposed itself as a majority in the country by the beginning of the 1970s, despite the fact that no real nation-wide census had been undertaken since 1932. In the politically Maronite-dominated state, claims for a more important Muslim political participation were supported and strengthened by the numerous and radicalized Palestinian refugee groups.[7]

At the heart of the conflict, the territory was quickly divided between the Kataeb (the Maronite armed palangists) and the Muslim Nationalists who confronted each other in the streets and slaughtered civilians. The Lebanese state, whose credibility was already weakened in the past few years by an internal political crisis and its sovereignty weaknesses, neither had the decisional capacity nor the military force to react: Beyruth was divided along the "green line," while slaughters, plundering, and violent confrontations continued. After the Maronite Lebanese President Frangieh called for the intervention of the Syrian army, the latter penetrated in the country and took control of much of its territory.

While violence was rising, the intervention of a great figure from the diaspora, Raymond Edde, showed from abroad the will of the Maronite diasporic community to resolve the internal crisis the country faced.

Both Phalangists and Syrians tried many times to silence Edde's voice, leading to his exile to Paris in 1976. From there, the key figure of the moderated Christians, who was also the son of the 1936 Lebanon's president, spoke up and prophesized the many mistakes made by the extreme-Maronite leadership, imposing himself as one of the voices of peace within the Maronite community.

As the antithesis of the war leaders that had been taking the lead of the Maronite's fight for recognition, Edde denounced their "incursive and aggressive aventurism."[8] Surviving to the many attacks on his life launched by his opponents – the Syrians, Pierre, and Bachir Jemayiil, as well as President Chamoun – he quickly became the symbol of hope and moderation within the Maronite community.

Before his exile, he took the leadership of the Lebanese National Bloc (LNB), a party funded by his father which aimed at the even distribution of power between Muslims and Christians in the frame of Lebanese Nationalism. During the war years, the party opposed to arm a militia and aligned itself with the Sunni side, maintaining a moderate position.[9] While being ruled from the diaspora, Edde's party became the example of collaboration between the Arabs and Christians uniting around the symbol of Lebanon's unity and fighting against occupation.

Aside from the civil war between Arabs and Maronites, the Christians themselves faced a deep divide. Phalangists were strongly opposed to negotiations with Syria, while the Maronites represented by President Frangieh favoured Syria's involvement in Lebanon's politics. In the meantime, Occidental powers and the UN tried to reestablish peace by sending military troops, while Syria ended up occupying a large part of Lebanon. It is in this political context and turmoil that Hezbollah was funded in 1982 by the Shi'ites in reaction to the Israeli invasions in 1978 and 1982 due to Palestinian Fedayeen attacks from Lebanon. Threatened by the rise in violence and by warlords and their private militias fighting to gain power over territory, thousands of Maronites were forced to flee abroad.[10]

The new migrants took part in the pre-existing diaspora and offered their support to the Christian community that remained in Lebanon. Some may argue that financial support from diaspora communities is a significant factor fueling ethnic conflicts. Undoubtedly, the solidarity linking the Maronite diaspora to the homeland Maronites generated remittances inflows coming from transnational Lebanese sources. This financial support was possibly used by Maronites armed groups, as most of the Maronites who fled from the horrors of the conflict certainly still clang to their ethnic prejudices. However, as we will see further in this chapter, a greater proportion of these remittances was allocated to reconstruction and peace-building projects in the less-violent stages of the conflict.

The Lebanese Maronites already present in the diaspora played a major role in helping the new migrants to work out an honorable economic situation for themselves by facilitating their introduction on the job market and their adaptation to the residence country. Their job and social network developed in three main activities: luxury restaurants, exiled press, and the Lebanese banking system.

Maronites also benefited from the long-standing Lebanese presence in France by easily obtaining visas and working permits as soon as they desired to leave Lebanon.[11] Especially in Occidental Europe, the Lebanese diaspora resulting of the civil war is described as a diasporic community "strong of its commercial experience and of its community network." It also benefits from the dynamic ethnic Lebanese economy, which consists of the "interconnection between different economic sector (bank, press, restaurants) from the diaspora in France and in the rest of the world."[12]

In France, more particularly, most of the income earned through activities of the diaspora abroad are directly transmitted to Lebanon.[13] This once again demonstrates the large input of diasporic remittances on the Maronite community in Lebanon, which possibly contributed to financing part of the weapons of the Maronite's paramilitary groups within the conflict. However, during the early Israeli involvement in Lebanon, much of the Christian militias' arms and military equipment was provided by the Jewish state.[14] It is difficult to assess whether or not the financial support offered by the Maronite diaspora shifted the balance of power in favour of the Christian community since many other outside actors interfered in the conflict and also provided resources to the sides. Identifying the diaspora's resources input among those brought by the Syrians, the Hezbollah, Israel, the Occidental powers such as France, the USA, the USSR, or Iran is a difficult task.

The peace plan adopted in 1989 intended to organize power sharing under the aegis of the Syrian troops. Some Christians approve it, as opposed to others who want secession from the Syrian government. It is at this moment that a Maronite general, Michel Aoun, takes military action to push the Syrian out of Lebanon. His efforts to preserve the country's independence made him be considered a hero to some and a war dangerous criminal to others. However, after an internal war broke out within the Maronite community, the Syrian intervened against the General Aoun's troops in 1990. Defeated, he finally fled to Paris and settled there.

Because of the Syrian guardianship, which turned the power balance in disfavour of the Christians who were discriminated and regularly attacked, many of them fled from the conflict.

In 1995, the Maronite patriarch and bishops urged the Maronites to stop fleeing Lebanon and called back the by-then estimated 900,000 Maronites who had left the country between 1975 and 1990. It is believed that by 1999, an estimated half of that number had returned to Lebanon, but the diaspora remains unquestionably large and of great influence.

At this point of the post-conflict stage, thousands of Maronites from the diaspora come back every year, despite the fact that most of them keep links abroad that would provide them with refuge and resources in case of renewed conflict.[15]

The civil war finalized in 1990, but the reconciliation and peace-building process was made difficult as ethnic cleavages and Syrian occupation remained. Hafez-al-Assad organized a political regime serving his interests by appointing the Lebanese political leaders he desired.[16]

In 1999, Raymon Edde raised his voice from the diaspora again by denouncing the Syrian government's political intrumentalization of Lebanon.

For him and much of the Maronite diaspora, the fact that Syria had decided to place voting booths on Lebanese territory for upcoming Syrian elections showed the extent to which it was using its illegitimate guardianship position over Lebanon by treating it as an annexed territory and almost as a Syrian province. More than ever, voices from the diaspora raised themselves to accuse Emile Lahoud of being a puppet of Syria.[17]

In February 2005, after the assassination of Prime Minister Rafik Hariri, which involved the Syrian secret services, marches were organized in the Lebanese capital to demand the withdrawal of Syria from Beyruth's internal affairs. This launched the Cedar Revolutions, which were supported throughout the world by the diaspora, whether it was in the Maronite or Muslim diasporic communitites.[18] Rafik Hariri was a Sunni-Muslim Lebanese businessman who worked for the reconstruction of Lebanon in the post-civil war era and donated most of his fortune to support education and the spreading of multiculturalism within the state. Claiming the withdrawal of Syrian troops, the Cedar Revolutions involved Christian and Arab Lebanese, multiconfessional politicians, grassroots movements, and the Maronite diaspora.

By supporting those who denounced Syria's blurry role in the assassination of the man who was seen as Lebanon's benefactor by the popular layers of the Lebanese society, the Maronite diaspora proved that the Lebanese people within the state or abroad were united around the same cause: Lebanese unity and nationalism.[19]

In this case, the diaspora worked as a voice-amplifying device to make the Lebanese people's claims be heard internationally. It helped remind the world to what extent the guardianship of Syria over Lebanon was a dysfunctional and a weakening element for the country's politics. This broader mobilization against Syria added international pressure on the state's leaders for their withdrawal.[20]

After the Security Council's demand for Syria's withdrawal, Michel Aoun, who had launched his political party in 1992 from his exile in France, returned to Lebanon. His party, called the Free Patriotic Movement (FPM), sought at the time the withdrawal of Syrian troops and the establishment of a Lebanese sovereign state.

In February 2006, the Maronite diaspora, fearing renewed hostilities between the communities, used many media platforms to launch an international campaign against Aoun's party, and especially used the internet through various Maronites' blogs and websites that presented politically committed op-eds, Lebanese scholars' articles from the diaspora, and exchanges of ideas on forums about General Aoun's political games. As a blogger writes it in one of his online articles, during the year 2006, "Aoun signed an agreement with Hezbollah as the latter slowly drifted away from the electoral alliance it had forged a few months earlier. The agreement served to create a 'Christian cover' for Hezbollah's arms. It backfired. Aoun's popularity began to slip, whether his followers like to admit it or not."[21]

Indeed, the general signed an agreement with the Hezbollah, suddenly changing his political strategy since his political-reform program faced strong opposition. The Christian diaspora used all the media at its disposal to express its fears that Aoun's political party was being instrumentalized by the Hezbollah to bypass the prohibition that was inflicted both on the Shi'ites party and on the media of the latter, being classified as a terrorist organization.[22]

As revealed by the Kuwaitian daily newspapers "*Al Seyassah,*" dozens of Lebanese organizations and institutions from the diaspora also raised their voices and launched campaigns to forbid Aoun's party in the United States and in Occidental areas.[23]

Another example of the contribution of the Maronite diaspora to maintain peace is the official intervention of both the World Maronite Union and the World Council for the Cedars Revolutions, which sought to awake public awareness about the general's dangerous political games transnationally through the media. Their intensive political activism aimed at demanding from the American administration that it "take efficient measures against the Hezbollah – FPM alliance."[24] They also asked from the American government that it forbid the penetration of Aoun's representatives attempting to manipulate the American opinion if favour of the Hezbollah on the American territory. The transnational actions of the diasporic Maronite organizations definitively had a great effect on Lebanon's internal politics.

As an answer, General Aoun decided to play on the same "transnational field" and issued a large "call to the Lebanese diaspora" in February 2009, thus revealing that he acknowledged the key role undertaken by the Maronite diaspora in affecting the civil war and its aftermath. The call's main purpose was to warn the diaspora of its possible manipulation by the "movement of the future," the party in power at the time he spoke.

In his call, he declared that he believed the intentions of the movement of the future were to "undertake the task of a targeted selection of certain Lebanese Christians living in diaspora in the hope that they will obtain game-changing results" in the upcoming elections by "having part of the emigrated voters travel to the country."[25] First warning the diaspora that "enticing them with a touristic stay in Lebanon is the price they pay for their votes," he also reminded them that it was the Movement of the Future and its allies that "forced the diaspora to emigrate" resorting to force during the civil war. He also referred to "their marginalization" on the political level and to the fact that the party and its allies "turned the diaspora into nationals devoid of any protection and rights."[26] Although the political context of this declaration does not enable us to consider it as an objective source of information, it draws our attention to the great transnational political power that the diaspora holds in its hands because it potentially is a great agent of change through the right of vote.

However, the vote in "abstensia" is a right whose Lebanese diaspora is still deprived of today, since the necessary administrative organization required for the emigrated people to vote in diaspora countries has been continuously postponed for political reasons.[27]

This transnational political power is coupled with the impact of globalization, which in this case enables to turn the diaspora into a *tangible and reachable political constitution* settled abroad, which has the power to change the balance of power by travelling from their residence countries to their homeland.

This relative power attributed to the Maronite diaspora is due to the peculiar demographic balance of Lebanon since the Lebanese diaspora is thought to be 14 million while the population of the homeland is estimated to be 4 million.[28]

The previous part looked at the Maronite Diasporic transnational politics and activism. To measure the diaspora's impact on the conflict, we will examine the remittances, the transfers of skills and knowledge, as well as the diaspora's political activism in its hosting countries to finally review all the means the diaspora used to influence the conflict, whether it was positively or negatively in terms of peaceful resolution.

Deescalation phase: Transnational politics and activism in the Maronite diaspora

Despite the fact that the number of Lebanese emigrants, about 4 to 6 million, is difficult to assess with accuracy, the Maronite presence in emigration countries has had tremendous effect on the Lebanese political, economic, and social life during the civil war and its aftermath.

The way the government looks at its "*Al intishar Al Lubani*" – "the Lebanese expansion" – reveals a lot about the impact of the latter. Nevertheless, the Lebanese government never had a developed diaspora policy to benefit fully from its ties with the Lebanese abroad.[29]

Lebanese migrants have always had solidarity ties with the homeland and strengthened those links. In order to strengthen this solidarity, the diasporas "preserve regular contacts with their homelands . . . create elaborate networks that permit and encourage exchanges of money, political support and cultural influence with their homelands and other segments of the diaspora whenever these exist."[30]

Regarding the economic relations, the Lebanese migrants, constituted mainly of Maronites, have largely contributed to their homeland's economical development by sending remittances, strengthening business relationships between their country of residence and their homeland, and "through philanthropic activities."[31] Expressing their solidarity during the protracted conflicts of 1975 to date, they sent important funds to support their community and built infrastructures, roads, community centers, municipal buildings, and churches whenever the political situation was stable enough to start reconstruction.[32]

Networking was probably the most valuable asset used by the Lebanese diaspora to help its homeland community during the protracted conflict. Whether it was in terms of social network, or in terms of finding new funds for remittances, it definitely helped adding resources to the Maronite party during the conflict.

On one hand, the diaspora's social network helped "sponsoring new emigrants" abroad and making their life easier in their new country of residence.[33] As already mentioned, a good example of this social networking is the case of the Maronite diaspora settled in France, whose importance, economic success, and social status have earned it a position in the French society, enabling it to help new emigrants granting visas and working permits easily during the 1970s.[34] Amir Abdulkarim speaks about a "family Lebanese emigration" and the appearance of a "migration market" in which the Lebanese diasporic communities invested heavily to support their relatives and loved families who intended to flee from the 1975 protracted conflict.[35]

However, where networking has revealed to be the most tangible valuable asset is through remittances and funds sent to the homeland Christian community.

The large monetary transfer that the emigrants send to their families accounts for an important part of the country's economy. Lebanese migrants send about "$ 4.9 billion dollars in 2005 and $ 5.6 billion in 2004."[36] The newspaper *The Business Year* refers to the Christian Lebanese overseas network as the element that enabled Lebanon to become the possessor one of "the highest remittances-to-GDP ratios anywhere in the world."[37] It is the size of the diaspora that has helped stabilize and restructure the homeland's economy in the aftermath of the conflict. Remittances acted as a major source of liquidity and FDI.

The internationalized banking system and economy managed to channel continuously the diaspora's financial inputs, during and after the civil war.

Fervent nationalism, strong solidarity, and family links explain the impact of the diasporic networking on the country's economy reconstruction in the aftermath of the conflict, thanks to the free flow of liquidities and hard currencies, flow of information regarding the stability of exchange rates and the development of the international banking system. These economic incentives benefited to the whole population in Lebanon and contributed to the stabilization of the social situation.

In the post-war turmoil, the diaspora contributed to the subscription of treasury bonds, which were issued in 1991 and targeted especially the diasporic communities. The aim was to use their assistance in order to reduce the debt, thus contributing to regulate the economic and social situation. In total, $ 35 million dollars were raised through that mechanism, showing how responsive the diasporic communities could be when the economic balance of Lebanon was at stake.[38] The halo effect of the diasporic contribution affected the whole economy, and benefited the whole population, regardless of their confessional belonging.

Guita Hourani, writing on the Lebanese diaspora and its homeland relations, summarized the networks linking Lebanese diasporas with Lebanon in Table 10.1.

The situation in the homeland intensely affects the diaspora and strengthens the emotional links that tie it to its homeland, leading the diasporic communities preexisting the 1975 conflict to extend their aid to the homeland and send more funds than they did before the turmoil. As mentioned by Guita Hourani, the 1975 civil war and the protracted conflicts up to date, have "rekindled quiescent association" between the Lebanese diaspora and the homeland.[39]

Sheffer speaks about this phenomenon by evoking the renewed and rekindled Lebanese Christian South Americans' commitment in Lebanon. From 1975 to date, they were very supportive of their social group within the conflict and continuously sent "funds to their families and transferred financial resources to support their factions in Lebanon."[40]

This transnational activism might have played a certain role in increasing tensions between the sides rather than trying to resolve grievances and tensions between them.

Nevertheless, the solidarity that ties the diaspora with its homeland ethnic group, together with the geographical distance separating them, create an environment in which the survival of the ethnic group and the diaspora's identity becomes prioritized to seeking solutions for peace.

As long as violence threatens an ethnic group, all its resources are dedicated to its survival rather than launching peace-building efforts, whose first effects would appear in the long term. This is possibly what explains why most of the peace-building efforts made by the Maronite diaspora intervene in the aftermath of the civil war, that is to say when grievances and tensions still predominate, but when terror and violence have both decreased significantly enough for the sides to dedicate time and resources to something different from striving for their own survival.

Aside from remittances, whose uses are unknown and effects hard to measure, the impact of the Maronite diaspora's investments and donations to philanthropic activities, together with reconstruction projects, undoubtedly had a positive effect on peace building.

Mostly, the post-war turmoil's environment laid the ground for a more involved activism on the part of the diaspora, whose donations helped promoting villages development in a desolated Lebanon.

In the 1980s and the 1990s, emigrants' remittances purposely dedicated to Lebanon's reconstruction enabled the building and renovation of many facilities and infrastructures destroyed by the civil war. In Ehden and Zgharta, two close cities in the northern region of the country, remittances allowed the building of the municipal palace, to renovate a public school, and to order sculptures to help commemorate important Lebanese personalities known for their patriotism through sculptures. These initiatives show the deep involvement of the diaspora in spreading hope and patriotism for the future of a united country they believed in.[41]

Table 10.1 Selected types of Lebanese Diaspora networks with homeland

Economic/Financial	Political	Social	Cultural	Religious
• Remittances • Tourism • Government bonds • Businesses • Property investments • Property improvements	• Lobbying groups • Overseas branches of main political parties and movements • Advocacy groups • Human rights organizations • Testimonies • Political media • Funding political candidates or groups	• Social remittances such as ideas and values • Village associations and organizations • Family associations • Development organizations • Philanthropic projects • Charitable organizations • Hospital support • Educational support • Village infrastructure • Municipal support • Village websites	• Cultural tourism • Cultural festivals • Musical exchanges • Educational exchanges • Internet websites • Blogs and other internet discussion groups • Printed media • Visual media • Satellite TV • Art exhibits • Theater • Sports exchanges	• Building religious edifices • Religious pilgrimages • Printed material • Visual material • Satellite TV programs • Religious ceremonies • Religious feasts • Religious websites

Source: Guita Hourani.

Philanthropic donations were also raised from the Lebanese Children Fund (LCF), an organization created by Francis Fares, a Lebanese youngster who fled from the civil war in 1976 and funded this association in the diaspora. Originally based in the United States, the LCF then opened offices in Canada, Dubai, and Lebanon to raise funds and donations from Lebanese diasporic communities.[42]

The destruction and casualties caused by the civil war and its turbulences have raised consciousness that the country was in serious need of investments in the public health sector. Unfortunately, the combination of the dysfunctional government and its internal debt made difficult any improvement. The global communication systems and the internet media helped spread the information that Lebanon was in need of investments in the health sector. The new media and long-distance communication played a major role in connecting the diaspora's communities with internal issues affecting Lebanon. It appeared to be a genuine source of information through which the Lebanese abroad based their understanding of the Lebanese internal situation. Blogs, forums, and Lebanese diaspora's websites, such as the one of the World Maronite Union, played a major role in raising awareness about the need of external investment in the health sector.

The Maronite migrants' contribution in the health sector restored the National Health System and benefited all communities. This is another example of the diaspora's mobilization for the reconstruction of Lebanon, and of its role in sending peace-building incentives to the rival sides remaining in the homeland by showing how the two communities could collaborate over important national issues. The diasporic communities, from both the Maronite and Arab sides, built hospitals and health centers and sent equipment and vehicles intended at saving civilians.[43]

Tourism and regular trips to Lebanon "in the years since the war ended" showed a rapid increase in the number of visitors, who happened to be from the diaspora, this latter consisting mainly of Maronites and Christian Lebanese. As Hourani writes it, the "pilgrimages" to the sacralized and idealized homeland are certainly a way to strengthen the diasporic communities' identification between their diasporic identity and their ancestors' homeland.[44] The tourism industry in the aftermath of the war contributed to developing the economy. In 2007, an article published in the *New York Times* clearly talked about this "ritual of return": "The Lebanese diaspora reverses itself on holidays, as the migrants who sustain the war-shattered Lebanese economy all year return from jobs across the globe to spend time with their families." The yearly visits of the diaspora are a confirmation of their support to "the families they helped sustain."[45]

The remittances supplied by the migrants played a major role in the country's reconstruction and became a vital element of the Lebanese consumer economy since they stand for about $1,400 per capita every year. Although Lebanon benefits from one of the "highest rates of remittances in the world," this does not compensate for the internal weaknesses of the country's development. The emigration has largely risen with the wealth generated by the oil monarchies, as many graduated Lebanese are being recruited by Gulf companies, thus depriving the country of its main natural resources – " its people." However, some see behind this phenomenon the effects of a "brain globalization" rather than a pure brain leak.[46]

Transnational political activism and lobbying is a renowned tool used by diasporas to affect conflict in the homeland. The Lebanese diaspora has been lobbying governments and international organizations from 1975 to date hoping to effect change in the Lebanese government and add pressure on Syrian and Israeli positions when necessary.[47] Numerous organizations focused on lobbying the US government for the major influence this actor possesses in the Middle East.[48]

Harouni mapped out many Lebanese Diasporic organizations, whose purpose was to lobby international organizations and governments in their host countries. The diaspora's organizations, which had a significant impact on transnational politics are "the Lebanese Information and Research Center, the American Lebanese League, The American Task for Lebanon, The Lebanese American Council for Democracy, The United States Committee for a Free Lebanon in the United States of America, the Association Franco-Libanaise in France, the Canadian Lebanese Association, Rassemblement Canadien pour le Liban and Grupo Parlamentar Brasileiro de Origem Libanesa and Confederaçao das Entidades Libano-Brasileiras en Brazil."[49]

Divisions and differences of political opinions within the diaspora make it difficult to identify each lobby group's community affiliation. Indeed, most of the diasporic organizations played a major role in lobbying for Lebanon's sovereignty and for the withdrawal of any foreign government within the state's affairs, regardless of the sectarian divisions within the country. However, most of the Maronite diasporic communities, when they were not lobbying for the state's unity and sovereignty, were putting pressure on governments to defend human rights in Lebanon and prevent the growing influence of Hezbollah over the national and international political sphere. The World Maronite Union and its roadmap for the Lebanese government,[50] political tribunes, calls, letter to the UN secretary,[51] and other demands to the American government, has had considerable influence both in terms of lobbying and in terms of providing most of its Maronite's diaspora readership with information regarding the war and its post-conflict turbulences.[52] The activism of the World Maronite Union has had a huge impact in shaping much of the Christian diaspora's decisions to support the Maronite community at home through the sending of remittances and investments in Lebanese liquidities to sustain the economy. The Union's website has proven to be a valuable platform to reach the Maronite diaspora and connect it together. Through the internet, the dissemination of information has allowed the various diasporic communities to take actions quickly from their country of residence by deciding to send money, build facilities, create philanthropic organizations, or launch peace-building initiatives between the Arab and Christian communities. However, the website has proven to have intensified the Maronite fight against the Hezbollah's growth.

Considerable aid from the United States has been provided to Christian-Lebanese personalities, as proves the recent testimony of Jeffrey Feltman, the Assistant Secretary of State for Near Eastern Affairs, before the US senate on 22 June 2010. He revealed that the American administration had given subsidies of about $500 million to Maronite Lebanese public figures in order to counter the Lebanese Hezbollah.[53]

Lobbying in their host countries, various Lebanese diasporas, in majority from the Maronite communities, played a major role in having bills supporting Lebanon's sovereignty approved in the US congress and in the Canadian Parliament.[54]

The power of communities' transnational activism abroad together with the interconnectivity of the media are other tools that work in favour of political activists wanting to bring about change. In comparison with internal activism, the risks linked to that transnational activism, are also lowered due to the geographical distance. Freedom of speech and assembly in countries of residence are rights which, if well used, can help communities to be heard transnationally by reaching higher layers of political leadership. The internationalized media in exposing the grievances of diasporic communities can be a central tool of political activism since they have the power to reveal what happens in the internal sphere of politics and bring it up to the international stage.

Dalia Abdelhady speaking of transnational involvement in the Lebanese diaspora in favour of the homeland in her book, first interviews a young Arab Lebanese activist living in the United States who reveals in a simple sentence why an emigrant being outside of Lebanon grants more power in effecting change in the homeland. He says that "a mere letter from a U.S. organization can be more effective in challenging Lebanese state oppression than political activism inside Lebanon." For him, "you get a letter of complaint from the U.S. State Department or a U.S. organization, and you get a couple of write-ups in *Time* magazine," which will in turn lead the Lebanese government to take action because they will feel "exposed."[55] Thus, we understand that this "exposure" is the very tool of threat that diaspora can use if their hosting countries possess enough prestige on the international stage to put pressure on their governments back home.

Abdelhady then interviews a Lebanese-American from the Maronite diasporic community who attempted to effect a change in people's minds in Lebanon by sending an equal amount of money to different confessional nonprofit organizations during the war: "a Maronite, an Orthodox, a Sunni, a Shiite, and a Jewish one."

From the diaspora can emanate moderated voices, which take actions designed at addressing sectarian divisions. The message sent by this equal money transfer was one of unity and peace. The "Friends of Lebanon" in New York played a major role in addressing those religious identity issues, splitting Lebanon during the civil war as the organization "comprised of Maronites, Druze, Sunnis, Shiites, and Greek Orthodox," challenging the traditional sectarian conflict norms at the time.[56] The initiative of the multi-confessional diasporic communities provided Lebanese people undergoing the conflict's torment with a tangible example on which they could rely to hope for peace and launch community-based peace-building initiatives within the country.

Most of the members of the Lebanese society have experienced emigration in their life, or have close relatives who were part of the diaspora, and thus can have understood the conflict from a different point of view during their stay abroad. The open-mindedness resulting from such an experience, together with the adaptation efforts made by Lebanese diasporic communities to integrate in their hosting countries require understanding and tolerance toward other communities, which are also necessary psychological elements to coexist with the rival group and resolve the conflict. In 1992, for instance, "8.59% of the deputies in Parliament were Lebanese with migrant experience."[57] Today, 20 percent of Lebanese deputies have been a migrant once. This very high ratio is the result of the migratory-movements that followed the 1975 protracted conflict. This stay abroad and the adaptation efforts it has required from the Lebanese migrants to integrate and live with different communities in their host countries have certainly had an impact on the migrants' views upon the conflict in the homeland and their wish to participate in the political life from the inside. Again, it appears difficult to measure the positive or negative impact it had on the spreading of peace-building incentives.

Conclusions

In the first stages of the conflict and at the peak of violence between the sides, it appears difficult to trace and apportion the contribution of the Maronite diaspora to peace-building or conflict-fueling inputs. It seems that the remittances and the help provided by the pre-existing diaspora was useful to only one side early in the conflict.

At these stages, financial transactions strengthened the economic asymmetry between the Christian and Muslim Arab-Nationalist side by providing the first group with a regular money input coming from abroad. On one hand, this money flow shows how the Maronite diaspora militated in favour of its faction in the conflict, and certainly helped the Maronite side buying arms and defending its interests in the civil war, but on another hand, it played a major role in preventing the whole Lebanese economy from crumbling both during the war and in its aftermath. The remittances accounted for a major part of the country's economy and contributed greatly to the country's reconstruction.

However, from the de-escalation phase to date, efforts are made for reconstruction, pressure from the outside is applied on any internal political actors that would allow the presence of Syria or the Hezbollah in Lebanon's internal affairs and financial solidarity intervenes in order to sustain the homeland's economy.

The diaspora's philanthropic activities help recontruct schools, hospitals, and community centers, which all impact positively on the communities' reconciliation in the aftermath of the war.

The interconnectivity existing between the media and international political organizations, such as the UN or Amnesty International, helps spread the impact of the diaspora's lobbying for peace-building actions. Political activism and solidarity online through blogs, forums, websites, and op-eds also represents a large part of how the Maronite diaspora intends to promote peace.

In addition, various voices from the diaspora, coming both from Maronite political figures and from Maronite nongovernmental organizations such as the World Maronite Union, provide the rival sides and parties interested in resolving the conflict with moderated opinions with which finding constructive solutions. Numerous attempts at finding stabilizing institutional solutions to enable political cohabitation within the government are provided by such institutions.

Fighting against the Hezbollah's growing influence in Lebanon is also a task that has been undertaken by many Maronite diasporic communities throughout the world. They militate to raise awareness and lobby in their host countries' governments against the spreading of the terror group's influence in Lebanon. One can grasp a sense of the immense political power of the diaspora by observing how the question of granting Lebanese citizenship to much of the diaspora continues to create confessional and community disputes. Indeed, as some argue, giving it the right to vote in "absentia" would reshape the demographic balance in favour of the Christian side since the Maronite represent the major part of the Lebanese migrants; thus destabilizing the Muslim majority.

Notes

1 E. Verdeil, G. Faour, S. Velut, *Atlas du Liban* online, retrieved on April 11, 2012 from http://ifpo.revues.org/415#tocto2n3
2 Ibid.
3 Ibid.
4 J.M. Brinkerhoff (2008). "Diaspora identity and the potential for violence: toward an identity-mobilization framework," *Identity*, 8: 1, p. 70.
5 E. Verdeil, G. Faour, S. Velut, *Atlas du Liban*, retrieved on April 12, 2012 from http://ifpo.revues.org/415#tocto2n3
6 Ibid.
7 A. Abdulkarim."les Libanais en France : évolution et originalité,", *Revue européenne des migrations internationales*, Vol. 9-N 1, pp. 113–129.
8 R. Naba. "Chrétiens d'orient: le singulier dester des chrétiens arabes,"*Centre de recherche sur la mondialisation*. Written on October 22. 2010, retrieved from http://www.mondialisation.ca/index.php?context=va&aid=21568
9 Switzerland: Federal Office for Migration, *Liban—Feuilles d'information sur les pays*, retrieved on April 12, 2012 from http://www.unhcr.org/refworld/docid/466fe6932.html From UNHCR UN Refugee Agency, refworld .1 July 1997.
10 J. Minahan (2002), *Encyclopedia of the Stateless Nations: L-R*, Greenwood, p 1197.
11 A. Abdulkarim (1996), "La diaspora libanaise en France: processus migratoire et économie ethnique," *Revue europeene de migrations internationales*, Vol. 13 (1), n, p. 223.
12 Ibid.
13 Ibid.
14 Ciel de Gloire et Batailles, l'histoire de l'aviation de 1914 à nos jours, History Website. Retrieved on April 12, 2012 from http://www.cieldegloire.com/batailles_israel_1982.php
15 J. Minahan, p. 1199.
16 S. Chautard (1997), Comprendre les conflicts au moyen orient, Studyrama, p. 206.
17 R. Naba, Chrétiens d'Orient: le singulier destin des chrétiens arabes, *Centre de Recherche pour la Mondialisation*, retrieved from Mondialisation.ca Website on April 11, 2012 from http://www.mondialisation.ca/index.php?context=va&aid=21568
18 S. Chautard, p 206.
19 Ibid.
20 Ibid.
21 "A separate state of mind, Lebanon" (blog)—retrieved on 6/09/12 from http://stateofmind13.com/tag/michel-aoun/
22 "Former General Aoun and Orange TV spread Iranian-inspired Jihadist propaganda," A. Cochran, October 11, 2007, retrieved from http://www.aramaic-dem.org/English/politik/071011.htm

23 Randa al-Fayçal, "Le hezbollah mène la plus importante guerre de l'ombre pour con-troler le Liban," *Media arabe Website,* October 4, 2012, retrieved from http://media rabe.info/spip.php?article1166
24 Randa Al-Fayçal, La diaspora Libanaise contre le CPL de Michel Aoun, *médiArabe. info Website,* retrieved on April 10, 2012 from http://ashomer.blogspot.fr/2008/04/la-diaspora-libanaise-contre-le-cpl-de.html
25 Appel Général de michel Aoun à la diaspora, February 17, 2009, retrieved on April 9, 2012 from http://www.carim.org/public/polsoctexts/PS3LEB003_FR.pdf
26 Ibid.
27 Ibid.
28 Foreign Commonwealth Office, Middle East and North Africa. *Databook on popula-tions,* last reviewed February 29, 2012, retrieved on April 12, 2012, from http://www.fco.gov.uk/en/travel-and-living-abroad/travel-advice-by-country/country-profile/middle-east-north-africa/lebanon
29 "Lebanese Diaspora and Homeland Relations, Guita Hourani"—paper for *Migration and refugee movements in the Middle East and North Africa.* The forced migration and refugee studies program the *American University in Cairo,* Egypt. October 23–25, 2007.
30 Sheffer, G. Middle Eastern Diasporas: Introduction and Readings, *Journal Middle East Review of International Affairs,* 1(2), July 1997, n.p. [http://meria.idc.ac.il/journal/1997/issue2/jvol1no2in.html].
31 G. Hourani, p. 4.
32 Ibid.
33 G. Hourani, p. 5.
34 A. Abdulkarim, p. 223.
35 Ibid.
36 *World Fact Book on Lebanon,* retrieved on April 12, 2012, from https://www.cia.gov/library/publications/the-world-factbook/geos/le.html
37 "Where the heart is," *The Business Year*, No author. No date. Retrieved on April 10, 2012, from http://www.thebusinessyear.com/publication.aspx?PubId=2&artId=12
38 G. Hournani, p. 6.
39 G. Hournani, p. 7.
40 G. Sheffer, "Diaspora Politics at Home Abroad," Cambridge University Press, New York, 2003, p. 208.
41 G. Hourani, p. 8 from *Capitaux d'Émigrés et Reconstruction du Liban, Le Commerce du Levant,* December 10, 1984, and H. Amery, "The Effects of Migration and Remittances on Two Lebanese Villages," Ph.D. dissertation, McMaster University, Canada, 1992.
42 *The Lebanese Children's Fund website,* retrieved on April 12, 2012 from http://www.lebanesechildrensfund.com/?page_id=4
43 Boutros Labaki, 2006, "The role of transnational communities in fostering develop-ment in countries of origin: The case of Lebanon," retrieved on April 12, 2012 from http://www.un.org/esa/population/meetings/EGM_Ittmig_Arab/Paper13_Labaki.pdf
44 G. Hourani, p. 11 and Batrouney, "Australian-Lebanese: Return Visits to Lebanon and Issues of Identity," in *Lebanese Diaspora: History, Racism and Belonging,* edited by Paul Tabar, Beirut, Lebanon: Lebanese American University, 2005.
45 R. F. Worth, "Beirut Journal" (December 24, 2007), *New York Times Middle East,* retrieved on April 12, 2012, from http://www.nytimes.com/2007/12/24/world/middleeast/24lebanon.html?_r=1
46 Ibid.
47 Ch. Besecker-Kassab, "Immigrant Use of Political Media in the U.S.: A Case Study of the Maronite Lebanese of South Florida," Ph.D. dissertation, University of Miami, 1992.
48 C. L. Gates, *Middle East Research and Information Project (MERIP) No. 73* (Dec. 1978), pp. 17–19, published by: *Middle East Research and Information Project (MERIP)*, The Lebanese Lobby in the US.
49 G. Hourani, p 10.

50 C. Jalkh, (2008). "A Roadmap for Free Lebanon" (1) retrieved on April 12, 2012, from http://www.10452lccc.com/freedom%20fighter2/charles30.12.07.htm
51 E. Sacre-abu arz, President of Guardian of the Cedars Party—Lebanese National Move-ment, Open Letter to the Secretary General of the UN, January 18, 2008, retrieved on April 13, 2012, from http://www.aramaic-dem.org/English/politik/080118.htm
52 *The Maronite Union website*, retrieved on 12/04/12 from http://www.aramaic-dem.org/English/politik/0.htm
53 R. Naqba.
54 G. Hourani, p. 11.
55 D. Abdelhady (2011), *The Lebanese Diaspora: the Arab Immigrant Experience in Montreal*, New York University Press, p.109.
56 Ibid.
57 G. Hourani, p 11.

References

D. Abdelhady. (2011). *The Lebanese diaspora: the Arab immigrant experience in Montreal.* New York University Press.

A. Abdulkarim. (1993). "Les Libanais en France: évolution et originalité," *Revue européenne des migrations internationales*, 9 (1), 113–129.

A. Abdulkarim. (1996). "La diaspora libanaise en France: processus migratoire et économie ethnique," *Revue europeene de migrations internationales*, 13 (1), 223–224.

Randa Al-Fayçal. (November 13, 2007). "Le hezbollah mène la plus importante guerre de l'ombre pour controler le Liban," *MédiaArabe.info*. Retrieved on April 10, 2012 from http://mediarabe.info/spip.php?article1166

Randa Al-Fayçal. (April 20, 2008). "La diaspora Libanaise contre le CPL de Michel Aoun," *MédiaArabe.info*. Retrieved on April 10, 2012 from http://ashomer.blogspot.fr/2008/04/la-diaspora-libanaise-contre-le-cpl-de.html

D. Bar Tal. (July 2007). "Sociopsychological foundations of Intractable Conflicts," *American Behavioral Scientist*, 50 (11), 1430–1453.

C. Besecker-Kassab. "Immigrant Use of Political Media in the U.S.: A Case Study of the Maronite Lebanese of South Florida," Ph.D. dissertation, University of Miami, 1992.

J. M. Brinkerhoff. (2008). Diaspora identity and the potential for violence: toward an identity-mobilization framework. *Identity*, 8(1), 16–45.

S. Chautard. (1997). Comprendre les conflicts au moyen orient, Studyrama.

Ciel de Gloire et Batailles. "l'histoire de l'aviation de 1914 à nos jours." Website. Retrieved on April 12, 2012, from http://www.cieldegloire.com/batailles_israel_1982.php

Cochran, A. (October 11, 2007). "Former General Aoun and orange TV spread Iranian-inspired Jihadist propaganda." *Aramean Democratic Organization online*. Retrieved on April 12, 2012, from http://www.aramaic-dem.org/English/politik/071011.htm

Foreign Commonwealth Office, Middle East and North Africa. "Databook on populations," Last reviewed February 29, 2012. Retrieved on April 12, 2012 from http://www.fco.gov.uk/en/travel-and-living-abroad/travel-advice-by-country/country-profile/middle-east-north-africa/lebanon

C. L. Gates. "Middle East Research and Information Project (MERIP)," No. 73 (December 1978), pp. 17–19. Published by: *Middle East Research and Information Project (MERIP)*, The Lebanese Lobby in the United States.

B. Labaki. (2006). "The role of transnational communities in fostering development in countries of origin: the case of Lebanon," retrieved on April 12, 2012 from http://www.un.org/esa/population/meetings/EGM_Ittmig_Arab/Paper13_Labaki.pdf

The Lebanese children's fund website, retrieved on April 12, 2012 from http://www.lebane sechildrensfund.com/?page_id=4

"Lebanese Diaspora and Homeland Relations, Guita Hourani" – paper for *Migration and Refugee Movements in the Middle East and North Africa.* The forced migration and refugee studies program at the American University in Cairo, Egypt. Oct 23–25, 2007.

The Maronite Union website, retrieved on April 12, 2012, from http://www.aramaic-dem. org/English/politik/0.htm

J. Minahan. (2002). *Encyclopedia of the Stateless Nations: L-R*, Greenwood.

R. Naba. (October 22, 2010). "Chrétiens d'orient: le singulier dester des chrétiens arabes,"*Mondialisation.ca Website, Centre de recherche sur la mondialisation.* Retrieved on April 11, 2012 from http://www.mondialisation.ca/index.php? context=va&aid=21568

G. Sheffer. (1986). *Modern Diasporas in International Politics.* Kent, Croom Helm.

G. Sheffer. "Middle Eastern Diasporas: Introduction and Readings," *Middle East Review of International Affairs*, 1(2), July 1997, n.p. [http://meria.idc.ac.il/journal/1997/issue2/ jvol1no2in.html].

G. Sheffer. (2003). *Diaspora Politics at Home Abroad.* Cambridge University Press: New York, 2003.

Smith and Stares. (2007). *Diasporas in Conflict: Peace-makers or Peace-wreckers?* United Nations University Press.

Switzerland: Federal Office for Migration, *Liban – Feuilles d'information sur les pays.* Retrieved on April 12, 2012 from http://www.unhcr.org/refworld/docid/466fe6932.html. From UNHCR UN refugee agency, refworld. July 1, 1997.

E. Verdeil, G. Faour, S. Velut. *Atlas du Liban online*, retrieved on April 11, 2012 from http://ifpo.revues.org/415#tocto2n3

"Where the heart is." *The Business Year.* No author. No date. Retrieved on April 10, 2012 from http://www.thebusinessyear.com/publication.aspx?PubId=2&artId=12

World Fact Book on Lebanon. Retrieved on April 12, 2012 from https://www.cia.gov/ library/publications/the-world-factbook/geos/le.html

R.F. Worth. (December 24, 2007). "Home On Holiday, The Lebanese Say, What Turmoil?" *New York Times Online,* retrieved on April 12, 2012 from http://www.nytimes. com/2007/12/24/world/middleeast/24lebanon.html?_r=1

Other Documents

"Appel Général de michel Aoun à la diaspora," 17/02/2009 – retrieved on April 9, 2012 from http://www.carim.org/public/polsoctexts/PS3LEB003_FR.pdf

C. Jalkh. (2008). "A Roadmap for Free Lebanon" (1) retrieved on April 12, 2012 from http://www.10452lccc.com/freedom%20fighter2/charles30.12.07.htm

E. Sacre (Abu arz), President of Guardian of the cedars party – Lebanese National Movement, Open Letter to the Secretary General of the UN, January 18, 2008. retrieved on April 13, 2012 from http://www.aramaic-dem.org/English/politik/080118.htm

Blog

"A separate state of mind," (March 14, 2012), "On the Maronite patriarch, Samir Geagea and Michael Aoun," retrieved on September 6, 2012 from http://stateofmind13.com/tag/ michel-aoun/

Part IV

Private Companies

11 The private sector's role in democracy

Abdulwahab Alkebsi

Introduction

In 2011, when Arab citizens took to the streets to demand greater dignity and freedom, they not only challenged governments throughout the Middle East and North Africa, but also irreversibly changed the discussion of democracy in the region. The new face of the Arab citizen – young, vibrant, educated, organized, connected, and hungry for democracy – replaced stereotypes of a people mired in authoritarianism. And claims that the Arab world did not want democracy were put to rest, as increasingly inescapable calls for reform first swept Tunisia and then reverberated across the Middle East. In weeks, citizens made clear that the same faces that had ruled them for decades would rule them no more.

And yet, despite these calls for democracy, the trying period that followed the uprisings has served as a reminder that consolidated democracy in the Middle East is not a *fait accompli.* It will likely take years – if not decades – for the dust to settle. And, when it does, a democratic outcome is not inevitable. The peril is that transitions and reforms will remove one class of corrupt cronies and authoritarian rulers, only to retain the same social contract between leader and citizen – with the people continuing to look to the government to provide public sector jobs rather than to provide an environment conducive for entrepreneurship and market-based prosperity.

With political uncertainty exacerbating economic challenges that in part fuelled the uprisings, it is not inconceivable that Arab countries may be tempted to follow the turn to populism that has proven fateful for other nascent democracies and post-revolutionary countries. Venezuela, Bolivia, and Iran have seen their economic freedom scores drop in the past decade so that they now find their states lingering at the bottom of ease of doing business and perception of corruption rankings. Anti-market policies have squandered natural resources, exacerbated income inequality, and undermined the development of civil society. Government handouts have kept the people dependent on the state, taking away the independence that is so necessary to hold the government accountable in a democratic system.

The picture does not have to be so dire for the Middle East. To be successful, democratic transitions and reform initiatives should include the voice of the private sector through a consultative process that also encourages participation from a broad range of society. If democratic, market-oriented reforms are applied properly, the region's countries may be able to foster a better business climate for the domestic private sector and attract foreign investors that will view a stable democratic state as an opportunity to do business based on the rule of law. A democracy that is thus able to promote prosperity for its citizens can be one that is more sustainable. And a state that is dependent on revenues generated from its citizens and businesses can become accountable to its citizens. In a region that is undergoing intense political change, the private sector should be a key state partner in the transition to and sustainment of democracy.

Interconnectedness of market economy and democracy

Democratic governance is the system most proven to improve the quality of life for citizens, and in doing so, support political stability. Democracy achieves these goals because its sustaining values support individual freedom, freedom of association, and institutions. The best democracies flourish in market economies because of the shared foundational principles of transparency, accountability, fairness, and responsibility. Civil liberties are intrinsically linked to economic freedoms; the pluralism that allows the formation of political parties also fosters associational life; and the institutions that support fair and transparent political contests also support economic competition.

Democratic and market-oriented reforms are therefore mutually reinforcing, and in truth, one system cannot exist without the other. As Nobel Laureate Douglass North explains, "The challenge is to create efficient markets – not simply economic markets, but first of all political ones . . . it is political markets that first put in place the economic rules of the game."[1] Put simply, the court that ensures one's civil suit is settled fairly is the same court that upholds one's property rights – essential for conducting business. The same system of governance that includes the public in decision-making, by definition, includes business among this diverse constituency.

Recognizing the benefits of democratic governance, and painfully aware of the challenges that face citizens without it, fostering and promoting democracy become priorities. There are two sides to democracy: elections and governance. The importance of the former has become an axiomatic truth for much of the world, and for good reason. A people's ability to select representatives for positions of authority lies at the heart of a functioning democracy. The latter must also receive its due attention. The quality of a democracy lies in allowing the people to guide everyday decision-making of those in power. The nature of institutions that govern elected and appointed officials, and the mechanisms available for citizens to participate in decision-making, become significant factors in a democracy's ability to deliver for its citizens.

As democracy scholar Larry Diamond suggests, "There is a common, core problem in all badly governed democracies: pervasive corruption, cronyism, clientelism, and abuse of power. To change the way government works means changing the way politics and society work, changing the values and expectations of how people will behave when they acquire power and control over resources. That, in turn, requires sustained attention to how public officials utilize their offices."[2] As part of civil society, the private sector has a dynamic role to play in combating these core problems and improving the democratic governance of elected officials and appointed decision-makers. It is in its interest to do so; only an enabling environment based on the shared values of democracy and market economy can foster sustained economic growth.

Middle East context

Without the development of democratic governance in the region, and without the participation of the private sector in decision-making, the Middle East's looming challenges will not be adequately met and political-economic transitions will fall short. Yet the region's private sector faces an array of challenges hindering its contribution to both. Ineffective public sectors and constrained private sectors have resulted in less democratic policymaking, more pervasive corruption, and poorer services for citizens.

The state and the public sector

According to the deteriorating social contract in the Middle East, citizens recognize the legitimacy of the government and tolerate curbs on their freedoms in return for jobs and services that the government provides. The people are trained to look to the public sector as the guarantor of jobs, yet particularly as populations grow, the government cannot live up to its end of the bargain. Former Egyptian President Gamal Nasser famously guaranteed a government job for every Egyptian university graduate. Contrary to his expectations, unemployment figures rose as bureaucracy increased, military spending expanded, and investment decreased.[3]

The state-guided capitalism that this social contract produces has proven to be unviable. State-guided capitalism and authoritarian governance only allow a country to catch up to standards that are already in sight. Once "economies are at the frontier where success is not so easy to generate – because there are no clear leaders to copy or follow – mistakes are easy to make."[4] State-guided capitalism stymies innovation and entrepreneurship, and results in a bloated bureaucracy and a population dependent on the state and public sector.

In the decade preceding the uprisings, popular pressure forced many authoritarian rulers to embark upon initial market-oriented reforms. After Ahmed Nazif became prime minister in 2004, Egypt began to reorganize its banking sector, reevaluate subsidies, and pursue privatization.[5] In Tunisia, the regime took steps to improve payment of taxes and trade across borders; investor protection was strengthened to a degree.[6] Yet even these half-hearted efforts to reform were systematically undermined. Pervasive corruption, weak rule of law, and non-existent or weak institutions of accountability allowed crony capitalists – not average citizens – to benefit from nascent economic reforms. Governments in the region may have taken up the rhetoric of privatization and increasing private sector employment. But, at the end of the day, they have been unwilling to upset the status quo and loosen their grip on power, resources, and decision-making. In other words, they have been unwilling to democratize.

The private sector

The private sector and particularly small and medium-sized enterprises (SMEs) are the generators of jobs and growth, not the state or public sector. To enable entrepreneurs who can establish and maintain their small businesses, the proper environment must be in place. How easy is it to start and grow a business? How strong is the rule of law, and how secure are property and contract rights? How are continued innovation and other productive activitities incentivized? These primary conditions maximize growth.[7] Yet such institutions and norms cannot simply be copied into a unique country context. Government must participate in a dialogue with the private sector so that it understands the business community's priority areas for reform and how such reforms might be implemented realistically.

Unfortunately, even such general prerequisites for sustained economic growth have gone unfulfilled in the Middle East. Entrepreneurs have faced myriad challenges related to starting, running, and – if necessary – closing their businesses. Inconsistent enforcement of contracts, complex licensing procedures and customs regulations, opaque government procurement rules, and limited access to capital are just a few of the common challenges that businesspeople have faced in the region. Even when "ease of doing business" indicators are addressed, general deficits in transparency, trust, market competition, and the rule of law mean that doing business in the Middle East has remained an uphill battle. The barriers that hamper entrepreneurship reflect deep governance failures that undermine both the prospects for democracy and the strength of economies in the region.

The potential for reform has never been higher for those living in the Middle East and North Africa. Elections, political party laws, constitutional reforms, and development of a free media are justified demands necessary for transitioning to democracy. However, these reforms will not automatically eliminate the long-standing obstacles to economic participation. Rather, states in the Middle East require deeper institutional changes that will not only support political reforms, but will also allow the private sector to participate in the political arena and contribute to the economy's development and stability. The alternative is unilateral decision-making and the likely populist policies enacted to placate citizens who are increasingly discontent about regimes' inability to enable prosperity. The vicious cycle of unemployment and discontent will continue.

The private sector's economic and democratic roles

The many faces of the private sector

Alternate uses of economic terms obscure the mutually beneficial relationship between democracy and market economy. Before entering into a discussion on the private sector's role in democracy, it is necessary to disabuse these misperceptions.[8] First, business is not a monolith. Diverse actors compose what is sometimes reduced to "the business community." Small and medium-sized business owners most certainly express different concerns about the environment for business than do state-owned enterprises or multinational corporations. And informal sector businesspeople, often neglected in political discussions, have interests unique to their extralegal context. Business cannot be considered a homogenous community.

Second, a private sector is not synonymous with a market economy. A private sector is something much simpler than a market economy because the latter "requires a complex institutional framework that goes beyond the presence of private enterprises."[9] Such a framework is born of a transparent political process that sets clear laws and regulations that govern the economy. This relates to the third myth concerning business, that if the government steps out of the way, a free market will develop. Contrary to this perception, government has a significant role to play in ensuring that the market operates based on laws and institutions. Without such guarantees, investors would not have confidence in the market and entrepreneurs would not have faith in the system, and therefore would not start businesses or generate jobs.

The diverse actors that make up the private sector in a market economy have a keen interest in ensuring that the democratic values of transparency, accountability, fairness, and responsibility become institutionalized – these same values underpin an enabling environment for economic growth. As such, the private sector has a dynamic role to play in initiatives that range from combating corruption to reforming the judiciary, and advocating for reduced legal and regulatory burdens to strengthening the enforcement capacity of government agencies. Such democratic reforms provide the best context for citizens to become successful in business.

Unfortunately, diverse private sector interests in Middle Eastern economies are not often articulated to policymakers. Large corporations will always have access to decision-makers, but small and medium-sized businesses, which compose the vast majority of the economy and employ the most citizens, only have their interests heard when individual voices are amplified by business associations. Associations are a significant democratic force, as they increase the participatory nature of governance and are a key tool to allow individuals facing similar challenges to present suggested reforms to elected and appointed officials.

Challenges to doing business

Business associations have a distinct incentive in reducing legal and regulatory burdens, which disproportionately affect the small and medium-sized business sector and the work of entrepreneurs. Removing legal and regulatory barriers to business has a direct influence on consolidating democratic governance and improving economic growth. As legal and regulatory burdens increase, opportunities for corruption also increase. For instance, bribes may be demanded to hasten the process of registering a business, or potential entrepreneurs may be discouraged from starting a new business because of severe bankruptcy and other market exit rules. Such consequences undermine the growth of the private sector and its ability to generate jobs, as well as the strength of the rule of law and transparency.

A primary topic of interest related to such reforms is the informal sector. Informality refers to businesspeople who perform *legitimate* work and provide *legal* goods but are confined to extralegal work because of a restrictive regulatory environment and the burden of entry into the formal sector. Common examples of informal sector workers in the Middle East are unlicensed street vendors and unregistered minibus drivers.

As economist Hernando de Soto and his team famously revealed more than a decade ago, it took 289 days (six hours each day) to register a business in Peru, and registration cost 31 times Peru's monthly minimum wage.[10] Conditions in the Middle East are not much different. A Survey of 500 Street Vendors in Egypt,[11] conducted by the Federation of Economic Development Associations (FEDA), revealed that only 8 percent had a vendor's license. A full 90 percent of them are willing to pay fees and taxes and comply with work standards if they are able to obtain the necessary licenses. They find the road to "legitimacy" too cumbersome and laden with obstacles and corruption. In such an environment, there are more disincentives to registering a business than there are advantages to doing so.

In addition to onerous regulatory barriers that discourage entrance into the formal economy, weak rule of law and weak or nonexistent property rights increase the occurrence of informal sector work and stymie economic growth. This is important because assets, not cold cash, drive entrepreneurship. It may be taken for granted that in the United States, a mortgage on an entrepreneur's house is the greatest source of start-up capital for a new business.[12] Yet in the Middle East, large amounts of capital are defective due to a lack of property rights: "Because the rights to these possessions are not adequately documented, these assets cannot readily be turned into capital, cannot be traded outside of narrow local circles where people know and trust each other, cannot be used as collateral for a loan, and cannot be used as a share against an investment."[13] The institutionalization of property rights is a complex process, but essential to the performance of a democracy and market economy, and to the strength of the rule of law.

Firm statistics on the size of the informal sector and the lost growth opportunities it represents are understandably difficult to collect. Yet in 2002, the ILO estimated that informal sector gross domestic product (GDP) was 27 percent of nonagricultural GDP in North Africa.[14] Hernando de Soto undertook an extensive study from the late 1990s to 2004,[15] after which his team concluded that the informal sector employed 9.6 million Egyptians, compared to the private sector's 6.8 million and the public sector's 5.9 million employees. His research team estimated that 92 percent of Egyptians had no legal title to their property. These facts led the team to estimate that the collective value of extralegal business and property was $248 billion (more than $400 billion in 2013 dollars). To put this in perspective, that figure is "30 times greater than the market value of the companies registered on the Cairo Stock Exchange and 55 times greater than the value of foreign direct investment in Egypt since Napoleon invaded."[16]

There are concrete, negative consequences of high rates of informality. Businesses that are limited to the informal sector have a cap on their growth potential due to their extralegal status. Weak rule of law and property rights make obtaining capital difficult, as taxes go unpaid and corruption becomes pervasive. Moreover, resources are allocated inefficiently as entrepreneurs make decisions based on the restrictions of a cumbersome regulatory environment, rather than on the natural flow of innovation. Informal sector work, on average, is not technology-intensive and relies on unskilled labor. And, as fewer companies participate in the formal market, the reduced competition lowers the quality and efficiency of goods and services.

Politically, denying economic opportunity to informal entrepreneurs and workers hinders democratic development. When excluded from the formal economy, citizens effectively become disenfranchised. They lack mechanisms to voice input on policies that could improve their businesses and local communities, and by extension, weaken the quality of governance in the country. At the same time, informal sector workers are at greater risk due to their extralegal status. They have difficulty securing basic services such as utility connections, leading to the illegal tapping of taxpayers' utility lines. Both the informal sector and formal sector are disadvantaged in such a context.

In the Middle East, the informal sector tends to be viewed as a problem rather than as an opportunity for the government to encourage more sustainable employment, build investor confidence, broaden the tax base while potentially lowering taxes, strengthen the formal financial sector, increase the welfare and security of marginalized groups, and empower women, who form a significant portion of informal operators.

Business associations: Strengthening democracy through transparent advocacy

When entrepreneurs, informal workers, and other businesspeople organize themselves in business associations and chambers of commerce, they can amplify their voices to advocate for reforms that improve the ease of doing business and quality of governance. Associations can participate in a constructive public-private dialogue with government by carrying a concrete agenda of recommendations to the government as a basis for discussion. In this way, "businesses can go beyond the immediate value of goods and services they deliver to their customers and provide greater value to the country as a whole. They can become an integral part of the complex institutional transformation necessary for democratic and entrepreneurial economies to flourish."[17]

Through participating in the advocacy process, business associations can transparently use their expertise to provide oversight of laws and policies and help to influence the shape of emerging public policy. Effective advocacy necessitates that business associations reach out to a diverse private sector, reconcile often diverging interests, and then represent and help the private sector participate in an open debate on policy. Well-planned and executed advocacy strengthens business support for democracy and pressures government to acknowledge and respond to democratic processes. Advocacy equips business association members with the information, motivation, and tools with which to protect and improve not only the business climate, but also democratic governance.

The private sector, through the business associations that represent its interests, can have a prominent role in initiatives such as identifying the sources of high business costs and barriers to formal business; raising awareness about these issues among the private sector, the public, and decision-makers; mobilizing businesspeople and citizens to advocate for legal and regulatory reforms to address these barriers and costs; proposing specific legal and regulatory reforms; and working with policymakers to understand the implementation of enacted reforms.

There is immense potential for democratic, market-oriented reform right now in the Middle East. As citizens articulate their desire for more rapid changes to long-standing policies, the private sector has an interest in ensuring that the new policies adopted will enhance its ability to innovate and create jobs. Failure to listen to these voices as articulated through business associations could lead states to adopt populist policies that result in capital flight, greater job loss, economic turmoil, and a return to unilateral decision-making.

The private sector has the knowledge and experience to ensure that demands for change are met with economic reforms that are substantive and based on sound thinking. Rather than the government imposing generic regulations, countries throughout the region must first understand the root causes of systemic problems. Who demands bribes? Who pays them? What are the barriers to entrepreneurship? How could government incentivize formal business registration? A public-private dialogue, facilitated by business associations, can work to answer these questions and contribute to implementable policies that will enable the private sector to create the high-value jobs that the youth are demanding all over the region.

Common ground: Fighting corruption

By advocating in an open and transparent manner, business associations model democratic practices. The alternative is dealing behind closed doors, crony capitalists, and the pervasive corruption that they generate – the hallmarks of authoritarian governance. As the majority of businesses stand to gain from a decrease in corruption, and governments realize that a corrupt regime reputation spurs public unease and instability, as well as withdrawal of international financial support, anti-corruption initiatives present a clear opportunity for public-private dialogue.

Corruption is an intentional conflict of interest that benefits both parties involved. As corruption becomes more pervasive in government and business, resources are poorly allocated, investors withdraw their capital, efficiency and innovation decline, policies do not serve local communities, and opportunities for employment decrease. While Qataris and Emiratis view their governments as moderately clean, the vast majority of citizens in the Middle East consider their governments corrupt. Out of a possible 10, Morocco, Algeria, Lebanon, Syria, Iran, Libya, Yemen, and Iraq scored a 3 or lower on the Transparency International 2010 Corruption Perceptions Index. Oman, Bahrain, Jordan, Saudi Arabia, Kuwait, and Tunisia scored between 4 and 5.[18] Yet international indices are not necessary to establish that regime corruption is on citizens' minds; corruption seemed to top the list of grievances in nearly every country that experienced an uprising in 2011. In countries in transition, this mistrust has hardly subsided. In 2012, the Corruption Perception Index scores for Egypt and Tunisia barely moved.

There are many causes of corruption, which make it seem difficult to address. Ambiguous, complex, and contradictory laws incentivize obviating legal barriers to doing business by paying bribes. Lagging enforcement of what is on the books fosters corruption as well. A general lack of transparency and accountability, and lack of competition, allow corruption to run rife, and low public-sector wages provide an incentive to supplement income with bribes. Democracy and a vibrant market economy cannot thrive in countries where corruption undermines their core values.

An anti-corruption strategy that investigates the demand-side of corruption (emanating from the public sector) and the supply-side of corruption (linked to the private sector) has the best chance of limiting corrupt practices. Only initiatives that join the public and private sectors in a discussion on institutional reforms – which must provide incentives that reward transparency and fairness and punish bribery and abuse of power – will be able to effectively combat both the supply and demand sides of corruption. Business associations and chambers of commerce play a direct role in changing incentive structures; entrepreneurs know from experience the inefficiencies of economic and legal structures and the opportunities for bribery that arise as a result. In this way, extensive international experience can be combined with valuable local knowledge to successfully combat corruption.

The private sector has diverse methods available to curb corruption. A large component of anti-corruption initiatives is simplifying the legal codes and regulations that govern opening, running, and closing businesses, along with paying taxes. Think tanks and nongovernmental organizations such as business associations can educate the public about the costs of corruption, while suggesting reforms to combat this issue. The business community can become compliant with internationally recognized accounting standards and can adhere to corporate governance guidelines such as those published by the Organisation for Economic Co-operation and Development (OECD) or local corporate governance codes and best practices manuals that have already been adopted in Bahrain, Egypt,

Lebanon, Oman, Tunisia, and other countries in the region. Companies can also adopt their own codes of ethics and transparency guidelines. And the private sector can work with the public sector to establish transparent guidelines that regulate how and when government agencies award subsidies and exemptions, and to clearly lay out rules regulating conflict of interest.

Conclusion

The private sector, particularly in the Middle East, has a dynamic role to play in heeding the calls for reform in the region, supporting democratic governance, and ultimately ensuring that the old social contract that held citizens dependent on the state is not renewed by new leaders but rather replaced with a democratic one. It is in the private sector's interest to step into this role, because democracy is good for business. Increasing broad public participation in decision-making to include members of the business community creates stakeholders that have a vested interest in supporting the mechanisms that make democracy and market economies function. Operating through business associations to collectively advocate for and advance reform is simply one way in which the private sector can encourage and strengthen democratic governance. Businesses can themselves be a model for reform when they adopt and adhere to corporate governance codes. And entrepreneurs and businesspeople can be individual agents of reform by pressing for their interconnected civic, political, and economic rights. A democracy cannot flourish and deliver dividends for its citizens unless it engages the private sector along these lines.

Notes

1 Douglass North. "Local Knowledge and Institutional Reform" (Center for International Private Enterprise, Economic Reform Feature Service, 26 August 2004), 2.
2 Larry Diamond. *The Spirit of Democracy* (New York: Times Books of Henry Holt & Company, 2008), 302–303.
3 Michael Haag. *Egypt* (London, United Kingdom: Carogan Guides, 1993), 31.
4 William J. Baumol, Robert E. Litan, and Carl J. Schramm. *Good Capitalism, Bad Capitalism and the Economics of Growth and Prosperity* (New Haven, Connecticut: Yale University Press, 2007), 69.
5 Lahcen Achy. "The Uncertain Future of Egypt's Economic Reforms," *Ahram Online*, 22 December 2010.
6 "Business Reforms in Tunisia" (International Finance Corporation and World Bank, Doing Business Indicators, 2008–2011).
7 Baumol, Litan, and Schramm, *Good Capitalism, Bad Capitalism*, 95–121.
8 John D. Sullivan. "The Business of Democracies that Deliver: Reflections on CIPE's 25th Anniversary" (Center for International Private Enterprise, Economic Reform Feature Service, 15 May 2009), 4.
9 Ibid, 4.
10 Hernando de Soto. *The Mystery of Capital* (New York: Basic Books, 2000), 20.
11 "Survey Analysis Report on Street Vendors" Federation of Economic Development Associations (2009).

12 Ibid, 6.
13 Ibid.
14 ILO, Women and men in the informal economy—a statistical picture 2002. In: Kristina Flodman Becker. "The Informal Economy" (Sida, 2004), 20.
15 Hernando de Soto. "Egypt's Economic Apartheid," *Wall Street Journal*, 3 February 2010.
16 Ibid.
17 Aleksandr Shkolnikov. "Beyond Individual Success Stories: Promoting Entrepreneurship through Institutional Reform" (Center for International Private Enterprise, Economic Reform Feature Service, 31 December 2010), 6.
18 "Corruption Perceptions Index" Transparency International (2010), 12.

12 The role of civil society and private business in the democratization process of Saudi Arabia

Safi Kaskas

The term 'democratization of Saudi Arabia' has a different meaning to different people. In fact, most Saudis consider democracy a western concept.[1]

Indeed, western (liberal) democracy has been identified as a form of government that allows citizens equal participation in the decisions that affect their lives, empowering every member of a community with the opportunity to contribute toward self-governance. Democracy, as a form of government, has been highly simplified, where individual views have been grouped into usually two opposing sides or parties, replacing popular direct sovereignty with a tiered system of representative democracy, highly diminishing the power of the individual citizen and his or her right to political self-determination.

Eventually democracy extends beyond the scope of the political arena into more intrinsic aspects of citizens' lives; the democratic process essentially affects the socio-economic performance of a community. Equality under the law, as well as in making the law, is at the essence of democracy. Naturally, granting all citizens equal participation means women are entitled to equal rights in governing themselves and playing a role in the political processes of the country. Further, countering poverty and extending basic rights into areas such as food, water, healthcare, and education to all citizens, is part of the democratization process.

The Kingdom of Saudi Arabia is an Islamic monarchy. However, as Caroline Montagu points out in her article 'Civil Society and the Voluntary Sector in Saudi Arabia,'[2] it is important in understanding the state and ruling monarchy to recognize that they are neither homogenous nor hegemonic. Therefore, although civil society in Saudi Arabia is not integrated as part of the overall political structure, there is an informal yet highly active relationship between them, which aims toward creating a healthier social environment.

Saudis, who have been held back culturally and pushed back historically from political participation have nonetheless taken certain initiatives to have a say on issues in terms related to their neighborhoods and immediate concerns, with the intention of creating a healthier social environment. It will be shown that the very existence of these initiatives, in the form of civil organizations (including businesses) have a direct bearing on the political level. In the absence of formal political pluralism, they provide a vehicle of communication between citizen and state. Indeed, the formal status, or lack thereof, of these civil groupings, is secondary to the substantive role they play both politically and socially. "Focusing studies of civil society exclusively on questions of legitimacy, consensus and hegemony may draw attention away from important cases in which the state's right to rule is not widely questioned but where the growth of civil society's institutions, nonetheless, dramatically affects the overall distribution of power."[3]

In developing societies, the middle class is usually the catalyst for social reform, even when the issues affect primarily the poor majority. In Saudi Arabia, private businessmen and merchant families are taking the lead in identifying key social issues and spearheading the formation of civil society groups in order to bring about change. Organizations established by individuals have created a safe forum where ideas are brought to the table, solutions are proposed, and decisions are taken by a majority vote. The bylaws of these organizations usually emphasize the election of the president and the board, help promote team spirit, and encourage participation in the decision-making process. Private citizens have demonstrated a powerful momentum in following up on ideas and moving them from paper to execution, in turn empowering the lower part of the political pyramid. Civil society organizations in Saudi Arabia almost doubled in number from 1990 to 2012, and the UNDP views them as the richest source of civic vitality in the Arab world, guiding citizens with an "invisible social hand" (Yom, 2005).[4]

In this way, civil society organizations are able to contribute to the process of democratization, by actually creating a mini-simulation of self-governance. According to a recent study, it appears that leading businessmen are the driving force for corporate social responsibility (CSR)[5] in the country. Private businesses have the formal structure, the funding and generally the vision to extend the reach of their projects beyond their direct surroundings and communities. Through their social projects, they have been able to identify issues that extend beyond the individual and local surroundings to problems that cut across social classes and regions. Given the fact that Saudi Arabia is essentially a country with different tribal, ethnic, and cultural origins – as yet unreconciled – these examples of social responsibility, and civil society groups in general, can override these differences, focusing on peoples' shared predicaments.

Regardless of the diversity, the Kingdom remains an Islamic country, governed by Shari'a law. Having been ingrained in the social structure of the country, it can be said that Islam pervades Saudi society. Thus, it is not surprising that the initiative for civil society, including private businesses, is not fueled by governmental, political, or even capital gains. In Saudi Arabia, all sustainability projects have socio-religious roots. Zakat (purification of capital) is actually the third of the five pillars governing Islam, wherein citizens are required to give 2.5 percent of their liquid assets annually to charity, and sadaqa (alms-giving) is a societal norm. Therefore, the subject of 'giving back' to the community is not the issue, but rather the mechanism. Traditionally, government organizations and departments have been responsible for conducting the charitable and welfare activities of the state. Recently, private businesses have become increasingly aware of the social responsibility they carry, as well as the opportunity they have to make a much more profound impact.

Saudi Arabian society has seen an unprecedented increase in demand for civic rights. As a result, many collaborative civil society initiatives have been undertaken to establish independent organizations working on public affairs issues. In response to these collaborative initiatives, the Saudi government has enacted legislation that addresses the issues of registering and supervising these organizations. In 2008, a draft Civil Society Organizations Law was passed by the Consultative Council, though it has yet to be approved by the Saudi Council of Ministers. Although a comprehensive framework law is needed in Saudi Arabia, the draft law as it stands is flawed. If enacted, the draft law would constrain the activities of civil society groups specifically by restricting cooperation with regional and international civil-society organizations[6].

Another unique form of informal social networking exists in various cities in Saudi Arabia and form an important part of the Saudi social capital. In 1925, the notables of Jeddah, consisting mostly of local merchants, decided to surrender the city to Abdulaziz Ibn Saud. Consequently, Ibn Saud was declared the new King of Hejaz, and Jeddah merchants gained great status with the new king, which guaranteed them a larger degree of freedom. The merchants' families, who were prominent in business even before the creation of Saudi Arabia and the unification of the peninsula, managed to maintain their old traditions of gathering within each neighborhood of Jeddah to discuss local problems and to organize volunteers for response to social needs.

The same tradition spread to Riyadh and to other cities. Today, weekly meetings are held in various neighborhoods. The talks (from personal experience), cover a variety of topics, ranging from religion to politics and media coverage of current events, and they welcome all those interested to partake and express their opinion, so as long as it is done in a respectful and constructive manner. The meetings usually go on from after the last prayer of Isha' until midnight and end with a lavish dinner for all attendees. Although these discussions do not necessarily lead to any tangible change or policy revision as such, on a micro-level, they do represent the essence of the ideology of democracy where every willing participating citizen is welcome to share his or her input.

Examples of typical weekly gatherings in Jeddah:

Saturday:
1. Sabtiat Al Manna' hosted by the notable writer Abdullah Almanna'
2. Sabtiat Al Radwan hosted by businessman Abdulbasit Radwan

Sunday
1. Ahadiat Ishki hosted by Dr. Anwar Ishki
2. Ahadiat Al Nasseef hosted by Dr. Abdullah Omar Nassef

Monday
1. Ithnayniat Khoja hosted by businessman Abdelmaksoud Khoja
2. Ithnayniat Al Bassan hosted by businessman Walid Al Bassam

Tuesday
1. Tholothiyat Attayeb, hosted by businessman Mohammad Said Attayeb (Abul Shayma')
2. Atholothiya Al Makkiya, hosted by Dr. Sami Ankawi

Thursday
1. Khamisiat businessman and writer Mohammad Omar Alamoudi

Friday
1. Al Jumawiya, hosted by businessman Dr. Abdulrahman Fakeeh

These weekly lectures and meetings represent a breeding ground of ideas, and reintroduce the concept of intellectual debate, which is a part of the Saudi culture that has been foregone by the country's educational system. Nomadic tribes, as well as Arabian scholars, have been known through the ages for their late-night gatherings, conversing democratically about art, music, politics, and issues directly affecting citizens. Saudis are still engaged in the same activities, informally, in these weekly meetings.

Another important form of civil participation is through the local Chambers of Commerce and Industry. The Council of Saudi Chambers was established in March 1980 in Riyadh to oversee and coordinate the regional chambers, and support the development of the private sector and enhance its role in national development.[7]

The Jeddah Chamber of Commerce is one of the most prevalent and active in terms of its breadth and depth in servicing the local community through the direction of the same local businessmen we discussed previously. The actual constitution of the Jeddah Chamber of Commerce and Industry (JCCI) is democratic, with electoral campaigns and voting required in attaining positions of office on the management board or part of the general secretariat. The JCCI is a case study in how civic life, when led by businessmen, is able to vary significantly from the regular community lifestyle, and even more so from the state-instilled system. For example, one of the vice-presidents of the JCCI is a woman, Dr. Lama Al Sulaiman, with at least two other female members of the JCCI serving on the board. The president of the JCCI oversees the main sectors of the JCCI, namely the Business and Committees Sector, the Business Sectors Support Division, the IT and Information sector, and finally, the Support and Services sector. However, more important are the specialized centers that the JCCI has established. There are seven specialized centers at the JCCI, including the Jeddah Business Development Center to support small independent businesses and the Jeddah Social Responsibility Center. In addition, the JCCI oversees the Jeddah Marketing Board, which is the organizing task force behind the Jeddah Economic Forum, a growing event that has seen top-tier speakers including heads of states and corporations over the years.

This center is also responsible for portraying the image of Jeddah as a tourism hotspot in the kingdom. Other specialized centers are the Jeddah Center for

Events and Forums, the Jeddah Law and Justice Center, Jeddah Job Development Center, Jeddah Training Center and the Khadeejah Bint Khuwailed Center. The Khadija Bint Khuwailed Women's Center has taken a prominent role in the Jeddah civil-society scene. The idea, which was first presented in 2000, materialized in 2004 as a forum for women to discuss their local issues, spearheaded by the voluntary work of a handful of Saudi middle-class women who began presentation and confidence-building classes for women.[8] The name of the center is attributed to the first wife of Prophet Muhammad, who prior to their marriage was, and who remained, an important businesswoman. Islam has always granted women equal rights in terms of business, property, and ownership, and have had these rights protected for more than 1,400 years. The Khadija Bint Khuwailed Center has appealed to the sensibility of the Saudi culture in establishing itself and its laws. Primarily, the purpose of the center is to facilitate women's dealings with the Chamber[9]; however, it has also been active in improving the laws and regulations in place that have restricted female business owners in the past based on the local culture. Previously, women were only allowed to operate businesses in certain industries, such as beauty and fashion; however, thanks to the perseverance and lobbying of the center, women are now able to trade in real estate, construction, contracting, and public services, which were all forbidden to women previously. The center was also pivotal in removing the requirement that a woman needed permission from her legal guardian in order to participate in a business venture. According to Ms. Basma Al-Omair, executive director of the center, they are currently working on removing the requirement that Saudi businesswomen must hire a male manager for their business if it is located in a mixed environment.[10] These issues and achievements, though small, cannot be diminished and are an important step toward opening up the business environment to free trade, but more importantly, this is a model of how private businesses have been able to directly and democratically achieve a fundamental change in laws through a civil association.

The civil outreach programs of the center also extend guidance to the society, and it is highly active in teaching Saudi women through discussion forums and seminars how to assume the responsibility of their role in society. The topics that are broached in these seminars do show the level of development and depth that the center has progressed, too. The first seminar held in March 2009 focused exclusively on job interview techniques and resume building, with women from the workforce sharing their own experiences about starting small businesses and being employed. In contrast, by November 2010, the topic of the Khadija Bint Khuwailed Center's forum was 'The Realistic Participation of Women in National Development.' At this event, prominent businesswomen shared their experiences alongside clerics and religious men who discussed the importance and benefit to society as a whole of the participation of females in the workplace. Although the forum did not result in any direct changes of regulations, the center's continued efforts to shed light on shocking statistics is essential in developing the psyche for acceptance of the Islamic concept that women have both the ability and the right to be successful in private business.

Another important forum and platform for civil association is the National Dialogue, which begun in 2003. The importance of the National Dialogue lies in the fact that it is able to cut across all three major national regions, bringing to light issues that are important to all citizens. However, Caroline Montagu does point out that instead of 'bringing together' citizens, the National Dialogue instead has highlighted the huge rift in ideology and demands of the Saudi people. By focusing on pluralism, individual rights, and minority rights, the National Dialogue makes differences stand out, such as during a session entitled 'Women's Rights Under Islam,' which saw an emotional and verbal outburst between conservative men and liberal women.[11] That, however, does not take away from the important role many men have played in emphasizing women's rights in the kingdom, and a great deal of development in women's rights can be attributed to educated private businessmen and professionals, who have paved the way, albeit less vocally than their female counterparts, for the execution of change. Montagu discusses how women could not have gotten so far in municipal election campaigns without the support of Shari 'a (Islamic law) judges.[12] These private individuals have identified the problems facing the society and have exercised their civil association individually in this respect. Though their effect may have been profound, the truth is that the reach of individual professionals remains limited and inconsistent.

However, of all the methods of civil participation available, private business initiatives could prove to be the most influential. Private businesses have the ability to reach across the nation, as well as the funding and organization in place to offer continued support and assistance. The concept of Corporate Social Responsibility (CSR) in Saudi Arabia is both old and new. CSR has unabashedly taken the corporate scene by storm, yet keeping in mind the social culture and religious background of the country, the challenge for CSR in Saudi Arabia has been changing the perspective of Corporate Responsibility from being one of charity to one of sustainability. Tamkeen Sustainability Advisors is the first Saudi consultancy firm to offer Corporate Social Responsibility consultancy and programs for private businesses in the kingdom. In January 2010, they released their study entitled 'The Evolution of CSR in Saudi Arabia,' which offers an interesting insight into how the concept of CSR has taken shape within private businesses in Saudi Arabia. Founder and Managing Director, Ms. Asya AlShaikh, pointed out in her opening to the study that 'CSR has evolved from being an alien concept to a buzzword in the corporate arena,' pointing out that Ms. AlShaikh's definition of CSR refers to sustainable responsibility and competitive sustainability in the kingdom.[13] The study highlights that although the social and religious context in the kingdom is the basis for performing good deeds, key issues such as a better workplace, health and safety standards, and good governance are being recognized as areas of interest to both the private and governmental sectors alike. Yet the study also recognizes that although CSR has gained momentum and popularity among private businesses, this momentum appears one-dimensional, with programs being able to cover a large range of topics, as well as being able to cut across regions, thus achieving depth; however, the issue remains that CSR in the kingdom has yet to achieve real depth. Despite the resources available to them, private businesses have failed to achieve their full potential and instill a meaningful impact in the society as a whole.

The main factor that limits CSR goals from achieving their full capacity appears to be the perception of CSR as a cost rather than an investment. Saudi companies assume that the greatest benefit from CSR for a company is reputation and image development. Whereas smaller businesses, and private businessmen and women from large and prominent Saudi merchant families, have been able to set up smaller sustainability projects in their communities, as a whole, CSR has adversely been unable to grasp the concept of sustainable giving as opposed to charitable projects, which is the traditional corporate responsibility concept. Saudi companies need to become more aware of the benefit in financial and social terms that they are able to bring about through their responsible behavior toward their employees, shareholders, and customers, as well as the benefit they could potentially be presenting toward social improvement. The best way for private businesses to achieve depth and impact through their civil service initiatives would be to align their initiatives with national development priorities. Although a few Saudi companies do consider national development priorities while setting the CSR direction, it is not the primary consideration.[14] Instead, private Saudi businesses opt to link their CSR philanthropy with issues that align with their company image or product. Yet more often than not, it is difficult to find a direct alignment between both, resulting in very superficial campaigns that provide only temporary relief. Breadth has been achieved, but the move from charity to a form of self-governing will come from active implementation with a vision to achieve goals; ideally, the goals that have been identified as part of the national development scheme. By aligning their strategies with national priorities, companies would be better equipped to further the democratization process in the country since they would be directly contributing to the betterment of their society through their own choice to participate in associational life.

The biggest players in CSR are the industrial, banking, and retail sectors, which have devoted their attention mainly to employee well-being, community development, and the environment. Private charities, on the other hand, have been more instrumental in combating more politically substantial issues, such as women empowerment, women representation in courts, changes in family law, political and human rights, unemployment, the medical impact of endogamy, family violence, disabilities, sexual abuse, and poverty.[15] Companies have opted out of tackling core problems, and the reality is that Saudi companies believe that the main reason CSR is not creating a meaningful impact on national development is due to a lack of support from the government and media.[16] Companies have cited this issue with regard to a lack of direction from the government. Only a minority of Saudi companies have attempted to use their CSR programs to help fulfill national development goals.

The Saudi government has yet to recognize the incredible potential that private businesses offer when it comes to positive contributions to society. Once the government is able to appreciate this, it will be able to identify the challenges facing private businesses in this regard, and will be able to provide the infrastructure as well as the facilities to help CSR programs set their goals parallel to national development priorities. Further, the government should offer subsidies, reim-bursements, and other incentives in order to motivate private businesses to take up national development needs as part of their philanthropic programs.

Similarly, Saudi companies have expressed a disappointment with the media when it comes to portraying CSR programs as charitable projects embarked on by private businesses, as opposed to linking CSR goals and achievements to national priority needs. Yet on the other hand, companies have credited the media with being the most important external driver for public awareness and response to private business initiatives.[17]

In addition to a lack of governmental direction and guidance, governmental regulations have also hindered the actual implementation of CSR. The regulatory framework has proved to be overly bureaucratic due to a lack of uniformity regard-ing regulation in Saudi law. This in turn, has brought to light problems regarding corruption, the legal and court system and an overall lack of support from various governmental agencies. Labor laws have left CSR departments facing problems of available qualified talent. Over the past decade, Saudi labor law has adopted a policy of 'Saudization,' trying to move away from expatriate workers in an attempt to reduce the local unemployment rate. As a result, implementation of this policy has become stringent, highly regulated, and enforced. Yet the output of the educational system, which as previously discussed is subpar, has left a vacuum between what is required, on the one hand, in terms of globally competitive talent that would be able to implement creative and forward-thinking solutions, and, on the other hand, the young graduates that have been trained through a system that does not encourage creativity.

The issue of education has plagued many debates on national development and self-governing. The government claimed that certain civil rights have not been supported by citizens, and have in some cases, such as the matter of legal-izing females driving, been shunned and rejected. The opposing argument is that citizens have not received adequate or appropriate education in order to be able to demand these rights. A recent article[18] by a female Saudi legal consultant, Tala Al-Hejailan, argues that the lack of women's rights and hence human rights in the kingdom stems from ignorance and misinterpretation of Islamic teachings. The article reiterates the point that Islam granted women rights regarding ownership, career, family, and education 1,400 years ago, whereas these rights were only achieved by women in the west at the beginning of the 20th century. Thus, she finds it shocking that it is these same women who are resistant to change base their arguments on Islamic teachings. The article highlights an important point; women in Saudi Arabia are not necessarily oppressed by their male counterparts per se, but are rather resistant to the 'ambush of westernized ideas regarding women.'[19] The Saudi government has been operational and attentive to the needs of women by providing scholarships for those who choose to pursue academic degrees abroad, as they have to men. In addition, the Saudization law does call for an increase in the employment of women. Therefore, Al-Hejailan makes the essential point: "As in a democracy, how can one change a system, in which the majority of people reject positive and necessary change?"[20] There has been an overall call for reform in the educational system, from 'radically Islamic' to 'Islamically Informative,' yet this has been slow to grasp.

Yet education is not the only factor causing resistance to change. Saudi Arabia is a country where people with the same education have very different opinions that are heavily influenced by culture and tradition. Even among the highly educated elite, many believe that radical cultural change is not appropriate for Saudi Arabia and the Saudi people. Saudis have gone from Bedouin life to living in the cities in less than 50 years. Yet through the process of urbanization, they have maintained their traditions and culture. In a post -9/11 era, there is a widely spread perception among Saudis that western morality is being aggressively imposed on them, in an attempt to strip Saudi Arabia of its identity. Many Saudis have become highly defensive in the face of what has been perceived as the heavy hand of America that has extended to other countries in the Arabian Gulf, tainting the authentic and pure lifestyle of their ancestors. This has made most Saudis resistant to the western model of democratization. While a western democratic model is not likely to be embraced in Saudi Arabia, that is not to say that a Saudi democratic model is not possible.

This rift in public opinion has left the ruling monarchy with a dilemma. A step toward westernization would be perceived as stripping Saudi of its Islamic identity, and as such, the monarchy has displayed that it would rather maintain the status quo than risk being perceived by its citizens as a western puppet. In order to avoid disturbance of the delicate balance, the state cannot display overt affection toward westernization and westernized democratization, and must practice restraint. Hence, the Saudi state has developed a policy of stability rather than volatility concerning implementing change, and this policy has truly played to Saudi Arabia's benefit. Although the state has moved very slowly in a western direction, the country has had time to adapt slowly to the changes that have been made, thus gaining stability. Although much progress is still required for Saudi Arabia, we must keep in mind that this relatively young country has brought together a variety of ideologies from its oil-rich, work-oriented eastern province, through its harsh desert capital, to its historical religious centers and trading cities in the west. Too much change too fast would not be received well. However, civil societies, especially east and west of the country, have been able to implement change at a much faster pace, by providing an alternative structure of instigating reform, yet still extending traditional morals and values throughout the population.

It must be pointed out that not all civil-society organizations are welcomed, and highly independent branches are shut down,[21] yet even the state has recognized that it can benefit from a 'bottom-up' approach to reform in a model where citizens, led by the example of private businesses, have taken the initiative to govern themselves.

As a result, we have seen a political enmeshing of the monarchy and civil societies, with many royals providing patronage at all levels of associational life. Although this may not be what is intrinsically expected, given the generally opposing directions of each force, we have seen primarily that the monarchy, like the citizens of Saudi Arabia, is not homogeneous.[22] Indeed, although CSR have identified that the government and regulatory framework as their main challenge in being effective, having a royal on board can be influential in pushing projects through in the right direction.

By western standards, Saudi Arabia has severe problems, not the least of which is the issue of women's rights. Religious conservatives continue to wield a club to keep Saudis in check. The judicial system is mired in tribal customs and the abuses of male guardianship have put a stranglehold on women's ability to find employment or travel. The unemployment rate is at least 10 percent and perhaps as high as 20 percent. Thousands of young Saudi men and women graduating from local universities have no job prospects, while others returning with applied science degrees from foreign universities find it easier to find employment. Only 10 percent of the Saudi population owns their own home.

As 2011 witnessed one revolution leading to another in countries neighboring Saudi Arabia, western analysts who compared Saudi Arabia to its neighbors failed to consider that not a single Arab country threatened with anti-government protests is, in fact, similar to the kingdom. Saudis, I observed, neither are worried about the near future nor are they seriously thinking about changing their system of governance.

The Saudi government recognizes that some of these issues are critical, and it is continuously trying to find solutions. On March 18, 2011, after Friday prayer, the king announced a new wave of benefits for the citizens. He thanked the citizens for their loyalty and called the youth the safety valve for the nation.

For the first time, the government agreed to establish unemployment allowances up to one year to help Saudis find jobs. University students studying abroad at their own expense will now receive scholarships. SR 1 billion ($266.6 million) has been added to the social-welfare rolls. SR 14 billion ($3.7 billion) will be available for home loans. The government also announced Tuesday, February 15, 2011, that it was setting aside SR 10 million ($2.6 million) to fund literary clubs and licensed NGOs.

What was actually missing from the king's address to his people was a road map to a constitutional monarchy that will enable the Saudi people to have constitutional rights at a point in the future and pull the rug from under the opposition.

Saudi Arabia does not require a revolution, but rather a progressive evolution in the functioning of the state, leading toward more social and political freedoms. Private businessmen have provided an alternative and a nonthreatening method of citizens' participation by opening up the avenues of civil societies. As civil society develops and becomes more sophisticated, especially CSR programs, the government will need to further cooperate with this channel and use it efficiently.

Notes

1 The electronic survey that we have conducted in 2010 showed that the majority of respondents considered democracy to be a western concept. However, the survey was repeated in February 2011, after the success of the Tunisian and the Egyptian

revolutions. It was found that a larger percentage of Saudis were more sympathetic since they identified democracy as a form of participatory government.

2   Caroline Montagu, "Civil Society and the Voluntary Sector in Saudi Arabia," *The Middle East Journal,* Winter 2010.

3   Joel S. Migdal, "Civil Society in Israel," in Ellis Goldberg, Resat Kasaba, and Joel S. Migdal, eds., *Rules and Rights in the Middle East Democracy, Law and Society* (Seattle: University of Washington Press, 1993), pp. 122–23, as cited by Caroline Montagu, "Civil Society and the Voluntary Sector in Saudi Arabia," *The Middle East Journal,* Winter 2010.

4   http://www.istr.org/conference/istanbul/WorkingPapers/Afif%20WP10.pdf

5   "The Evolution of CSR in Saudi Arabia," A Study by Tamkeen Sustainability Advisors, January 2010, p. 7.

6   http://www.icnl.org/knowledge/ngolawmonitor/pdf/SaudiArabia.pdf

7   About the Council, Council of Saudi Chambers, http://www.saudichambers.org.sa/2_1276_ENU_HTML.htm

8   Caroline Montagu, "Civil Society and the Voluntary Sector in Saudi Arabia," *The Middle East Journal,* Winter 2010.

9   About the Center, Khadija Bint Khuwailed Center, JCCI http://www.jcci.org.sa/JCCI/EN/Specialized+Centers/Khadija+Bint+Khuwailid+Center/About+The+Center/?cnName={C3B92370–5714–4325-BCD1–555BA1CCB0C4}

10   Lulwa Shalhoub, "Rocky Road Ahead for Saudi Women Studying Abroad," *Arab News,* June 2010 http://arabnews.com/supplement_archives/top_20_supplement/article 66314.ece

11   Caroline Montagu, "Civil Society and the Voluntary Sector in Saudi Arabia," *The Middle East Journal,* Winter 2010.

12   Ibid.

13   "The Evolution of CSR in Saudi Arabia," A Study by Tamkeen Sustainability Advisors, January 2010, p. 2.

14   "The Evolution of CSR in Saudi Arabia," A Study by Tamkeen Sustainability Advisors, January 2010, p. 5.

15   Caroline Montagu, "Civil Society and the Voluntary Sector in Saudi Arabia," *The Middle East Journal,* Winter 2010.

16   "The Evolution of CSR in Saudi Arabia," A Study by Tamkeen Sustainability Advisors, January 2010, p. 6.

17   "The Evolution of CSR in Saudi Arabia," A Study by Tamkeen Sustainability Advisors, January 2010, p. 8.

18   Tala Al-Hejailan, "Education Key to Women's Rights," *Arab News,* April 2011, http://arabnews.com/opinion/columns/article340848.ece

19   Ibid.

20   Ibid.

21   Caroline Montagu, "Civil Society and the Voluntary Sector in Saudi Arabia," *The Middle East Journal,* Winter 2010.

22   Ibid.

References

"About the Center," Khadija Bint Khuwailed Center, JCCI http://www.jcci.org.sa/JCCI/EN/Specialized+Centers/Khadija+Bint+Khuwailid+Center/About+The+Center/?cnName={C3B92370–5714–4325-BCD1–555BA1CCB0C4}

"About the Council," Council of Saudi Chambers, http://www.saudichambers.org.sa/2_1276_ENU_HTML.htm

Tala Al-Hejailan, "Education Key To Women's Rights," *Arab News,* April 2011. http://arabnews.com/opinion/columns/article340848.ece http://data.un.org/CountryProfile.aspx?crName=SAUDI%20ARABIA

The Central Department of Statistics. The Ministry of Economy and Planning.

"The Evolution of CSR in Saudi Arabia," A Study by Tamkeen Sustainability Advisors, January 2010.

Joel S. Migdal, "Civil Society in Israel," in Ellis Goldberg, Resat Kasaba, and Joel S. Migdal, eds., *Rules and Rights in the Middle East Democracy, Law and Society* (Seattle: University of Washington Press, 1993), pp. 122–123, as cited by Caroline Montagu, "Civil Society and the Voluntary Sector in Saudi Arabia," *The Middle East Journal,* Winter 2010.

Caroline Montagu, "Civil Society and the Voluntary Sector in Saudi Arabia," *The Middle East Journal,* Winter 2010.

Ursula Lindsey, "Saudi Arabia's Education Reforms Emphasize Training for Jobs," *The Chronicle of Higher Education,* October 2010, http://chronicle.com/article/Saudi-Arabias-Education/124771/

Lulwa Shalhoub, "Rocky Road Ahead for Saudi Women Studying Abroad," *Arab News,* June 2010. http://arabnews.com/supplement_archives/top_20_supplement/article66314.ece

"Voluntary Work in Civil Society: Saudi Women Volunteers as Social Capital," paper presented at the Ninth International Conference of the International Society for Third Sector Research (Kadir Has University, Istanbul, Turkey, July 7–10, 2010, by Suad Afif. http://www.istr.org/conference/istanbul/WorkingPapers/Afif%20WP10.pdf

13 Post-conflict reconstruction and the private sector in Iraq

Benjamin MacQueen

Introduction

The role of the private sector and, more specifically, external private sector actors, in Iraqi reconstruction represents the implementation of an unabashed neo-liberal model of deregulation and almost unfettered international access to Iraq's economic resources. As such, the Iraqi economy now functions with little state control and is dependent on the actions of foreign investors. While this raises an obvious critique of the role of the private sector in post-conflict reconstruction in terms of local control over economic development, it need not necessarily undermine the rationale for private sector involvement in reconstruction processes. This chapter examines the role of the private sector in Iraq in order to highlight how the implementation of this specific model works to the detriment of the economic, social, and political well-being of the majority of Iraqi citizens. However, it also contains lessons on 'what not to do' in terms of managing the relationship between political and economic reconstruction and how external private sector involvement can be better managed.

Post-conflict reconstruction and the private sector

Post-conflict reconstruction can be understood as "a set of transitional reconstruction activities . . . designed to lay the foundation for longer-term developments such as democratisation, economic development and social justice" (Suhrke *et al* 2002, p. 876). These efforts are driven by foreign governments and multilateral agencies such as the UN and the World Bank, often in partnership with a range of private-sector actors, notably multinational corporations (MNCs). Here, the restoration of governance is the focus of the reconstruction process. The development or redevelopment of the institutions of governance focuses on strengthening the executive, judicial, and legislative branches, as well as the armed forces, the civil service, and regulatory mechanisms. The logic here is to create institutions that have integrity so that they may withstand future crises. Once political institutions are seen as integral by both citizens and political elites, they become invested in this new arrangement, enhancing the prospects for operating within this system in a nonviolent way rather than resorting to anti-systemic and/or violent means (Elkins and Sides 2007, p. 693).

Put simply, post-conflict reconstruction is a process designed to undermine violence through the fostering of political, social, and economic stability. Here, the development of new institutions is critical to the maintenance of this stability and should ideally be guided by the needs and interests of the majority of citizens. This requires promoting attachment among the citizenry to these new institutions. Maximizing legitimacy for these new arrangements is an intensely difficult task. This is particularly so when a community is divided along ethnic, ideological, religious lines, or more often than not, some combination of these, characteristic features of communities in conflict. Such divisions almost always impose themselves on processes of political reconstruction, which has to deal with the legacy of fragile colonial political constructions established over multi-ethnic societies (Premdas 2004, p. 252). Therefore, what we often see today is an effort to reconstruct political institutions where the institutions themselves previously had minimal levels of state attachment with the presence of significant external involvement.

Economic reform and reconstruction is a key part of this dynamic, and of particular concern to external actors. Institutions such as the World Bank are central, focused on the need for external financial support in the initial post-conflict period. However, this task is complicated by the lack of absorptive capacity on the part of the state that has been affected by violence and is compounded by the difficulty in attracting foreign investment to a post-conflict country. This raises the dilemma where post-conflict states struggle to "fully absorb reconstruction aid" yet are unable to "attract much private investment . . . sectors that could offset the state's low absorptive capacity" (Schwartz *et al* 2004, p. i). It is here that the role of the private sector and particularly external private investors such as MNCs are bought into reconstruction processes, backed by agencies such as the World Bank.

The World Bank's stated aims are two-fold, to "provide interim services that help ameliorate the hardships caused by the conflict" and to "put in place policies which will shorten the non-investment gap as much as possible and which will lead to sustainable service provision and growth" (Schwartz *et al* 2004, p. 5). In this, the World Bank is focused on managing government regulation to promote long-term concessions that would mitigate poor risk ratings as an incentive for foreign investment. This is designed to "shorten the non-investment gap" between the end of aid programs and the commencement of foreign direct investment (Schwartz *et al* 2004, p. 4).

The role of the World Bank, MNCs and the private sector more generally in reconstruction processes is not without controversy. Views are often polarized between how the private sector can "prolong conflict, obstruct peacemaking and lead to an exploitation of natural resources to the detriment of peace, development and social progress' or alternatively how the private sector can provide the 'economic instruments to provide incentives for peace" (Berdal & Mousavizadeh 2010, p. 37). Further than this, it is argued that there are potentially divergent priorities between what political reconstruction should seek to achieve and what external investment may require. Specifically, MNCs, the World Bank and other institutions seek stability as surety for returns on potential investments in post-conflict states (Berdal & Mousavizadeh 2010, p. 40–41). However, uncertainly and fragility are hallmarks of these environments. Indeed, efforts at political reconstruction to promote democracy are likely to foster continued uncertainty and instability, particularly in the short term where private investment is needed to supplant aid programs. As such, the drive for stability to promote investment may undercut moves to promote political reform leading to greater democratisation.

It is here that critical focus on the neo-liberal model guiding the World Bank and foreign investment comes into stark relief. Neo-liberal views of development are centered on four categories that shape policy choices and priorities. These are the centrality of the individual as a rational actor, an unrestricted global market as the best mechanism for the distribution of wealth to these individuals, limiting the role of the state's potential to distort the logic of the market, and democratic systems that would, ideally, act to limit the potential for the state to interfere in the market (Hindess 2002, p. 198; Wool 2007, p. 460; Williams 2008, p. 20; Dodge 2009, p. 1275). In simpler terms, neo-liberalism focuses on unhindered individual choice in an unrestricted market place where the exercise of state power is to be minimized as much as possible, particularly in relation to economic activity. In terms of reconstruction, this relationship, rather than aid or development assistance, is posited as the quickest means for recovery.

These priorities are evident in the World Bank's stated goals, and the impacts of this on regulatory environments for state reconstruction. This has its roots in the various debt crises of the 1970s and 1980s where both the World Bank and International Monetary Fund (IMF) were endowed with sweeping powers to promote aggressively 'market reliance' in the developing world (Agnew & Corbridge 1995, p. 198; Dodge 2010, p. 1275). Here, free-market reforms were tied to "legal provisions for foreign investment . . . private property rights (and) zero subsidies for food and essential services" as key steps in enhancing what has become commonly known as 'good governance' (Guttal 2005, p. 77). In cases of post-conflict reconstruction, this philosophy became the template for guiding the design of new political institutions, ones that would have built-in limits on state regulatory capacity and be judged by predetermined parameters for economic and political progress.

These terms of debate have evolved since the end of the Cold War, where issues are increasingly framed in terms of peacekeeping, peace-building, and humanitarian assistance. This has been an important step in recognizing the human impact of conflict and political chaos, and one that has stepped back from the overtly negative view of the state and particularly state regulation in reconstruction environments (Berdal & Mousavizadeh 2010, p. 44). This has been reflected in general normative shifts toward an emphasis on human security that includes references to economic certainty and meeting basic human needs.

However, reconstruction in Iraq since 2003, and particularly the efforts to limit state regulation on foreign direct investment, stands as an exception. Indeed, the US-led reconstruction process here represents the high water mark of an ultra-neo-liberal model of reconstruction. Putting aside the flawed legal rationale for the invasion and occupation of Iraq based on allegations of possession of weapons of mass destruction in violation of UN Security Council Resolution 1441, the philosophical justification for the Bush administration centered on a particular notion of *freedom*. This notion of freedom was articulated around a neo-liberal logic that would catalyze similar processes across the Arab and Muslim world, undercutting perceived hostility to the United States. More than this, the critical view of the state embodied in the neo-liberal doctrine of the Bush administration helped justify the targeting and systematic dismantling of the state of Iraq, despite facing a non-state enemy in the form of Al Qaeda. This has created an exceptional environment in Iraq in terms of the role of the private sector in post-conflict reconstruction, one that contains many negative lessons, but lessons nonetheless.

Reconstruction in Iraq and the private sector

The vision of what Iraqi reconstruction would look like was clearly identified by L. Paul Bremer, head of the Coalition Provisional Authority (CPA) that ruled Iraq through 2003 and 2004, when he stated that the

> removal of Saddam Hussein offers Iraqis hope for a better economic future. For a free Iraq to thrive, its economy must be transformed – and this will require the wholesale reallocation of resources and people from state control to private enterprise, the promotion of free trade, and the mobilization of domestic foreign capital (Bremer 2003).

This was dubbed "Operation Iraqi Prosperity," a vital ancillary to the military actions ("Operation Iraqi Freedom") against Saddam Hussein's regime. Indeed, it may be argued that the process of wholesale economic reform spoken about by Bremer was more of a defining feature of this intervention than the military action itself. Here, the private sector was to play the central role in Iraqi reconstruction where reconstruction would be governed by the creation of an unfettered free market.

US-led reconstruction in Iraq was not implemented in a vacuum. The condition of the Iraqi state that the United States found when it installed the CPA in April 2003 was a skeleton structure. Ravaged by several decades of harsh dictatorship and 13 years of international sanctions, the Iraqi state was barely functional on the eve of the US-led invasion. As the "shock and awe" campaign led by the United States wreaked further destruction on the country, the country's fragility quickly became evident. The rapid collapse of the formal Iraqi resistance in the initial stages of the conflict was compounded by the three weeks of intense looting across the country that stripped Iraq of its basic infrastructure. Hospitals and ministries were looted, the regular army disintegrated, and the civil service ceased to function (Phillips 2005, p. 135). Even Bremer, the architect of the reconstruction policy in Iraq after 2003, commented that he had no idea "how utterly broken the country was" upon his arrival in Baghdad (Bremer & McConnell 2006, p. 18).

There were some signs in this early phase that the United States would seek to try to revive salvageable parts of the pre-2003 Iraqi state; however, this would be subject to a particular model of state behavior. As Toby Dodge has identified, the CPA sought to implement a form of 'structural adjustment' modeled on the World Bank and IMF programs of the 1980s and 1990s backed by US military force (Dodge 2010, p. 1,278). Iraqi institutions would be revived or maintained as tools to supply the necessary social and political order in which sweeping economic reform would take place. In the words of then-Secretary of State Condoleezza Rice, new leadership would be bought in but "we were going to keep the body in place" (quoted in Gordon 2004). However, this program was quickly supplanted by a more literalist implementation of neo-liberal reforms led by the CPA, quickly followed by the collapse of the security environment that undermined the legitimacy of the new political institutions.

The key examples of this doctrine in practice were the disbanding of the Iraqi army and the so-called de-Ba'athification policy (General Order Number 1). Despite claims from Bremer that there was no formal edict to dismantle the Iraqi security services, the CPA both encouraged the disintegration of the regular Iraqi army and the more formal liquidation of the Republican Guard (Bremer & McConnell 2006, p. 49; Chebab 2006, pp. 55–56). The immediate effect of this was not just a collapse of formal resistance to the US presence in the first weeks and months after the invasion, but also a removal of any insulation between the Iraqi people and US troops. This led to growing frustration and resentment toward the United States among Iraqis as insecurity and disaggregated violence spread throughout the country toward the end of 2003.

Compounding this situation was the perhaps more famous edict, de-Ba'athification, that removed all upper-ranking members of the Ba'ath Party from any government employment (Coalition Provisional Authority 2003a). This stripped Iraqi state ministries of their entire upper level of management, depriving the new governing body of people with essential on-the-ground knowledge to help provide basic services. Combined with the looting and general insecurity that virtually destroyed Iraq's physical infrastructure, this loss of expertise left the state in ruins. In addition, the sacking of more than 100,000 public servants, and the decommissioning of an estimated 300,000 Iraqi soldiers created a huge pool of unemployed, disenfranchised people, many of whom saw armed resistance to the United States and violent confrontation with perceived sectarian enemies as their only means of survival.

As such, almost immediately, the Iraqi state was systematically dismantled. In this context, further attempts at political reconstruction were profoundly mismanaged. The drafting of the new constitution through 2004 and 2005 was subject to heavy US influence and then was substantially amended after its ratification in 2005, under pressure from sectarian and religious leaders (MacQueen and Akbarzadeh 2008, p. 63). The fragility of the constitution and any remnants of state integrity were further undermined with its virtual abandonment in 2005 in favor of a power-sharing arrangement based on the implementation of a *de facto* confessional quota system in Parliament. This has hindered the potential for the new government and its institutions to gain popular legitimacy as "government ministries were farmed out to various parties without any significant oversight over the way the ministries conducted their daily business" (Kadhim 2010).

Private sector-led 'reconstruction'?

In terms of the private sector, the CPA combined its dismantling of government institutions with a range of free-market reforms that deprived any current or future Iraqi government from controlling key aspects of foreign investment. General Order Number 39, issued in September 2003, saw "complete foreign ownership of Iraqi companies and assets (apart from natural resources), total overseas remittance of profits and some of the lowest taxes in the world" (Coalition Provisional Authority 2003b; Medani 2004, p. 28). Order 39 was framed in the language of humanitarian intervention, and as such, sets the framework for how private sector involvement in Iraqi reconstruction would be managed. Here, the order cited United Nations Security Council Resolution 1483 that lifted the previous sanctions on Iraq imposed after the 1990 invasion of Kuwait and called for international assistance in reconstruction. However, the priorities of the CPA and Order 39 imposed a particular interpretation on implementing the UN's call for assistance in "promoting economic reconstruction and the conditions for sustainable development" (United Nations Security Council 2003). The rationale for reform of the foreign investment laws in Iraq as articulated in Order 39 focused on its

> transition from a non-transparent centrally planned economy to a market economy characterized by sustainable economic growth through the establishment of a dynamic private sector, and the need to enact institutional and legal reforms to give it effect (Coalition Provisional Authority 2003b).

This statement framed the subsequent set of edicts that replaced all existing foreign investment law in Iraq. For instance, the order removed any limits on foreign ownership of Iraqi businesses with the exception of the "primary extraction and initial processing" of natural resources, allowed foreign companies to transfer money out of Iraq without consultation, extended real estate leases for foreign firms, and prohibited the Iraqi government from being able to exercise legal authority over companies in dispute unless the companies requested government assistance (Coalition Provisional Authority 2003b). In addition, it limited the ability of future Iraqi governments to make substantial changes to these laws, as well as made this subject to any international agreement that "provides for more favorable terms with respect to foreign investors" (Coalition Provisional Authority 2003b).

Reconstruction, deregulation, decentralization, and oil

Reform of the Iraqi oil industry captures many of the conflicting trends that have resulted from reconstruction in Iraq and the role of the private sector. Iraq is still without a formal law governing the oil industry; however, there is a draft law guided by the principles established in Order 39. The draft law is premised on four elements: (1) removal of state regulations from the industry; (2) separating existing oil operations from new projects with new operations being the exclusive domain of the private sector; (3) large increases in output; and (4) privatization of the downstream industry (Mahdi 2007, p. 14). In this, efforts toward privatization of the industry and moves to decentralize remaining decision-making powers away from the central government and to regional and local authorities are critical.

The draft law itself emerged after the end of CPA administration, a move interpreted by some as an attempt to "avoid accusations of a US attempt to control Iraq's oil," a process in contrast to decisions on "banking, investment and commercial laws" that were taken under CPA auspices guided by Order 39 (Khadduri 2004; Mahdi 2007, p. 15). Here, the United States was careful not to move too rapidly for fear of a collapse of the local oil industry as, in the words of Secretary of Defense Rumsfeld, "The bulk of the funds for Iraq's reconstruction will come from Iraqis – from oil revenues" (quoted in Gilmore 2003). However, moves toward dismantling state control were evident from the beginning, where high-level oil executives were immediately housed in Iraq's new Oil Ministry in an 'advisory' capacity (Mahdi 2007, p. 15).

With the arrival of the first post-CPA government, the process of drafting a new law for the oil industry began. It immediately reflected the preference for a heavily deregulated system with the initial draft permitting long-term contracts with foreign oil companies "whereby foreign companies will control and manage Iraq's oil resources for up to 25 years" (Mahdi 2007, p. 11). Successive Iraqi governments, along with the United States, have argued that the draft law does not provide for the full privatization of the industry, but a system of joint ownership between the Iraqi government and foreign oil companies. However, this system of joint ownership has given these companies an effective veto over both future oil policy and the contracting process. In terms of policy, the lack of a clear law, and the stripping of regulatory powers, has seen production levels increase dramatically causing a drop in the price of oil, affecting the ability of this income to be used for reconstruction purposes. In addition, the provisions of Order 39 allow foreign oil companies to store funds in banks overseas, with no compulsion to re-invest these in reconstruction programs in Iraq (Mahdi 2009).

The issue that has caused the most political controversy in Iraq is not the sale of the state's most valuable asset, but the effort to shift the remaining decision-making powers over the future of Iraq's oil industry from the federal to the state and local levels. In this regard, debate over Iraq's draft oil law has not only caught up in, but also actually exacerbated, the regional and sectarian conflicts across the country. The relationship between the central government and regional authorities in Iraq is still undefined. Indeed, a clear decision on how the state should be structured (federally, centrally, some other form) has been consciously avoided by successive Iraqi governments in order to avoid the potential for conflict over access to resources. Efforts at decentralization of the oil industry, as outlined in the draft law, have added to the confusion over the status of regional versus central powers. Indeed, both decentralization and deregulation have fostered instability with the potential for violence. This has mitigated the process of reconstruction through weakening political coordination and coherence and diverting much needed resources away from the provision of essential services (Mahdi 2007, p. 20).

Iraq and lessons learned for reconstruction

The neo-liberal logic that has guided reconstruction in Iraq, and the role of the private sector in this process, teaches a series of negative lessons. The standardized parameters of deregulation and the focus on private sector-led development are not suitable for a state that has been under harsh authoritarian rule since the 1970s and effectively been at war since 1980. The problems affecting the Iraqi state are more profound than debates over the "relative efficiency of private versus public sectors" and deeper than reliance on often fickle foreign investment can address (Mahdi 2007, p. 12). Indeed, the shock associated with adjustment from a wartime, state-led economy to one of the most deregulated economic environments in the world has caused great disruption to the already fragile structure of Iraqi economic life.

Here, the reconstruction process implemented by the US government, the CPA, and agencies such as USAID have worked against the rebuilding of Iraq's physical infrastructure, as well as undermining the development of a cohesive national political system in the country. With private control over key industries, overseas companies have been unhindered in sourcing foreign labor for projects in Iraq as a means save money through lower wages, as well as to subvert the potential for efforts at unionization. Indeed, the first act of the CPA, Order 1, banned strikes and led to the detention of the leaders of Iraq's largest union (Coalition Provisional Authority 2003a). This fed into the growing number of unemployed in Iraq, a key recruitment pool for the various insurgent groups, as well as solidifying the view of the US and Iraqi governments as "exploitative rather than liberationary" (Medani 2004, p. 31).

This has been compounded since 2003 through the largely noncompetitive nature of bidding contracts for key reconstruction processes facilitated through Order 39. The major companies, such as Bechtel and Halliburton, alongside private security contractors such as Xe Services (formerly Blackwater Industries) saw investment priorities set by foreign businesses rather than by Iraqis themselves. Where Iraqi government officials have been involved, they have been accused of benefitting financially and politically from restricting competition and enforcing the provisions of Order 1 relating to the organisation of labor.

The lack of Iraqi participation in the new Iraqi economy and reconstruction efforts has fed into the burgeoning "shadow economy," one that itself has links within successive Iraqi governments. Combined with an unrestricted formal economy, the growth of the shadow economy more and more deprives the state of any form of tax revenue that may be used to fund reconstruction projects, and further undermines popular legitimacy in the new Iraqi political system.

As such, what we have seen at work in Iraq can be described as a form of 'kinetic' neo-liberalism where the state is required not only to limit its role in the private sector, but also to actively enforce this vision (Dodge 2009, p. 263). In other words, the new Iraqi state was not just to have a limited role, but intentionally designed to prohibit actively any intervention by any force other than unregulated capital in the Iraqi economy. This has had deeply negative consequences where the external private sector, seen as the engine of reconstruction, has helped create an environment that increasingly shifts wealth out of the country, ignores urgent reconstruction projects that aren't profitable, feeds confusion over the relationship between the central government and regional authorities, and undermines any potential for generating popular legitimacy for the new system.

References

Agnew, John & Corbridge, Stuart. 1995. *Mastering Space: Hegemony, Territory and International Political Economy.* London: Routledge.

Berdal, Mats & Mousavizadeh, Nader. 2010. "Investing for Peace: The Private Sector and the Challenges of Peacebuilding." *Survival* 52 (2): 37–58.

Bremer, L. Paul. 2003. "Operation Iraqi Prosperity." *The Wall Street Journal* (June 20).

Bremer, L. Paul & McConnell, Malcolm. 2006. *My Year in Iraq: the Struggle to Build a Future of Hope* (New York: Simon & Schuster).

Chebab, Zaki. 2006. *Iraq Ablaze: Inside the Iraqi Insurgency* (London: I. B. Tauris).

Coalition Provisional Authority. 2003a. *Coalition Provisional Authority Order Number 1: De-Ba'athification of Iraqi Society.* Available at: www.iraqcoalition.org/regulations/20031220_CPAORD_39_Foreign_Investment_.pdf (accessed January 21, 2011).

Coalition Provisional Authority. 2003b. *Coalition Provisional Authority Order Number 39: Foreign Investment.* Available at: www.iraqcoalition.org/regulations/20031220_CPAORD_39_Foreign_Investment_.pdf (accessed January 21, 2011).

Dodge, Toby. 2009. "Coming Face to Face with Bloody Reality: Liberal Common Sense and the Ideological Failure of the Bush Doctrine in Iraq." *International Politics* 46 (2): 253–275.

Dodge, Toby. 2010. "The Ideological Roots of Failure: the Application of Kinetic Neo-Liberalism to Iraq." *International Affairs* 86 (6): 1269–1286.

Elkins, Zachary & Sides, John. 2007. "Can Institutions Build Unity in Multiethnic States?" *American Political Science Review* 101 (4): 693–708.

Gilmore, Gerry J. 2003. "Bulk of Iraq Reconstruction Monies 'Will Come from Iraqis,' Rumsfeld Says." Available at www.defense.gov/news/newsarticle.aspx?id=28388 (accessed January 13, 2011).

Gordon, Michael. 2004. '"Catastrophic Success': The Strategy to Secure Iraq Did Not Foresee a 2nd War." *The New York Times* (October 19).

Guttal, Shamali. 2005. "The Politics of Post-war/Post-Conflict Reconstruction." *Development* 48 (3): 73–81.

Hindess, Barry. 2002. "Neo-liberal Citizenship." *Citizenship Studies* 6 (2): 127–143.

Kadhim, Abbas. 2010. "Iraq's Quest for Democracy amid Massive Corruption." Available at: www.carnegieendowment.org/arb/?fa=show&article=40278 (accessed March 17, 2011).

Khadduri, Walid. 2004. "The Iraqi Oil Industry: A Look Ahead." *Middle East Economic Survey* 47: 48.

MacQueen, Benjamin & Akbarzadeh, Shahram. 2008. "Islamic Reformism and Human Rights in Iraq: Gender Equality and Religious Freedom" in Akbarzadeh, Shahram & MacQueen, Benjamin (eds.), *Islam and Human Rights in Practice: Perspectives Across the Ummah* (London: Routledge), pp. 52–74.

Mahdi, Kamil. 2007a. "Iraq's Oil Law: Parsing the Fine Print." *World Policy Journal* 24 (2): 11–23.

Mahdi, Kamil. 2007b. "Neoliberalism, Conflict and an Oil Economy: The Case of Iraq." *Arab Studies Quarterly* 29 (1): pp. 1–20.

Mahdi, Kamil. 2009. "An Undesirable Alliance: The New Appearance of Iraq's Occupation." *Globalizations* 6 (1): 139–143.

Medani, Khalid Mustafa. 2004. "State Building in Reverse: The Neo-Liberal 'Reconstruction' of Iraq." *Middle East Report* 232: 28–35.

Phillips, David L. 2004. *Losing Iraq: Inside the Post-war Reconstruction Fiasco* (Boulder: Westview Press).

Premdas, Ralph R. "The Guyana Ethnic Quagmire: Problems and Solutions for Reconciliation." *Nationalism and Ethnic Politics* 10 (2): 251–268.

Schwartz, Jordan; Hahn, Shelly & Bannon, Ian. 2004. *The Private Sector's Role in the Provision of Infrastructure in Post-Conflict Countries: Patterns and Policy Options* (Washington D.C.: The World Bank).

Suhrke, Astri; Harpviken, Berg & Strand, Arne. "After Bonn: Conflictual Peace Building." *Third World Quarterly* 23 (5): 875–891.

United Nations Security Council. 2003. "United Nations Security Council Resolution 1483." Available at: daccess-dds-ny.un.org/doc/UNDOC/GEN/N03/368/53/PDF/N0336853.pdf?OpenElement (accessed January 13, 2011).

Williams, Michael C. 2008. *The World Bank and Social Transformation in International Politics: Liberalism, Governance and Sovereignty.* (London: Routledge).

Wool, Zoe H. 2007. "Operationalizing Iraqi Freedom: Governmentality, Neo-liberalism and New Public Management in the War in Iraq." *International Journal of Sociology and Social Policy* 27 (11): 460–468.

Index

For Product Safety Concerns and Information please contact our EU
representative GPSR@taylorandfrancis.com
Taylor & Francis Verlag GmbH, Kaufingerstraße 24, 80331 München, Germany

www.ingramcontent.com/pod-product-compliance
Lightning Source LLC
Chambersburg PA
CBHW050642280326
41932CB00015B/2747